CHARLES R. SWINDOLL

SWINDOLL'S
LIVING
INSIGHTS

NEW TESTAMENT COMMENTARY

PHILIPPIANS, COLOSSIANS, PHILEMON

Tyndale House Publishers, Inc.
Carol Stream, Illinois

Swindoll's Living Insights New Testament Commentary, Volume 9

Visit Tyndale online at www.tyndale.com.

Insights on Philippians, Colossians, Philemon copyright © 2017 by Charles R. Swindoll, Inc.

Cover photograph of mosaic copyright © Christian Mueller/Shutterstock. All rights reserved.

Photograph of notebook copyright © jcsmilly/Shutterstock. All rights reserved.

Unless otherwise noted, all artwork copyright © Tyndale House Publishers, Inc. All rights reserved.

All images are the property of their respective copyright holders and all rights are reserved.

Maps copyright © 2017 by Tyndale House Publishers, Inc. All rights reserved.

Designed by Nicole Grimes

Published in association with Yates & Yates, LLP (www.yates2.com).

Scripture quotations marked NASB are taken from the New American Standard Bible,® copyright © 1960, 1962, 1963, 1968, 1971, 1972, 1973, 1975, 1977, 1995 by The Lockman Foundation, La Habra, Calif. Used by permission. All rights reserved. For permission to quote information, visit http://www.lockman.org.

Scripture quotations marked NLT are taken from the *Holy Bible,* New Living Translation, copyright © 1996, 2004, 2015 by Tyndale House Foundation. Used by permission of Tyndale House Publishers, Inc., Carol Stream, Illinois 60188. All rights reserved.

Scripture quotations marked ESV are taken from *The Holy Bible*, English Standard Version® (ESV®), copyright © 2001 by Crossway, a publishing ministry of Good News Publishers. Used by permission. All rights reserved.

Scripture quotations marked NIV are taken from the Holy Bible, *New International Version,® NIV.®* Copyright © 1973, 1978, 1984, 2011 by Biblica, Inc.® Used by permission. All rights reserved worldwide.

Scripture quotations marked MSG are taken from *THE MESSAGE*, copyright © 1993, 1994, 1995, 1996, 2000, 2001, 2002 by Eugene H. Peterson. Used by permission of NavPress. All rights reserved. Represented by Tyndale House Publishers, Inc.

The "NASB," "NAS," "New American Standard Bible," and "New American Standard" trademarks are registered in the United States Patent and Trademark Office by The Lockman Foundation. Use of these trademarks requires the permission of The Lockman Foundation.

TYNDALE, Tyndale's quill logo, *New Living Translation*, and *NLT* are registered trademarks of Tyndale House Publishers, Inc.

ISBN 978-1-4143-9383-4   Hardcover

Printed in China

23 22 21 20 19 18 17
7   6   5   4   3   2   1

CONTENTS

AUTHOR'S PREFACE

For more than sixty years I have loved the Bible. It was that love for the Scriptures, mixed with a clear call into the gospel ministry during my tour of duty in the Marine Corps, that resulted in my going to Dallas Theological Seminary to prepare for a lifetime of ministry. During those four great years I had the privilege of studying under outstanding men of God, who also loved God's Word. They not only held the inerrant Word of God in high esteem, they taught it carefully, preached it passionately, and modeled it consistently. A week never passes without my giving thanks to God for the grand heritage that has been mine to claim! I am forever indebted to those fine theologians and mentors, who cultivated in me a strong commitment to the understanding, exposition, and application of God's truth.

For more than fifty years I have been engaged in doing just that—*and how I love it!* I confess without hesitation that I am addicted to the examination and the proclamation of the Scriptures. Because of this, books have played a major role in my life for as long as I have been in ministry—especially those volumes that explain the truths and enhance my understanding of what God has written. Through these many years I have collected a large personal library, which has proven invaluable as I have sought to remain a faithful student of the Bible. To the end of my days, my major goal in life is to communicate the Word with accuracy, insight, clarity, and practicality. Without informative and reliable books to turn to, I would have "run dry" decades ago.

Among my favorite and most well-worn volumes are those that have enabled me to get a better grasp of the biblical text. Like most expositors, I am forever searching for literary tools that I can use to hone my gifts and sharpen my skills. For me, that means finding resources that make the complicated simple and easy to understand, that offer insightful comments and word pictures that enable me to see the relevance of sacred truth in light of my twenty-first-century world, and that drive those truths home to my heart in ways I do not easily forget. When I come across such books, they wind up in my hands as I devour them and then place them in my library for further reference . . . and, believe me, I often return to them. What a relief it is to have these resources to turn to when I lack fresh insight, or when I need just the right story or illustration, or when I get stuck in the tangled text and cannot find my way out. For the serious expositor, a library is essential. As a mentor of mine once said, "Where else can you have ten thousand professors at your fingertips?"

In recent years I have discovered there are not nearly enough resources like those I just described. It was such a discovery that prompted me to consider becoming a part of the answer instead of lamenting the problem. But the solution would result in a huge undertaking. A writing project that covers all of the books and letters of the New Testament seemed overwhelming and intimidating. A rush of relief came when I realized that during the past fifty-plus years I've taught and preached through most of the New Testament. In my files were folders filled with notes from those messages that were just lying there, waiting to be brought out of hiding, given a fresh and relevant touch in light of today's needs, and applied to fit into the lives of men and women who long for a fresh word from the Lord. *That did it!* I began to work on plans to turn all of those notes into this commentary on the New Testament.

I must express my gratitude to Mike Svigel for his tireless and devoted efforts, serving as my hands-on, day-to-day editor. He has done superb work as we have walked our way through the verses and chapters of all twenty-seven New Testament books. It has been a pleasure to see how he has taken my original material and helped me shape it into a style that remains true to the text of the Scriptures, at the same time interestingly and creatively developed, and all the while allowing my voice to come through in a natural and easy-to-read manner.

I need to add sincere words of appreciation to the congregations I have served in various parts of these United States for more than five decades. It has been my good fortune to be the recipient of their love, support, encouragement, patience, and frequent words of affirmation as I have fulfilled my calling to stand and deliver God's message year after year. The sheep from all those flocks have endeared themselves to this shepherd in more ways than I can put into words . . . and none more than those I currently serve with delight at Stonebriar Community Church in Frisco, Texas.

Finally, I must thank my wife, Cynthia, for her understanding of my addiction to studying, to preaching, and to writing. Never has she discouraged me from staying at it. Never has she failed to urge me in the pursuit of doing my very best. On the contrary, her affectionate support personally, and her own commitment to excellence in leading Insight for Living for more than three and a half decades, have combined to keep me faithful to my calling "in season and out of season." Without her devotion to me and apart from our mutual partnership throughout our lifetime of ministry together, Swindoll's Living Insights would never have been undertaken.

I am grateful that it has now found its way into your hands and, ultimately, onto the shelves of your library. My continued hope and prayer is that you will find these volumes helpful in your own study and personal application of the Bible. May they help you come to realize, as I have over these many years, that God's Word is as timeless as it is true.

> The grass withers, the flower fades,
> But the word of our God stands forever. (Isa. 40:8, NASB)

Chuck Swindoll
Frisco, Texas

THE STRONG'S NUMBERING SYSTEM

Swindoll's Living Insights New Testament Commentary uses the Strong's word-study numbering system to give both newer and more advanced Bible students alike quicker, more convenient access to helpful original-language tools (e.g., concordances, lexicons, and theological dictionaries). The Strong's numbering system, made popular by the *Strong's Exhaustive Concordance of the Bible,* is used with the majority of biblical Greek and Hebrew reference works. Those who are unfamiliar with the ancient Hebrew, Aramaic, and Greek alphabets can quickly find information on a given word by looking up the appropriate index number. Advanced students will find the system helpful because it allows them to quickly find the lexical form of obscure conjugations and inflections.

When a Greek word is mentioned in the text, the Strong's number is included in square brackets after the Greek word. So in the example of the Greek word *agapē* [26], "love," the number is used with Greek tools keyed to the Strong's system.

On occasion, a Hebrew word is mentioned in the text. The Strong's Hebrew numbers are completely separate from the Greek numbers, so Hebrew numbers are prefixed with a letter "H." So, for example, the Hebrew word *kapporet* [H3727], "mercy seat," comes from *kopher* [H3722], "to ransom," "to secure favor through a gift."

INSIGHTS ON PHILIPPIANS

It's usually difficult to capture the essence

of a letter in one word, but in the case of

Philippians, that one word is joy. *Paul didn't*

write to answer any profound theological

question, solve some knotty practical

problem, or deal with a specific sin. Instead,

he wrote to express and encourage joy.

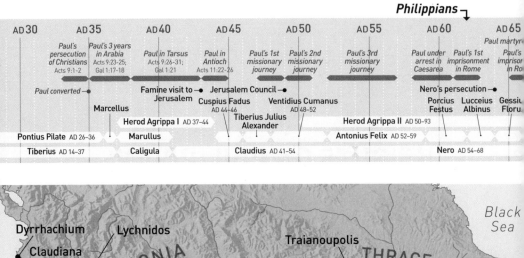

The Egnatian Way. Philippi was located in eastern Macedonia, just off the coast of the Aegean Sea, on the Egnatian Way.

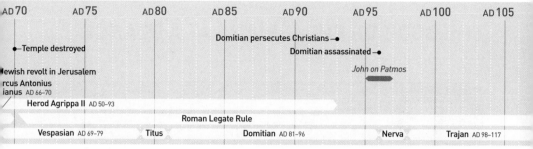

AD 70   AD 75   AD 80   AD 85   AD 90   AD 95   AD 100   AD 105

Domitian persecutes Christians —●
●—Temple destroyed   Domitian assassinated —●

Jewish revolt in Jerusalem   John on Patmos
rcus Antonius
ianus AD 66–70
    Herod Agrippa II AD 50–93

                    Roman Legate Rule
Vespasian AD 69–79   Titus   Domitian AD 81–96   Nerva   Trajan AD 98–117

PHILIPPIANS

INTRODUCTION

S ome of you may be old enough to remember singing—perhaps in Sunday school or at summer camp—that old song that starts out like this:

> "I've got the joy, joy, joy, joy down in my heart."
> "Where?"
> "Down in my heart!"
> "Where?"
> "Down in my heart!"

Do you know why we rarely sing that in church? Because it just doesn't sound right when it's sung with a frown. I don't want to seem ultranegative, but have you noticed the look on the faces of many in the Sunday-morning crowds? One word comes to mind—*grim*. As a close friend of mine used to say to his congregation, "Many of you have the joy so deep down in your heart that your face hasn't found out yet!"

There are exceptions. I've seen joyful believers and rejoicing congregations. I'm thankful that I've had the privilege to serve such congregations for most of my ministry. But sadly, truly joyful Christians are a rare species . . . and they seem to be facing extinction today.

Now, to be clear, when I say "joyful Christians," I'm not talking about silly Christians or foolish Christians. I'm not talking about Christians who think everything's a joke. And I'm certainly not talking about sarcastic or cynical or sneering Christians. I'm in search of Christians who are genuinely *joyful*—the kind of joyful that looks a lot more like contentment and peace than simply excitement or happiness.

What about you? Are you one of the joyful remnant? Or have you forgotten how good it is to smile? Have your burdens caused your

THE BOOK OF PHILIPPIANS AT A GLANCE

SECTION	JOY IN LIVING	JOY IN SERVING
PASSAGE	1:1-30	2:1-30
THEMES	Joy in spite of unfulfilled desires Joy in spite of circumstances Joy in spite of conflicts	Right attitude Right theology Right models
KEY TERMS	Joy, to rejoice	
	Prayer/supplication Day of Christ	Form To Make Empty

JOY IN SHARING	JOY IN RESTING
3:1-21	4:1-23
A warning	Unity
A testimony	Peace
A goal	Contentment
A command	

To regard	
Righteousness	To Worry
Mutilation/circumcision	Peace

QUICK FACTS ON PHILIPPIANS

Who wrote it? Paul, with Timothy (Phil. 1:1).

Where was it written? Rome, where Paul was under house arrest (Acts 28:16, 30-31).

When was it written? Around AD 62, during Paul's house arrest in Rome while he awaited a hearing before Caesar (Acts 28:16-31).

Why was it written? To encourage believers to find Christ-centered, Spirit-empowered joy in living, serving, sharing, and resting.

shoulders to droop and your back to slouch? Honestly, when was the last time you really let the joy of the Lord change your countenance?

If you're like most people, you could probably use a healthy dose of real joy.

Thankfully, that's the theme of the book of Philippians. From the first word to the last, Paul's letter is saturated with joy. Talk about a message desperately needed today! In our world of downers and disappointments, setbacks and failures, tragedies and disasters, how easy it is to let despair take over.

I can't think of anything that reveals the person and work of Jesus Christ in the lives of believers more than the manifestation of joy. It's the Christian's most obvious advertisement that he or she has something that can make a real difference in a world scraping for just an ounce of contentment and happiness.

THE BACKGROUND OF PHILIPPIANS

I've never spent time in jail, but I've visited a few, and I know many men and women who are heavily involved in prison ministry. Along with hospitals and cemeteries, jails are among the most joyless places on earth. How strange it seems, then—from a completely worldly perspective—that Paul and Silas were singing for joy while chained up in a dingy prison in the city of Philippi.

On one occasion, having been arrested, beaten with rods, and thrown into jail, Paul and Silas had every reason to be bitter. They could have been angry at their enemies, unhappy with their circumstances, even upset with God for allowing it all to happen. But instead, come midnight, the beleaguered apostle and his associate were singing joyous praises to God—with every tormented prisoner and every sour-faced guard within earshot (Acts 16:22-25).

Fast-forward a dozen years. Paul is again under arrest—this time not languishing in a dank cell awaiting an uncertain punishment, but under house arrest in his own rented home in the city of Rome (Acts 28:30-31). Between AD 61 and AD 63, Paul was forced to stay put in the great capital of the Roman Empire while he waited for a hearing before Caesar's court. But he wasn't cut off from the outside world. Even though a soldier was guarding him day and night (Acts 28:16), Paul enjoyed a measure of freedom that enabled him to continue his teaching and writing ministry.

During this lengthy stay, Paul drafted the four letters that New Testament scholars call the "Prison Epistles": Ephesians, Philippians, Colossians, and Philemon. The first is considered a "circular letter," addressed to the church in Ephesus but written to a more general audience with the intent that it would be circulated among the churches in Asia Minor.[1] As such, Paul discussed some very deep theological issues that would be doctrinally foundational and practically fruitful for many believers. The shorter letter to the Colossians shares some similar themes with Ephesians, but Paul clearly wrote it to a specific church with particular challenges from false teachers, even though he expected it to be passed around to other churches (Col. 4:16). Although brief in comparison to other New Testament letters, Paul's pointed letter to Philemon—a leader in the church of Colossae—dealt with the specific issue of what to do with a certain runaway slave, Onesimus, who had become a Christian.

Philippians was sent separately to Macedonia instead of Asia Minor and is unique not only when compared to the other three Prison Epistles but also within the New Testament itself. For example, unlike most New Testament books, there aren't any major problem passages for scholarly puzzle solvers to wring their hands over. It's a pretty straightforward presentation with an easy-to-follow argument. Remarkably, the letter doesn't contain a single Old Testament quotation, perhaps indicating that its original audience was mostly comprised of Gentile Christians and few Jewish believers. Also, Philippians sustains the theme of joy throughout the letter, using the word in each of its four chapters and mentioning "joy" or the related verb "rejoice" a dozen times throughout. Finally, Jesus Christ is mentioned over forty times in this letter, with the obvious implication that Jesus and joy go hand in hand. Overall, Philippians comes across as warm, encouraging, and affirming, the most positive of all Paul's letters . . . even though he wrote it while under arrest!

THE AUTHOR, AUDIENCE, AND OCCASION OF PHILIPPIANS

Philippians 1:1 leaves no doubt that Paul authored this letter with the assistance of his longtime companion Timothy, who had been with

PHILIPPI IN THE FIRST CENTURY

PHILIPPIANS 1:1

Founded in the fourth century BC in a region rich with silver and gold, the settlement that would come to be known as Philippi was originally given the name Crenides (Greek for "fountains"). Within a few years, however, in 356 BC, Philip II of Macedon, father of Alexander the Great, named the new city after himself: Philippi.[2]

In the year 42 BC Julius Caesar's assassins, Brutus and Cassius, were defeated in battle just outside the city. After the war, Philippi was designated a Roman colony.[3] When Paul and Silas planted the church in Philippi (around AD 49), the city was populated mostly by natives of nearby Thrace and Greece, but it also contained Romans, Egyptians, and some Jews.[4] Situated on the Egnatian Way, the major highway running east–west, Philippi was a city that traded in both goods and cultures. This led to a mixture of religious traditions, including the worship of Greek and Roman gods and goddesses as well as foreign gods from Asia Minor to Egypt—at least thirty-five different deities were worshiped in that one city.[5] Because Philippi was a Roman colony, emperor worship was also prevalent there.[6]

It was into this confused religious milieu that Paul, Silas, Timothy, and the chronicler Luke carried the light of the gospel during Paul's

© Barry Beitzel

The east–west **Egnatian Way** passed through Philippi and connected it with the nearby port city of Neapolis, guaranteeing a steady stream of both commerce and great intellectual variety.

second missionary journey. While the team was in Troas, Paul had a vision of a man saying, "Come over to Macedonia and help us" (Acts 16:9). In response, they traveled by sea to Neapolis, a port city just a few hours from Philippi. Philippi was a city of about ten thousand residents at the time.[7] Luke describes it as "a leading city of the district of Macedonia, a Roman colony" (Acts 16:12).

The first convert to Christ in Philippi was Lydia, who was originally from Thyatira. She was a businesswoman who sold purple fabric (Acts 16:14-15). From her house Paul continued to add to the fledgling church. After a brief episode of imprisonment in Philippi that resulted in a jailer's conversion (Acts 16:22-36), the local authorities forced Paul and Silas to leave the city (Acts 16:37-39), but not before Paul provided encouragement to the newly planted church that was meeting in Lydia's house (Acts 16:40).

It appears that Luke, who had accompanied Paul, Silas, and Timothy to Philippi, stayed behind longer to continue to strengthen the church in the forced absence of Paul and Silas.[8] Later, Paul again visited the city of Philippi and the region of Macedonia to give the believers "much exhortation" (Acts 20:2). In fact, while most of his traveling companions, including Timothy and Tychicus, went on ahead to Troas, Paul stayed behind with Luke for several days to observe the Passover with the church (Acts 20:6).

The same church in Philippi received a letter from Polycarp, the famous bishop of Smyrna, around AD 110, in which Polycarp wrote, "The secure root of your faith, being proclaimed from ancient times, still continues and bears fruit to our Lord Jesus Christ" (Polycarp, *To the Philippians* 1.2).[9] How encouraging to know that Paul's efforts had not been in vain! A Christian presence tied to that original church plant in Philippi continued to flourish for centuries until its light was dimmed when Muslim forces flooded the region in the late medieval period.

© Barry Beitzel

Excavations of the **ruins of Philippi** reveal a large Roman city straddling the Egnatian Way, complete with a hilltop acropolis, a large forum in the center of town, a spacious theater, and public baths.

OVERJOYED: THE THEME OF JOY IN PHILIPPIANS

I thank my God in all my remembrance of you, always offering prayer with joy in my every prayer for you all. (1:3-4)

Christ is proclaimed; and in this I rejoice. Yes, and I will rejoice. (1:18)

I know that I will remain and continue with you all for your progress and joy in the faith. (1:25)

Make my joy complete by being of the same mind, maintaining the same love, united in spirit, intent on one purpose. (2:2)

I rejoice and share my joy with you all. (2:17)

Rejoice in the same way and share your joy with me. (2:18)

When you see him again you may rejoice. (2:28)

Receive him then in the Lord with all joy. (2:29)

My brethren, rejoice in the Lord. (3:1)

My beloved brethren whom I long to see, my joy and crown. (4:1)

Rejoice in the Lord always; again I will say, rejoice! (4:4)

But I rejoiced in the Lord greatly. (4:10)

Paul when the church at Philippi was established (see Acts 16). Though there have been a few scholars who propose alternate locations for the composition of Philippians, the majority hold that Paul wrote this letter while under house arrest in Rome.[10] This is my view too.

The audience is clear: Paul wrote this letter to the church in Philippi, a city in Macedonia on the northern shore of the Aegean Sea (see "Philippi in the First Century," pages 8-9). Because of the relatively small Jewish population in Philippi during the first century, the majority of Christians in the Philippian church were Gentiles—Romans, Greeks, local Thracians, and perhaps displaced peoples from Asia Minor and Egypt.

By the time Paul wrote Philippians, the church had been in existence for over a decade and had steadily grown from its humble beginnings as a small house church in Lydia's home (see Acts 16:40). In Philippians 1:1, Paul mentions not only "the saints" but also a plurality of leadership: "overseers and deacons." This suggests a church of dozens of members. Even in its infancy, however, the Philippian church was known for its generosity in rendering financial aid to Paul's mission (4:15-16).

Paul wrote this letter first to thank the Philippians for their support of his ministry (4:14-16). They had distinguished themselves in self-sacrificial giving. Second, he wrote to give them a general warning against false teachings (3:2, 17-19). Third, he wrote to encourage them to stand firm and strive for the faith (1:27-28). Finally, he wrote to encourage the Philippians to rejoice in the Lord, despite their outward circumstances—to find Christ-centered, Spirit-empowered joy in living, serving, sharing, and resting.

REJOICE IN THE LORD . . . ALWAYS!

It's usually difficult to capture the essence of a letter in one word, but in the case of Philippians, that one word is *joy*. Paul didn't write to answer any profound theological question, solve some knotty practical problem, or deal with a specific sin. Instead, he wrote to express and encourage joy. In a way, the book of Philippians is a showcase of joy. Like a treasure on display in the center of a gallery, joy can be examined from several angles to better appreciate its brilliance. Each of the four chapters reveals one of the distinct facets of that joy.

In chapter 1 we learn there is *joy in living*, even when we don't get what we want (1:6-7), when there are difficult circumstances (1:12-14), or when there are conflicts (1:21-30). To find joy in living, there has to be something more than good feelings and comfortable settings. That something is actually *Someone*—the Lord Jesus Christ (1:21). In chapter 2, we learn there is *joy in serving*. It starts with the right attitude—humility (2:3-8); it's maintained through right theology (2:12-13); and it's encouraged by the right models, such as Christ, Timothy, and Epaphroditus (2:5-8, 19-23, 25-30). In chapter 3, we learn there is *joy in sharing*. Paul shares a warning (3:1-2), a testimony (3:3-11), a goal for living (3:12-16), and a command (3:17-21). Finally, in chapter 4, we learn there is *joy in resting*. In one of the finest passages ever written on contentment, Paul explains how to find a joy in resting that's not undermined by circumstances (4:6-7, 10-13).

Philippians truly is a precious gem of joy, one that shines with enthusiasm and pulsates with encouragement. As we study its principles and adopt its precepts, it can turn our drab lives into brilliant jewels as well—jewels that shine with a living, serving, sharing, and resting light in a world that desperately needs it.

KEY TERMS IN PHILIPPIANS

chara (χαρά) [5479] "joy," "cheerfulness," "calm delight,"
  "gladness"; *chairō* (χαίρω) [5463] "to be cheerful,"
  "to rejoice," "to be glad"
These two sister terms—the noun *chara* and the verb *chairō*—are used fourteen times in this four-chapter book of Philippians. If you're musically trained, you've probably heard of "grace notes"—little incidental notes that add charm to a piece of music. One commentator on Philippians refers to Paul's use of "joy" and "rejoice" as "joy notes." He writes, "The addition of each joy note develops the theme of joy. As we read through the letter, our understanding of the source and nature of joy expands."[11]

phroneō (φρονέω) [5426] "to regard," "to feel,"
  "to think about"
In Philippians 2:2, Paul uses the verb *phroneō* twice: "Make my joy complete by being of the same mind (*phroneō*), maintaining the same love, united in spirit, intent on one purpose (*phroneō*)." This verse gives a good indication of the kinds of nuances this single word can have: "mind" (as in "opinion") or "purpose" (as in "intention"). And in Philippians 1:7, the emphasis seems to be on emotion: "For it is only right for me to feel (*phroneō*) this way about you all." Though it often appears in English translations as a noun, it's actually a verb, which suggests that our opinions, thoughts, and even feelings are acts of the will and are thus able to be changed and conformed to the humble, self-sacrificial mind of Christ (2:5).

JOY IN LIVING
(PHILIPPIANS 1:1-30)

Paul wrote his letter to the Philippians *to encourage them to find Christ-centered, Spirit-empowered joy in living, serving, sharing, and resting.* Though it contains sound doctrine and practical insights that have proven to be relevant throughout the centuries, Philippians is not primarily a theological treatise, but a loving letter of friendship from one brother in Christ to his extended spiritual family. Even when he warns the Philippians about false teaching, he does so warmly and graciously, expecting the best from his readers.

In chapter 1 this theme of joy is exemplified as Paul encourages the Philippians to find Christ-centered, Spirit-empowered joy in living—even when things don't seem to be going their way. It opens with Paul's cheerful admission that his prayers for the Philippians always kindle the warmth of joy in his heart (1:3-4). He also demonstrates personal joy and optimism in the midst of challenges and difficult circumstances that are beyond his control (1:6-14).

This is a message every generation of believers needs to hear! Whether we face conflicts or setbacks, we can find joy in living if Jesus Christ is the source and center of our lives. Regardless of whether we continue on in this world, striving for the gospel, or we pass on to the next to be with Christ, we're to keep our focus on Him, the source of our joy (1:21-25).

KEY TERMS IN PHILIPPIANS 1:1-30

proseuchē; deēsis (προσευχή; δέησις) [4335; 1162]
   "prayer," "supplication," "petition"
These two words are often coupled in both the Greek Old Testament (called the Septuagint) and the New Testament (1 Kgs. 8:54; 2 Chr. 6:29; Eph. 6:18; 1 Tim. 2:1). The first term, *proseuchē*—and its verb form, *proseuchomai* (Phil. 1:9)—refers to general addresses to God. Meanwhile, the noun *deēsis* refers to particular "requests" or specific "supplications"

---

and is often an "urgent request to meet a need."[1] In Philippians 1:4 Paul uses the latter term twice, indicating an intimate knowledge of the Philippians and a deep interest in their particular, urgent needs. Likewise, the Philippians themselves were offering their own supplications on behalf of Paul (Phil. 1:19), confirming the uniquely close relationship Paul had with the Philippian church.

hēmera Christou (ἡμέρα Χριστοῦ) [2250 + 5547] "day of Christ"

The ominous phrase "day of the Lord" (hēmera kuriou [2250 + 2962]) occurs throughout the Greek Old Testament and the New Testament in reference to a period of divine judgment upon the earth (Joel 2:1-10; 1 Thes. 5:2; 2 Pet. 3:10). However, the phrase "day of Christ" found in Philippians 1:6, 10; and 2:16 emphasizes the hope of deliverance and reward. This makes sense in the context of the positive, uplifting tone of Paul's letter to the Philippians—that even when addressing prophetic events, he keeps the focus on the positive hope for believers rather than the negative consequences of judgment for unbelievers.

Confident Enough to Be Joyful
PHILIPPIANS 1:1-11

NASB

[1] Paul and Timothy, bond-servants of Christ Jesus,

To all the [a]saints in Christ Jesus who are in Philippi, [b]including the overseers and deacons: [2] Grace to you and peace from God our Father and the Lord Jesus Christ.

[3] I thank my God in all my remembrance of you, [4] always offering prayer with joy in my every prayer for you all, [5] in view of your [a]participation in the gospel from the first day until now. [6] For I am confident of this very thing, that He who began a good work in you will perfect it until the day of Christ Jesus. [7a] For it is only right for me to feel this way about you all, because I have you

NLT

[1] This letter is from Paul and Timothy, slaves of Christ Jesus.

I am writing to all of God's holy people in Philippi who belong to Christ Jesus, including the church leaders* and deacons.

[2] May God our Father and the Lord Jesus Christ give you grace and peace.

[3] Every time I think of you, I give thanks to my God. [4] Whenever I pray, I make my requests for all of you with joy, [5] for you have been my partners in spreading the Good News about Christ from the time you first heard it until now. [6] And I am certain that God, who began the good work within you, will continue his work until it is finally finished on the day when Christ Jesus returns.

[7] So it is right that I should feel as I do about all of you, for you have a special place in my heart. You share

in my heart, since both in my [b]imprisonment and in the defense and confirmation of the gospel, you all are partakers of grace with me. [8]For God is my witness, how I long for you all with the [a]affection of Christ Jesus. [9]And this I pray, that your love may abound still more and more in real knowledge and all discernment, [10]so that you may [a]approve the things that are excellent, in order to be sincere and blameless [b]until the day of Christ; [11]having been filled with the fruit of righteousness which *comes* through Jesus Christ, to the glory and praise of God.

1:1 [a]Or *holy ones* [b]Lit *with*   1:5 [a]Or *sharing in the preaching of the gospel*   1:7 [a]Lit *Just as it is right* [b]Lit *bonds*   1:8 [a]Lit *inward parts*   1:10 [a]Or *discover;* or *distinguish between the things which differ* [b]Or *for*

with me the special favor of God, both in my imprisonment and in defending and confirming the truth of the Good News. [8]God knows how much I love you and long for you with the tender compassion of Christ Jesus.

[9]I pray that your love will overflow more and more, and that you will keep on growing in knowledge and understanding. [10]For I want you to understand what really matters, so that you may live pure and blameless lives until the day of Christ's return. [11]May you always be filled with the fruit of your salvation—the righteous character produced in your life by Jesus Christ*—for this will bring much glory and praise to God.

1:1 Or *overseers,* or *bishops.*   1:11 Greek *with the fruit of righteousness through Jesus Christ.*

Ours is a frivolous age with lots of shallow, empty laughter . . . but very little real joy.

Most people stumble around in perpetual confusion—darkness, really. As they seek genuine joy, they satisfy themselves with only occasional glimpses of light—and artificial light at that. Occasionally, it's sad to say, some of the light they're attracted to is a consuming fire. It destroys their lives rather than illuminating their minds or warming their hearts.

Paul would have understood this plight as he, too, groped around in darkness until that glorious day when the light of the gospel of Christ shone brightly into his life (Acts 9:1-19). From that day on, although he often experienced suffering, he rarely let the darkening fog of discouragement cloud his mind or drive out the light of joy.

His letter to the Philippians, embossed with unfading joy on every page, is proof that, for Paul, joy was more than a fleeting emotion; it was part of his ingrained character. How could that be? It's because he was confident that God was at work, that God was in complete control, and that God allowed all things to occur for one ultimate purpose—His greater glory.

Paul understood that joy doesn't depend on our circumstances, our possessions, or other people. Joy is an attitude of the heart determined by confidence in God. Paul knew that he had no control over the struggles and strife of life. But by yielding to the Spirit's work in his soul, Paul's trust and hope in God could guide him like an inner compass, keeping him on joy's course regardless of how strong the gale-force winds blew.

Poet Ella Wheeler Wilcox put this idea beautifully in her poem "The Winds of Fate":

> One ship drives east and another drives west
> With the self-same winds that blow;
>   'Tis the set of the sails
>   And not the gales
> That tells them the way to go.[2]

In the first chapter of Paul's joy-filled letter to the Philippians, we come face-to-face with his bold, joyous confidence, setting the trajectory for more to come. He extends a warm greeting to the Philippians in 1:1-2, offers up joyful thanksgiving in 1:3-8, and lifts them up in prayer in 1:9-11.

— 1:1-2 —

As he does in all his letters, Paul begins with a customary gracious greeting. When the Philippians took the scroll from the hand of Epaphroditus and unrolled it (see 2:25; 4:18), the first words they would have seen in the Greek text were "Paul and Timothy" (1:1). These were not strangers, not remote leaders governing impersonally from a distance through go-betweens—these were loving shepherds and beloved friends.

Though sometimes the inclusion of multiple names could indicate a sort of coauthorship (e.g., 1 Thessalonians), in the case of Philippians, Timothy probably wasn't involved in the actual composition of the letter itself. Throughout the letter Paul uses the first-person singular, indicating that he's personally the source of the words. Why is Timothy included then? Because the Philippians would have had fond memories of that wet-behind-the-ears "intern" who had just joined Paul and Silas prior to their original arrival in Philippi (see Acts 16). Timothy had been there when Paul shared the gospel with Lydia at the place of prayer by the river, when Paul cast the spirit of divination out of a slave girl and caused a great upheaval among the pagans of Philippi, when Paul and Silas were dragged off to prison as a result, and when the fledgling church grew despite their founding apostle and prophet being beaten and jailed. No doubt Timothy had been forced to step up and begin to lead the best he could in the absence of Paul and Silas. Now, over a decade later, Timothy was still at Paul's side as a "kindred spirit" of "proven worth" (Phil. 2:20, 22).

Today, icons, statues, and paintings of apostles tend to portray people like Paul and Timothy as larger-than-life heroes. If they aren't bulked up and poised for epic action, their faces glow, halos orbit their heads, and miracles flow from the tips of their fingers. What a contrast to Paul's own humble, self-demoting label "bond-servants of Christ Jesus" (1:1)! The term Paul uses, *doulos* [1401], means "one who serves another to the disregard of his own interests."[3]

Paul then identifies those to whom he writes: both the membership of the church in Philippi ("saints in Christ Jesus") and the leadership ("overseers and deacons"). The Greek word translated "overseers" (*episkopos* [1985]) refers to a group of leaders keeping a watchful eye over those in their charge. In the Septuagint (the Greek translation of the Old Testament), an *episkopos* was one who served as judge, as treasurer, or as supervisor of the priests and the Levites serving in the temple. Elsewhere in the New Testament, Peter calls Jesus the *episkopos* of our souls (1 Pet. 2:25). In this sense, the church official designated by this term is someone charged to "shepherd" (*poimainō* [4165]) the church, to serve as an undershepherd to the Lord, leading His flock on His behalf and under His authority. Paul listed the qualifications of an "overseer" in a letter to Timothy, who was serving in Ephesus at the time (1 Tim. 3:2-7).

The deacons, in turn, assisted the overseers in various ministry-related tasks. The term *diakonos* [1249] carries the idea of serving obediently, willingly, and submissively from a heart of humility. The Latin translation of the Greek term *diakonos* is *minister*, from which we get this particular title. In the New Testament, *diakonos* can refer to a servant with a certain mission (Rom. 15:8), a personal assistant (Matt. 22:13), or a person in the office of "minister" in a local church (Phil. 1:1). Acts 6:1-6 recounts the appointment of the first deacons in the church. Paul uses the term for "minister" in the general sense of a self-sacrificing servant in the kingdom of Christ.

The church in Philippi, of course, had multiple people appointed to both offices—overseers/elders and deacons/ministers (Phil. 1:1). They were tasked with the "equipping of the saints for the work of service, to the building up of the body of Christ" (Eph. 4:12). From the youngest to the oldest, from the recently baptized believers to Philippi's first converts, from followers to leaders, Paul calls them all "saints" (Phil. 1:1) and blesses them equally: "Grace to you and peace from God our

ORIGINAL CHURCH LEADERSHIP: OVERSEERS AND DEACONS

PHILIPPIANS 1:1

Today we hear a number of terms used to refer to the leaders of our churches: pastors, elders, overseers, superintendents, directors, co-ordinators, facilitators, ministers, priests, bishops . . . the list goes on. But in the early church only a few terms were used to describe what were essentially two levels of leadership: overseers (or elders) and deacons (or ministers). When an apostle planted a local church, a team of overseers/elders was appointed in it to serve as the shepherds, preachers, teachers, and general decision makers of the church—the leaders. The ministers/deacons were appointed to assist the leaders in the work of the ministry.[4]

The noun *episkopos* refers to an "overseer" (traditionally "bishop") (1 Tim. 3:2; Titus 1:7). In the New Testament, the term could be interchangeable with the word for "elders" (Acts 20:17, 28). When the original apostles exercised direct oversight in the churches, the offices of "elder", "pastor", and "overseer" all referred to the same type of leader. After the first-century era of the apostles, the office of a senior overseeing elder developed to help stabilize church authority. It is this position that in later centuries would develop into the episcopacy, the authority of a single bishop over a number of churches.[5]

However, in the New Testament period, "elder", "pastor", and "overseer" all represented one calling with the same responsibility to shepherd the flock. All three of these terms are used together in Acts 20:17, 28. In that account, Paul calls the "elders" of the church of Ephesus to meet him in Miletus, then he instructs them, "Be on guard for yourselves and for all the flock, among which the Holy Spirit has made you overseers (*episkopos*), to shepherd (*poimainō*) the church of God which He purchased with His own blood" (Acts 20:28).

Father and the Lord Jesus Christ" (1:2). Though this was a standard greeting in Paul's letters, it's a profoundly deep theological statement. Grace and peace are essential blessings for living the Christian life and especially for carrying out Christian ministry. These things can't be conjured from within; they are gifts of God through Jesus Christ.

— 1:3-8 —

Paul's fond memories of the Philippians prompted him to follow his gracious greeting with joyous thankfulness and prayer (1:3-4). Regarding the Philippians, he had no regrets, no ill feelings, no unresolved conflicts. His heart was filled with joy as he reminisced on the times he had spent with them—their first meeting over a decade earlier when the church was planted (Acts 16) and another gathering during his third missionary journey (Acts 20).

But his thankfulness and joy were not inspired by mere nostalgia. Paul indicates in Philippians 1:5 that the Philippians were participating "in the gospel from the first day until now." Their commitment to Christ and the proclamation of His word never let up, not for a moment.

I wonder how many pastors could say that about churches where they have served. Or how many saints could say it about longtime Christian friends? Like most of us, Paul experienced some great disappointments, from churches and from individual brothers and sisters in Christ. But not from the Philippians. The thought of them didn't make his stomach churn; rather, it prompted him to thankfulness, joy, and prayer.

Because of the Philippians' past perseverance and present passion, Paul was confident in their future faithfulness (1:6). He had no doubt that God was at work in Philippi, that He had plans for that church, and that He was in control and would see them through to the end. The Greek verb translated "perfect" in 1:6 is *epiteleō* [2005], which means "to bring about a result according to plan or objective."[6] God had begun the work of spiritual growth, of ministry participation, and of faithful Christian witness among these believers. And He would stay at it until He called them home or until Christ stepped back into this world to reward them for their Spirit-enabled labor.

Paul exposes his deep feelings in 1:7-8. Far from being a cold, get-it-done apostle, Paul didn't hesitate to share his deep emotions. He always had the Philippians "in his heart" (1:7). G. Walter Hansen unpacks the meaning of this phrase nicely: "When Paul tells his friends that he has them in his heart, he is expressing more than a sentimental feeling; he is stating the commitment of his heart to give his life for his friends."[7] Their commitment to him through thick and thin and their participation in the gospel ministry only served to strengthen his own heartfelt commitment to them. They were more than friends. They were lifelong partners in Christ.

Because of this, Paul yearned for them—*all of them* (1:8). Notice how many times Paul repeated the word "all" in 1:1-8:

- He greeted *all* the saints. (1:1)
- He thanked God in *all* his remembrance. (1:3)
- He prayed for *all* of them. (1:4)

- He felt strongly about them *all*. (1:7)
- They were *all* fellow partakers of grace. (1:7)
- He affectionately longed for them *all*. (1:8)

From the family of Lydia to the Roman jailer's household, from the elders and deacons to the new believers, the deep love Paul felt for the church in Philippi made his heart leap in his chest as he yearned to spend time with them again.

— 1:9-11 —

This profound thankfulness and love led to specific prayers for the Philippians, as it should for us. Christians shouldn't just say, "You're in our thoughts." We should say, "You're in our prayers"—and we should mean it! Paul certainly did. His deep, joyful contemplation of the Philippians prompted him to pray for some specific things, things that can only come from God.

First, he prayed that their love would continue to grow and would be characterized by "real knowledge and all discernment" (1:9). I like to picture love like a river. It needs to be guided by the banks of knowledge and discernment. Paul isn't telling the Philippians to let their love blind them to truth and righteousness so they end up overlooking sin and compromising holiness. That's a false interpretation of "love" we often see in the world today. True Christian love is guided by the best interest of others. With true knowledge and discernment, love learns to spot the phony, the wrong, the evil. It learns to "approve the things that are excellent" (1:10). This love, guided by wisdom, will preserve believers in righteousness until "the day of Christ"—the Second Coming, when the Lord Jesus will reward them for faithfulness.

Second, Paul prayed that they would be filled with the "fruit of righteousness" (1:11). Don't confuse this with self-righteousness, personal piety, or self-motivated works. Paul is referring to the righteousness of Christ working in us by the indwelling Holy Spirit to produce fruit in our lives (see Gal. 5:22-23). The result of such good works empowered by God will be "the glory and praise of God" (Phil. 1:11)—*not* our own praise and glory. Jesus said essentially the same thing: "Let your light shine before men in such a way that they may see your good works, and glorify your Father who is in heaven" (Matt. 5:16).

What a solid basis for abiding joy! When Paul scanned the ten-year life span of the body of Christ in Philippi, he had every reason to rejoice in confidence, as expressed in thanksgiving, prayer, and praise.

APPLICATION: PHILIPPIANS 1:1-11

Setting Your Sails for the Harbors of Joy

The second stanza of Wilcox's "The Winds of Fate" provides another reminder about setting our sails for joy:

Like the winds of the sea are the winds of fate,
As we voyage along through life;
'Tis the set of a soul
That decides its goal,
And not the calm or the strife.[8]

While I don't believe in fate, I do believe that apart from a confidence in the providential care of God, the winds of strife can easily capsize our vessels and leave our souls drowning in despair. To set the course of our souls to experience genuine joy, let's recall a few principles from Paul's opening words in Philippians 1.

First, *confidence brings joy when we focus on the things for which we're thankful.* Paul could have looked back ten years in Philippi and recalled the demon-possessed woman frustrating their preaching. He could have remembered his arrest and beatings. He could have dwelled on his imprisonment and expulsion from the city. Instead, he recalled the positives about the Philippians: their conversion, their faithfulness, their growth and participation in ministry, and their continued perseverance.

Second, *confidence brings joy when we let God be God.* Paul had every confidence that the work *God* had begun in the past among the Philippians, *God* would bring to completion in the future. This meant *God* would continue to work in the present. Let me make this personal. When I stop trying to play God in my own life and instead let Him accomplish my spiritual growth in His own way, I'll look differently at the winds of strife that blow through my life. And while I'm at it, I need to stop trying to play God in other people's lives through constant worry, anxiety, and manipulation. What we need is to pray with confidence in every circumstance that comes our way—and thank God for His promise to navigate us through it.

Third, *confidence brings joy when we keep love within its proper limits.* Those limits are knowledge and discernment. Asking two questions can help us here: To whom should we direct our love? And how can we best express that love? I've learned that loving our children doesn't mean giving them everything they want. In fact, it often means giving them what they don't want. The same is true of spouses, friends, colleagues, and those to whom we minister. But that takes knowledge—intimate knowledge of the person and their strengths and weaknesses, needs and desires. It also takes discernment—how, when, and where to meet those real needs.

How are your sails set today? Are they tattered and torn? Are you a victim of relentless storms of strife? In need of the mending only Christ can provide? Have you lowered your sails in defeat, surrendering to the gale-force winds? Or have you confidently hoisted them to the top of the mast to open yourself to the Spirit's wind guiding you where He wills? Let me encourage you to take this step with confidence: Set your sails and mark a course for the harbors of joy.

What a Way to Live!
PHILIPPIANS 1:12-20

NASB

¹²Now I want you to know, brethren, that my circumstances have turned out for the greater progress of the gospel, ¹³so that my ᵃimprisonment in *the cause of* Christ has become well known throughout the whole ᵇpraetorian guard and to everyone else, ¹⁴and that most of the ᵃbrethren, trusting in the Lord because of my ᵇimprisonment, have far more courage to speak the word of God without fear. ¹⁵Some, to be sure, are preaching Christ even ᵃfrom envy and strife, but some also ᵃfrom good will; ¹⁶the latter *do it* out of love, knowing that I am appointed for the defense of the gospel; ¹⁷the former proclaim Christ out of selfish ambition ᵃrather than from pure motives, thinking to cause me distress in my ᵇimprisonment. ¹⁸What then? Only that in every way, whether in pretense or in truth, Christ is proclaimed; and in this I rejoice.

NLT

¹²And I want you to know, my dear brothers and sisters,* that everything that has happened to me here has helped to spread the Good News. ¹³For everyone here, including the whole palace guard,* knows that I am in chains because of Christ. ¹⁴And because of my imprisonment, most of the believers* here have gained confidence and boldly speak God's message* without fear.

¹⁵It's true that some are preaching out of jealousy and rivalry. But others preach about Christ with pure motives. ¹⁶They preach because they love me, for they know I have been appointed to defend the Good News. ¹⁷Those others do not have pure motives as they preach about Christ. They preach with selfish ambition, not sincerely, intending to make my chains more painful to me. ¹⁸But that doesn't matter. Whether their motives are false or genuine, the message about Christ is being preached

Yes, and I will rejoice, [19]for I know that this will turn out for my [a]deliverance through your [b]prayers and the provision of the Spirit of Jesus Christ, [20]according to my earnest expectation and hope, that I will not be put to shame in anything, but *that* with all boldness, Christ will even now, as always, be exalted in my body, whether by life or by death.

1:13 [a]Lit *bonds* [b]Or *governor's palace* 1:14 [a]Or *brethren in the Lord, trusting because of my bonds* [b]Lit *bonds* 1:15 [a]Lit *because of* 1:17 [a]Lit *not sincerely* [b]Lit *bonds* 1:19 [a]Or *salvation* [b]Lit *supplication*

either way, so I rejoice. And I will continue to rejoice. [19]For I know that as you pray for me and the Spirit of Jesus Christ helps me, this will lead to my deliverance.

[20]For I fully expect and hope that I will never be ashamed, but that I will continue to be bold for Christ, as I have been in the past. And I trust that my life will bring honor to Christ, whether I live or die.

1:12 Greek *brothers.* 1:13 Greek *including all the Praetorium.* 1:14a Greek *brothers in the Lord.* 1:14b Some manuscripts read *speak the message.*

Holocaust survivor Viktor Frankl observed, "Everything can be taken from a man but one thing: the last of the human freedoms—to choose one's attitude in any given set of circumstances."[9]

If we pursue happiness instead of choosing joy, we'll become, as Frankl put it, "plaything[s] of circumstance."[10] Our inner peace will be tossed back and forth according to the whim of events beyond our control. But if we choose our attitude—the one basic freedom that can't be taken away from us—we can choose joy even in the midst of the cruelest of circumstances.

I am convinced that joy does not come from without, but from within. A life of calm, peaceful satisfaction, a positive attitude, a contented spirit—these aren't dependent on circumstances but on our mind-set. The way I see it, there are two types of people:

NEGATIVE MIND-SET PEOPLE	POSITIVE MIND-SET PEOPLE
• Those who need certain *things* before they can be happy • Those who are dependent on *others* to provide happiness • Those who see happiness as being "out there"—always future	• Those who need virtually *nothing* tangible to have inner joy • Those who depend on *Christ* to give them joy by the Holy Spirit • Those who choose to experience joy now, making it a present reality

It's not enough, though, simply to say, "I choose to be happy. I choose joy." The Bible's not a self-help manual to stir up your inner power of positive thinking. That's rubbish. When I talk about a "positive mind-set," I'm talking about the joyful disposition that comes from the renewal of the mind by the Holy Spirit (Rom. 12:2). That's the internal work of God. But God also uses external means to reinforce His work in us, like when we intentionally set our minds on the things of God (Phil. 4:8).

In Philippians 1:12-20, Paul embodies the decision to live a joyful life in spite of troubling circumstances. Remember who it is we're talking about. He wanted to go to Rome as a preacher. Instead, he went as a prisoner. As a Roman citizen he had the right to be treated with fairness and justice. Instead, he had been mistreated, falsely accused, and unjustly arrested. On top of all this, during his journey to Rome he was shipwrecked! If anybody had a right to look at the world through dim lenses, complaining that he had been victimized, it was Paul. But even through all this, he did not complain. He was confident, despite hardship (1:12-14); joyful, in spite of others' ill will (1:15-18); and hopeful, regardless of uncertainties (1:19-20).

— 1:12-14 —

In light of the chain of events leading to his imprisonment, Paul was convinced that his circumstances had turned out "for the greater progress of the gospel" (1:12). I love that! There's no pouting, no "woe is me" mentality. Rather than viewing his chains as intolerable restrictions, he saw them as God-appointed megaphones to get the message of the gospel into the imperial barracks. Because of his imprisonment under the ever-watching eyes of Roman soldiers, the cause of Christ had become known "throughout the whole praetorian guard" (1:13). In other words, the gospel had penetrated into places it never would have without Paul's "tragic" arrest.

Think about it. With each changing of the guard came a new opportunity for sharing Christ, for telling his compelling story of conversion. How he was once a persecutor of Christians. How he had met the Lord Jesus face-to-face. How he had gone from enemy to emissary overnight. For two years the guards heard Paul pray, preach, and dictate letters. They listened as he conversed with others about the consequences of sin and offered a new start by grace alone through faith alone in Christ alone. In this way, the gospel penetrated the imperial barracks like an arrow through armor.

None of this could have happened had Paul chosen despair instead of joy. Instead of asking, "Why did this have to happen to me?" he asked, "How has this resulted for God's benefit?" He rejoiced that the unfair circumstances that were brought about by those trying to silence him ended up amplifying the proclamation of the gospel far and wide. His own positive attitude during imprisonment encouraged those who were still free. They could put up with more, suffer more, speak out more . . . and spread the gospel with far more courage than they had before (1:14).

What Paul's enemies had intended as a deathblow to Paul's ministry had breathed new life into the church worldwide! I wonder if the words of the ancient patriarch Joseph ever entered Paul's mind as he reflected on his circumstances with a smile: "As for you, you meant evil against me, but God meant it for good in order to bring about this present result, to preserve many people alive" (Gen. 50:20).

— 1:15-18 —

Besides being confident even in the midst of hardship, Paul was also joyful in spite of what other people did to harm him. While Paul was stuck under house arrest, he had to count on others to carry on the work of spreading the gospel beyond the cities he and other apostles had already reached. Many had picked up the torch and were bearing it honorably in the same spirit of self-sacrificial love as Paul had. I think of Timothy, Luke, Mark, and others who were faithful to Paul's cause.

But with Paul stuck in a pit stop, his absence also encouraged others to infringe on his mission field with less honorable motives. Some began preaching the gospel not because the love of Christ compelled them, but because they saw a gap in the market and an opportunity to do what Paul had done and to get a little of the glory they thought Paul had received.

I can imagine that, as Paul's faithful friends visited him in his rented home and saw the unbelievably optimistic attitude he had, they may have become a little frustrated. Let me employ a little creative license:

Paul smiles widely, eyeing the Roman guard sitting nearby. "Isn't it amazing how God's working through all this?" He waves his hand around his home then gestures toward the soldier. "Did you hear what Claudius here said? The guards were talking about Jesus last night! The guards!"

"Huh?" Luke lifts his pen from the paper on which he had been writing since lunch, ignoring everything that had been going on all afternoon. "Oh, yeah. Sure, that's true." He sets down his pen. "But think of all the places where you could be taking the gospel." He points down at his paper. "I've been writing this account for that court official, Theophilus, all about the adventures we've already had. It's so amazing! So thrilling! I know there's more ahead. You still haven't made it to Spain like you wanted. But you're stuck

here. We have to get you out of Rome as soon as we can. I have this plan—"

Paul interrupts Luke with a wave of his hand. "Luke, so many other workers are rolling up their sleeves and digging in. I think being 'stuck' here may be a good thing. It's actually gotten people off their seats and serving. I feel like a lot of those guys were a little intimidated by me. Now they're boldly preaching in my place!"

Luke takes a deep breath. "About that . . ."

"Yes?"

"Well," Luke says, "you need to know that there are some, well—" he pauses, searching for the right word. "Let's just call them 'less than sincere' people preaching out there. Not that they're spreading heresy. It just seems like they're trying to make a name for themselves. Mark thinks they're driven by envy—envy of you and of each other. They're actually acting like it's a big competition, to see who can plant more churches. I even think a few might be trying to nudge you out a little while you're stuck here. All the more reason for us to figure out a way to get you out as soon as possible."

Paul lets out a long sigh and responds, "Hmmm. You know what, Luke? So what if some are preaching with wrong motives? So what if some are a little too interested in themselves? So what if there are some who are taking shots at me while I'm out of pocket? None of that matters. What matters is this." He leans in and looks Luke right in the eyes. "Christ is being preached, even more than when I was out there myself. And that thought alone is enough to make me rejoice!"

Although we have no official record, a conversation like this could have taken place. We do know Paul had been made aware of some fresh contenders out in the field—some preaching Christ "from envy and strife" and "selfish ambition," while others preaching with pure motives (1:15-17). In either case, Paul concedes, Christ is being preached (1:18).

But isn't this a contradiction in Paul's teaching? Didn't he strongly condemn those who were preaching a "different gospel" in Galatia (Gal. 1:6-9)? Is he now fine with false preaching? No! In Galatians, the apostle was denouncing those who garbled the gospel message into a message of works. They were preaching heresy. In Philippians, he's rejoicing that despite the impure motives of some, the authentic good news about the true Jesus is still being proclaimed.

A heretic with sincere motives is still preaching a gospel that has no power to save anyone. But a presentation of the truth, even by those who aren't living in accordance with it, still has the power to bring a person to faith. Never forget: It's the work of the Holy Spirit, not His empowered preachers, that saves people.

— 1:19-20 —

So far we've seen Paul model for us a particular lifestyle by his remaining confident through hardship (1:12-14) and by his choosing to be joyful in spite of others who might otherwise rob him of reasons to rejoice (1:15-18). Now, Paul shows us how to be hopeful, regardless of uncertainties (1:19-20).

With the gospel spreading and people proclaiming Christ, not simply in spite of Paul's imprisonment but because of it, Paul was greatly encouraged. This helped boost his trust in God instead of deflating his confidence. Yes, Paul's future was filled with countless uncertainties. I'm sure some reminded Paul that his own legal situation in Rome could conceivably take any number of negative—even tragic—turns. But Paul chose to be hopeful in spite of the uncertainties. He was confident that the Philippians' prayers and the Lord's provision would ultimately result in his deliverance, likely referring to a literal release from prison (1:19).

But what if he wasn't set free? What if his opponents somehow rigged the system, like they had done in the case of Jesus Christ? What if Paul faced the same path as his Lord? Despite these uncertainties, his hope remained. He was unafraid and unashamed. Whether he lived or died, he knew that Christ would be exalted (1:20).

APPLICATION: PHILIPPIANS 1:12-20

Three Truths to Help You Live Well

The secret to living well is the same as the secret to having joy: the centrality of Jesus Christ. Keeping Him as our top priority in life will give us great joy. Many people today are in a relentless but empty pursuit of happiness through other means. If that's you, *STOP!* True happiness is the cultivation of a Christ-empowered life.

When Christ is the center, not only does He replace anxiety, fear, and insecurity with contentment, but He also impacts our perspective regarding the three areas of concern Paul has been describing in this section. The three truths outlined below correspond to these three areas and will help us live well even when we suffer.

First, *when Christ is the center, He changes our attitude toward our circumstances.* I once read that one of the requirements for working alongside Mother Teresa in her ministry in India was a joyful attitude toward life. Surrounded by so much pain and suffering, there was nothing in the appearance of their work that would make somebody feel anything but sadness and sorrow. But their inner joy reached out to those in need and took them in, washed their wounds, and set them on the road to recovery. Those who live with an internal, abiding joy can't help but seek to conform their attitudes toward circumstances to their deep-seated convictions. It's transformative. Choose today to serve with joy rather than suffer under circumstances.

Second, *when Christ is the center, He delivers us from our preoccupation with how others view us.* The more Christ means to us, the less other people's opinions mean. We'll care less about how many "friends" or "followers" we have on social media. We'll care nothing about how many "likes" we get on something we post. How silly we've become! Over the years I've been bothered less and less about pleasing others, not because I care less about people, but because I care more about Christ—His priorities, His passions, His pursuits, and His plan for me. If I make Christ the center, He delivers me from my preoccupations with others. Choose today to care more about the mind of Christ than the opinions of others.

Third, *when Christ is the center, He calms our fears about ourselves and our futures.* People frequently say when worried, "I might die!" Let me tell you: Unless you happen to be among the generation that sees the Lord return, there's no "might" about it. You will die. So will I. Death has it out for all of us. It may not be for years, or it may be soon. You don't know, and you can't know. The last thing you should do is worry about when you'll die; instead, you should focus on how you'll live. If Christ is the center, it doesn't matter whether we live long or short lives, whether we die sooner or later. What matters is that we love Him, serve Him, and rejoice in His salvation *today*. Christ will take care of our tomorrows. Choose today to think more about focusing on Christ, His death, and His resurrection than about fretting over your own life and death.

Isn't it amazing that when the person of Christ is in full focus, centrally located in our hearts and minds, everything starts to make sense? Order emerges out of chaos. Clarity out of confusion. Life from death.

Between a Rock and a Hard Place
PHILIPPIANS 1:21-30

NASB

21For to me, to live is Christ and to die is gain. 22aBut if *I am* to live *on* in the flesh, this *will mean* fruitful labor for me; and I do not know bwhich to choose. 23But I am hard-pressed from both *directions,* having the desire to depart and be with Christ, for *that* is very much better; 24yet to remain on in the flesh is more necessary for your sake. 25Convinced of this, I know that I will remain and continue with you all for your progress and joy ain the faith, 26so that your proud confidence in me may abound in Christ Jesus through my coming to you again.

27Only conduct yourselves in a manner worthy of the gospel of Christ, so that whether I come and see you or remain absent, I will hear of you that you are standing firm in one spirit, with one amind striving together for the faith of the gospel; 28in no way alarmed by *your* opponents— which is a sign of destruction for them, but of salvation for you, and that *too,* from God. 29For to you it has been granted for Christ's sake, not only to believe in Him, but also to suffer for His sake, 30experiencing the same conflict which you saw in me, and now hear *to be* in me.

1:22 aOr *But if to live in the flesh, this will be fruitful labor for me, then I* bLit *what I shall choose*
1:25 aLit *of*   **1:27** aLit *soul*

NLT

21For to me, living means living for Christ, and dying is even better. 22But if I live, I can do more fruitful work for Christ. So I really don't know which is better. 23I'm torn between two desires: I long to go and be with Christ, which would be far better for me. 24But for your sakes, it is better that I continue to live.

25Knowing this, I am convinced that I will remain alive so I can continue to help all of you grow and experience the joy of your faith. 26And when I come to you again, you will have even more reason to take pride in Christ Jesus because of what he is doing through me.

27Above all, you must live as citizens of heaven, conducting yourselves in a manner worthy of the Good News about Christ. Then, whether I come and see you again or only hear about you, I will know that you are standing together with one spirit and one purpose, fighting together for the faith, which is the Good News. 28Don't be intimidated in any way by your enemies. This will be a sign to them that they are going to be destroyed, but that you are going to be saved, even by God himself. 29For you have been given not only the privilege of trusting in Christ but also the privilege of suffering for him. 30We are in this struggle together. You have seen my struggle in the past, and you know that I am still in the midst of it.

Have you ever waffled between two different—and reasonable—opinions, unable to decide which one to hold? Or thrown your hands up in frustration because you couldn't land on a conclusive decision between two equally favorable options? Or driven your friends and family mad seeking their advice about which course of action to take? Or wrung your hands over a decision, worried that you were about to make the wrong one?

Welcome to the club. We've all been there. And by "all," I mean all. From Adam to us, humans have been finding themselves repeatedly "stuck between a rock and a hard place," facing difficult dilemmas. I'm not talking about choosing between what is morally good or evil. There should be no wrestling with that. I'm talking about head-scratching predicaments that don't fit into a simple "this is right and that's wrong" approach. I'm talking about those gray areas that can't be reduced to convenient black-and-white options. By "dilemmas" I mean decisions for which there are pros and cons on either side. No matter which box you check or which path you take, something will be lost and something will be gained.

In Philippians 1:21-30, we encounter an emotional dilemma in Paul's mind. It was prompted by his absolute love for and devotion to Christ. On the one hand, in his heart of hearts, he longed to be with Christ personally—to walk and talk with Him in paradise. What a great blessing to be with the Lord! But on the other hand, he deeply longed to labor for Him, to invite others into a relationship with Him, and to represent Him as an ambassador of grace to a needy world.

Obviously, Paul couldn't have both. But which did he desire more?

More importantly, how did the dilemma draw him closer to Christ? And how did its resolution result in encouragement both for him and for us?

— 1:21-26 —

Paul's joyful attitude in the midst of unfavorable conditions was a direct result of placing Christ at the center of his life (1:12-20). In fact, because his whole being revolved around Christ, Paul could honestly say that "whether by life or by death" Christ would be exalted through him (1:20). He sums up this radically Christ-focused approach to life in one of the most profound but puzzling statements in the letter: "For to me, to live is Christ and to die is gain" (1:21).

Paul's real dilemma begins in 1:22 with the word *but*. He longed to be with the Lord in glory . . . *but* he also wanted to live on in the flesh

ON THE OTHER HAND: *SYNKRISIS* IN PAUL

PHILIPPIANS 1:21-26

"I do not know which to choose" (1:22).

In this section, Paul employs a rhetorical device known as *synkrisis*, a this-or-that, compare-and-contrast style that is exercised before arriving at a decision. It's a deliberative device intended to help the author shepherd the readers toward the same conclusion. But besides simply weighing a decision and resolving a dilemma, Paul is doing something even more profound here with *synkrisis*—something that contributes to his overall theme of finding abiding joy in the Christ-centered life.

One commentator notes that *synkrisis* "in ancient Hellenistic writings is sometimes applied to life and death (although in pagan texts it usually carries a tone of profound pessimism about human life)."[11] In a stunning twist, however, Paul's application of *synkrisis* is disarmingly *optimistic*! Whereas those without Christ have no hope—either in life or in death—Paul's twist on this rhetorical device demonstrates that the hope of the Christian faith resolves the human dilemma of life and death by seeing the Christ-centered positives in both. To live? That's to focus fully on Christ and serving Him. To die? That's to be with Christ and behold His face. Or, as Paul has it, "To live is Christ and to die is gain" (1:21).

so he could continue to bear fruit in ministry. Wedged between a rock and a hard place, Paul didn't know which to choose—not that he really had a say in the matter.[12] Paul wasn't contemplating suicide. He wasn't talking about taking his life into his own hands. He was facing a hearing before Caesar's court that could end up with his beheading—as it actually did about five years later. He was at the mercy of the court at the human level, and at the mercy of the sovereign God at the divine level. Nevertheless, as Paul contemplated either outcome—freedom or martyrdom—he thought, "If I had to pick, I'm not sure which I'd choose!"

As in all dilemmas, both alternatives had benefits and liabilities. Paul ponders these in 1:22-24. If Paul were to depart, he would be with Christ immediately (1:23). No longer would he endure stonings, beatings, imprisonments, perils, hunger, or restless nights (see 2 Cor. 11:23-27). The nagging "thorn in the flesh" that had dogged him every day would be gone (2 Cor. 12:7). Instead, he would experience rest and repose in the presence of Christ (2 Cor. 5:8).

On the other hand, Paul's death would leave dozens of disciples without their mentor, hundreds of spiritual children without their father in Christ, and the universal body of Christ without this foundational apostle. Unbelievers would be without his compelling witness to the Resurrection. Believers would be bereft of his encouragement and inspiration (Phil. 1:24).

	BENEFITS	LIABILITIES
TO DEPART (DEATH)	• Die as a martyr in imitation of Christ • Instantly be with Christ in glory • Be free from the pain of this world	• Be absent from those who needed him • No longer be a living witness for Christ • Leave a gap among the apostles
TO REMAIN (LIFE)	• Continue to have fruitful labor in ministry • Provide security and hope to believers • Train the next generation of leaders	• Absent from physical presence of Christ • Absent from heavenly glory • Continue in the suffering of this world

Like any believer suffering great hardship, pain, and the lingering threat of death, Paul longed to be with Christ. But having weighed both prospects, he became convinced that the best path would be to remain for the sake of the "progress and joy" of the Philippians (1:25). In this way, his life became an imitation of Christ, not by following Him in suffering and death, but by surrendering his own interests (to be with Christ) for the sake of others.

In the end, of course, Paul didn't have to choose life or death. This matter was chosen for him by the sovereign plan and purpose of God. This is why he wrote, "I know that I will remain and continue with you all" (1:25). Somehow it had been revealed to him that he would not, in fact, suffer the punishment of death but would be released to visit the Philippians yet again (1:26). How did he know this? It's possible that it had been revealed to him prophetically by the Holy Spirit, just as Peter's imminent execution had been made clear by Christ (2 Pet. 1:14). It's also possible that the Lord had allowed Paul to catch word through the Roman soldiers of the court's disposition concerning his case.[13] Whatever the source of his confidence that the dilemma would resolve itself with his release, it was well with his soul.

— 1:27-30 —

Paul was convinced that he would ultimately be released to continue to serve Christ and minister to the churches, but the timing and manner of his release was uncertain. Though he longed to see the Philippians and had every intention of doing so, he knew that God was the only One whose opinion counted and whose itinerary would come to pass. So, in case his visit was delayed, he wanted to hear that the Philippians were conducting themselves "in a manner worthy of the gospel of Christ" (1:27).

The Greek term translated "conduct yourselves," *politeuomai* [4176], has the sense of behaving as a proper citizen.[14] Later Paul uses the noun form, *politeuma* [4175], when he tells the Philippians, "Our citizenship is in heaven" (3:20). Regardless of how Paul's dilemma would ultimately work out, the responsibility of every Christian is the same: to live as citizens of heaven, not of this world system. What does it look like to live as a citizen of God's heavenly kingdom while here on earth?

First, *we stay together in one spirit and mind* (1:27). We are to live in unity and harmony with each other. We must avoid backbiting, gossiping, stirring up trouble, complaining, fighting, nagging, and all the other negative behaviors that break fellowship and bruise concord. We're to be the vaccine to discord and the antidote to schism, promoting peace and health in the body of Christ rather than debilitating it with poison.

Second, *we strive together for the faith of the gospel* (1:27). The Greek term translated "strive together" is *synathleō* [4866]. From the same root that gives us the word *athlete*, the term brings to mind the image of struggling side by side in a battle like gladiators or soldiers.[15] It's a blood-sweat-and-tears kind of term that implies courage, solidarity, and fighting to the finish.

Third, *we stand together without becoming alarmed by the opposition* (1:28). We should never go out looking for trouble, but when opponents step in our paths, we shouldn't be startled. When they get in our faces, we shouldn't flinch. When critics croon their taunts against the truth, we have no reason to shy away. Instead, we can stare them down in joyful calm. You want to see an opponent crumble? Respond to their angry attacks with joy.

Sadly, I've known many Christians who are scared to death every time a highbrow archaeologist digs up some artifact they claim disproves the Bible. Or they're afraid when a smiling cultist knocks on their door shoving heretical propaganda in their noses. Or they almost jump out of the airplane when the person in the seat next to them asks if they actually believe the Bible they're reading. But there's no reason to be alarmed. Respond with calm confidence and disarming joy.

When we stay together, strive together, and stand together, our united front will draw a clear line in the sand between the spiritual victors and the defeated foes of Christ. Commentator F. F. Bruce explains Paul's thought in 1:28-29:

> The presence of opposition, Paul assures them, shows that they are on the right path in their active gospel witness. It is a token of salvation to them, as it is a token of perdition for their opponents. . . . God is the author of the gospel: those who defend it may therefore expect deliverance and victory from him as surely as those who resist it may expect to incur his judgment.[16]

Opposition—even the kind that results in persecution and suffering—reminds us, as it did for Paul, that we belong to King Jesus and are conducting ourselves as citizens of His kingdom.

Did you notice that when Paul's dilemma was resolved (1:25-26), he gained complete clarity in how to move forward in confident joy? At first stuck between a rock and a hard place, as soon as he was out, the rock became his foundation and the hard place became his strength. When we can embrace joy in the midst of all circumstances—even in the midst of seemingly unsolvable dilemmas—we find ourselves lifted above the fray, gaining a new heavenly perspective for continuing our earthly walk.

APPLICATION: PHILIPPIANS 1:21-30

Dealing with Dilemmas

When I was younger, making decisions was hard, especially choosing between what looked like equally reasonable options. I thought that with age it would get a lot easier. I was happy to acquire a little gray hair if it meant my decisions would be more black and white.

I've logged over fifty years of ministry, and I've learned from experience that just because I may be older and wiser, dealing with dilemmas doesn't necessarily become easier. Some things in life simply aren't easy to decide, and there can be benefits and liabilities on both sides. We will all face dilemmas for the rest of our lives.

In fact, I've thought about this matter of dilemmas for quite some time. I've faced them so often and helped others talk through them so many times that I've been able to categorize them into three different groups.

First, there are *volitional dilemmas*. This is when you want to do two different things at the same time. Suppose you and your spouse want to start a family, but you have two more years of graduate school. You want both, but you feel you must choose. Not an easy decision. Or you have two job offers, and both are very attractive. You want both, but that's impossible. Those are volitional dilemmas.

Second, there are *emotional dilemmas*. You have conflicting feelings about a difficult situation. Years ago, our younger son discovered that his dog had a terrible skin disease. No matter what he did to try to relieve the dog's suffering, it didn't help. It became obvious that the misery of the dog was great, and it forced my son into an emotional dilemma. Should he keep the dog and let the misery go on, or should he put the dog to sleep?

Third, there are what I'll call *geographical dilemmas*. I've faced this several times over my years of ministry. The last big move was leaving California for Texas back in 1994. We loved California, our friends, our church, and the climate; but we also felt drawn to Texas, our old stomping grounds, the ministry opportunities, and the fresh start. We couldn't have both. A California-to-Texas commute was out of the question! So it was a dilemma. Do we stay or do we go?

As God has helped me work through these and countless other dilemmas throughout my life, He has also used the dilemmas to work in me, learning to trust Him, wrestle with Him in prayer, and praise Him for His constant guidance through the gray. Working through those tough decisions has also equipped me to sit down with others who are stuck between a rock and a hard place.

When we're dealing with our own dilemmas, we need to take that opportunity to place Christ as our top priority. It's so easy to get stuck between "this or that" and forget what's most important in life—"to live is Christ" (1:21). As we evaluate two reasonable options, we should ask ourselves questions like: Which of these is more Christlike? Which will bring Him greater glory? Which will better advance the proclamation of the gospel? In that process our own personal priorities will diminish and Christ will be honored.

JOY IN SERVING
(PHILIPPIANS 2:1-30)

Paul's letter to the Philippians spotlights Jesus as the source of a joyful life—authentic, abiding joy that manifests itself in living for others, serving others, sharing with others, and resting in Him. This joy is available to all believers, despite outward circumstances that could crush the spirits of those who have no source of hope.

The purposes of Christian ministry are to introduce people to Jesus Christ, to encourage them to become more like Him, and to equip them to serve others along the same path of faith, love, and hope. The second chapter of Paul's letter to the church in Philippi focuses on the person of Christ as a model to follow in joyous service to others.

The key to this joy in serving is Christlike humility based on a right understanding of the person and work of Christ (2:1-11). This lifestyle finds its source of power not in ourselves, but in the inner working of God (2:12-18). It's also exemplified and encouraged by others who model Christlike, self-sacrificial service (2:19-30).

KEY TERMS IN PHILIPPIANS 2:1-30

morphē (μορφή) [3444] "form," "shape," "external appearance"

In modern lingo, the verb *morph* has come to mean "change shape." It's a shortened form of "metamorphose." But the Greek noun *morphē* simply refers to the "outward appearance" of something.[1] The assumption is that the appearance is consistent with the nature of the thing. In Philippians 2:6-7, the term is used to describe the external condition or appearance that characterized both Christ's heavenly existence in "the form (*morphē*) of God" and His earthly existence after the Incarnation in "the form (*morphē*) of a bond-servant." In this case, the outward manifestation of His divine glory was veiled, and only His outward appearance of full humanity was seen.[2]

kenoō (**κενόω**) [2758] "to make empty," "to nullify," "to divest"

The verb *kenoō* is used to vividly and dramatically describe the selfless humility that Christ exhibited when He veiled His heavenly glory in the Incarnation to live a life in the form of a servant (2:7). In ancient Greek, the verb was mostly used figuratively in the sense of rendering something void (Rom. 4:14) or ineffective (1 Cor. 1:17). When Philippians 2:7 says that Christ "emptied Himself," that doesn't mean He rid Himself of deity or the attributes of deity, but that He humbly set aside the glorious external manifestation of His heavenly existence in order to live among us.

A Christlike Descent into Greatness
PHILIPPIANS 2:1-11

NASB

¹Therefore if there is any encouragement in Christ, if there is any consolation of love, if there is any fellowship of the Spirit, if any ªaffection and compassion, ²make my joy complete ªby being of the same mind, maintaining the same love, united in spirit, intent on one purpose. ³Do nothing ªfrom ᵇselfishness or empty conceit, but with humility of mind regard one another as more important than yourselves; ⁴do not *merely* look out for your own personal interests, but also for the interests of others. ⁵Have this attitude ªin yourselves which was also in Christ Jesus, ⁶who, although He existed in the form of God, did not regard equality with God a thing to be ªgrasped, ⁷but ªemptied Himself, taking the form of a bond-servant, *and* being made in the likeness of

NLT

¹Is there any encouragement from belonging to Christ? Any comfort from his love? Any fellowship together in the Spirit? Are your hearts tender and compassionate? ²Then make me truly happy by agreeing wholeheartedly with each other, loving one another, and working together with one mind and purpose.

³Don't be selfish; don't try to impress others. Be humble, thinking of others as better than yourselves. ⁴Don't look out only for your own interests, but take an interest in others, too.

⁵You must have the same attitude that Christ Jesus had.

⁶ Though he was God,*
　he did not think of equality
　　with God
　as something to cling to.
⁷ Instead, he gave up his divine
　　privileges*;
　he took the humble position
　　of a slave*
　and was born as a human
　　being.

NASB

men. [8]Being found in appearance as a man, He humbled Himself by becoming obedient to the point of death, even death [a]on a cross. [9]For this reason also, God highly exalted Him, and bestowed on Him the name which is above every name, [10]so that at the name of Jesus EVERY KNEE WILL BOW, of those who are in heaven and on earth and under the earth, [11]and that every tongue will confess that Jesus Christ is Lord, to the glory of God the Father.

2:1 [a]Lit *inward parts*   **2:2** [a]Lit *that you be*   **2:3** [a]Lit *according to*   [b]Or *contentiousness*   **2:5** [a]Or *among*   **2:6** [a]I.e. utilized or asserted   **2:7** [a]I.e. laid aside His privileges   **2:8** [a]Lit *of*

NLT

When he appeared in human form,*

[8] he humbled himself in obedience to God
and died a criminal's death on a cross.

[9] Therefore, God elevated him to the place of highest honor
and gave him the name above all other names,

[10] that at the name of Jesus every knee should bow,
in heaven and on earth and under the earth,

[11] and every tongue declare that Jesus Christ is Lord,
to the glory of God the Father.

2:6 Or *Being in the form of God.*   **2:7a** Greek *he emptied himself.*   **2:7b** Or *the form of a slave.*   **2:7c** Some English translations put this phrase in verse 8.

To move forward from the first chapter to the second chapter of Paul's letter to the Philippians, we need to take a step backward to Philippians 1:21, which is a key verse for the epistle: "For to me, to live is Christ and to die is gain." Paul knew that to experience martyrdom and to be ushered into the presence of Christ would be a great gain. But he also knew that God had much more work for him to do in the here and now and that he was called to encourage others to live like Christ.

But how do we truly live like Him? How do we possibly begin to take even one small step closer toward the greatness Christ exhibited as the God-man? Is there a certain series of deeds we need to do? Fruitless! Do we attempt to mimic His miracles? Impossible! Do we become little gods or little messiahs to conform to His divine nature? Blasphemy! No. We're told in the first part of Philippians 2 what it will take. It's actually quite simple, really. In fact, we can reduce it to just two words: selfless humility.

But just because it's simple doesn't mean it's easy. Genuine Christlikeness means embodying and expressing a virtue that's rarely seen on earth. But when it is, we can begin to experience what it is to live as He lived.

— 2:1-4 —

"What's the secret to a great life?" People have pondered this question for millennia—since long before there was a self-help section at a bookstore . . . or twinkle-eyed preachers trading in shallow "believe in yourself" platitudes . . . or cabinets full of supplements and drugs to increase our energy or enhance our effectiveness.

The Bible's answer to that question isn't long, convoluted, or complex. As already indicated, we can sum it up in two words: selfless humility. Not the kind we conjure through mantras or summon through meditation or instill through methods of behavior modification. This is a supernatural kind of selfless humility that has its source in our identification with and imitation of Christ. It results in love, fellowship, affection, compassion, unity, service, and joy. Of all the virtues Christ embodied, selfless humility seems to sum up well His overall character. Jesus Himself said as much to His disciples: "Whoever wishes to become great among you shall be your servant, and whoever wishes to be first among you shall be your slave; just as the Son of Man did not come to be served, but to serve, and to give His life a ransom for many" (Matt. 20:26-28).

Christ taught—through word and action—a descent into greatness. Paul unpacks this principle in Philippians 2:1-11, but he begins in 2:1-4 with the tangible results of Christlike selfless humility before focusing on the example of it in 2:5-11.

In the Greek text of 2:1-4, there is only one imperative: "Make my joy complete" (2:2). In 2:1 a logical (and theological) basis or motivation for the command is given. Paul uses what Greek scholars call a "first class condition." The four "ifs" in 2:1 aren't meant to communicate uncertainty, as if Paul wasn't sure whether there was encouragement in Christ, consolation of love, fellowship of the Spirit, or affection and compassion in the Christian life. Rather, these things are assumed to be true. The "if" clauses imply a logical or reasonable relationship: *Because* these things are true, *then* there should be an attendant effect.[3] It's like a dad saying to his son, "If you're my son, and if I'm your father, and if you're only seven, and if I'm the head of this home, then clean your room."

On the other side of the pivotal command ("make my joy complete") stand four means by which Paul's joy may be filled through the Philippians' response. In fact, the requests in 2:2 mirror the positive assertions in 2:1.

Because these are true:		by doing these:
encouragement in Christ	**then make my joy complete**	being of the same mind
consolation of love		maintaining the same love
fellowship of the Spirit		being united in spirit
affection and compassion		being intent on one purpose

"Being of the same mind" (2:2) doesn't mean that all believers are expected to agree on every minor issue of doctrine, conform to a dress code, or suppress individuality. It means they're to get along, agreeing on the supremacy of Christ and the centrality of the fundamentals of the faith. Paul encourages them, in light of their spiritual oneness in Christ, to be in harmony, not discord . . . in unity, not uniformity. In this Christlike unity, believers can maintain selfless love toward each other and direct their purposes toward the same goal—proclaiming Christ and helping others grow in their relationship with Him.

The great Bible teacher of yesteryear Harry Ironside offers this insight on how the church can achieve a Philippians 2:2 style of unity amid diversity:

> It is very evident that Christians will never see eye to eye on all points. We are so largely influenced by habits, by environment, by education, by the measure of intellectual and spiritual apprehension to which we have attained, that it is an impossibility to find any number of people who look at everything from the same standpoint. How then can such be of one mind? . . . The "mind of Christ" is the lowly mind. And, if we are all of this mind, we shall walk together in love, considering one another, and seeking rather to be helpers of one another's faith, than challenging each other's convictions.[4]

The "one mind" Paul urges for the Philippians—and for us—to have is one of selfless humility. But how is such a feat accomplished? Paul provides some snapshots of selfless humility in 2:3-4. Those who embody this Christlike virtue will not let selfishness or conceit motivate their attitudes, words, or actions. They will regard others as more important than themselves. They won't limit their focus to just their own interests. They'll give attention to the needs of others. But saying you'll behave this way and actually doing it are two different things. This is why Paul turns next to the crux of selfless humility: the person and work of Christ.

— 2:5-11 —

Jesus Christ is the supreme example and source of true selfless humility. In one of the most eloquent passages of Scripture, rightly regarded as a hymn sung in celebration of Christ's person and work,[5] Paul describes Christ's glorious life both before and after His selfless humility was expressed in His incarnation and death on the cross. In 2:5 Paul sets up the hymn, which is then relayed in 2:6-11. He says, "Have this attitude in yourselves which was also in Christ Jesus" (2:5). To understand the extent of selfless humility expected of followers of Christ, we look to the One who is humility incarnate. When we reflect on His person and work, letting this reflection inform our minds and invade our hearts, it will transform our lives by the power of the Holy Spirit.

This Christ hymn can be outlined in three basic movements:

- the Son of God in glory before coming to earth (2:6)
- the Son of God in selfless humility on earth (2:7-8)
- the Son of God in glory after leaving earth (2:9-11)

The Son of God in glory before coming to earth (2:6). Prior to the Incarnation, before the fully divine Son of God—the second person of the eternal Trinity—took on a fully human nature, He existed in eternity in equality with God the Father and God the Holy Spirit. According to commentator Richard Melick, the phrase "He existed in the form of God" means He had "an outward appearance consistent with what is true. The form perfectly expresses the inner reality."[6] This preincarnate existence is further described by the next phrase: "equality with God." Before coming to earth, the Son was fully divine in nature and attributes.

This idea of the full deity of the Son of God is taught elsewhere in the New Testament. Jesus prayed, "Father, glorify Me together with Yourself, with the glory which I had with You before the world was" (John 17:5). In describing Jesus, the apostle John wrote, "In the beginning was the Word, and the Word was with God, and the Word was God" (John 1:1). The author of Hebrews affirms that God the Son is "the radiance of [God's] glory and the exact representation of His nature" (Heb. 1:3).

But what does it mean that Christ "did not regard equality with God a thing to be grasped" (Phil. 2:6)? The noun translated "thing to be grasped," *harpagmos* [725], occurs only here in the New Testament. Outside the New Testament, in negative contexts, it refers to the act of robbery or the loot gained by plundering.[7] Clearly this isn't the meaning in Philippians 2:6. Christ couldn't have tried to rob God of His divine power; divine power was something the Son possessed by being the eternal Son of the eternal Father.

Positively, the noun *harpagmos* could mean something like "a great benefit" or "a favorable lot," like the glory, honor, power, and title that a prince might have by being the son of a king.[8] In this case, the statement that Christ did not regard "equality with God" to be a *harpagmos* would mean that even though as eternal Son the glory, honor, power, and title of deity are His, He did not take the attitude of a spoiled brat who basked in His own glory. Hansen translates this enigmatic verse along these lines: "The one existing in the form of God did not consider it an advantage to exploit to be equal to God."[9] Though he could have clutched the heavenly glory He had with the Father before time and space came into being—and He had every right to do so—He didn't. Christ voluntarily acted with an attitude of selfless humility, not with an air of self-focused superiority.

Along these lines, I like the words of Clement, the late first-century leader of the church of Rome—who may be the same "Clement" described as one of Paul's fellow workers in Philippians 4:3. In his own letter urging Christians to humility, he seems to be reflecting on Paul's Christ hymn of Philippians 2 when he writes: "For Christ is of those who are humble-minded, not of those who exalt themselves over his flock. The scepter of the majesty of God, the Lord Jesus Christ, did not come with the pomp of arrogance or pride (although he could have) but with humble-mindedness" (*1 Clement* 16.1-2).[10] Think about this. God the Son—eternal, all-powerful—didn't regard His exalted position as something to be grasped. Nothing within Him tempted Him to exploit His preeminent position as absolute Sovereign over all. Why not? Because of His perfect love for humanity manifested in selfless humility.

In a state of absolute perfection and full control, Jesus willingly stepped out of His rightful realm of glory for the sake of humanity. Though encompassed by an angelic chorus of perpetual praise, the Son unselfishly came to dwell among those who would curse and abuse Him. Though enwrapped in the radiant light of His own divine glory, God the Son put a veil of flesh over His glory—not diminishing it or extinguishing it, but concealing it—all on behalf of a cold, dark world that sought to plunge Him into the shadow of death.

What an incomprehensible, unfathomable example of selfless humility!

The Son of God in selfless humility on earth (2:7-8). The second movement of Paul's Christ hymn portrays the heavenly Sovereign as

EXCURSUS: DID CHRIST EMPTY HIMSELF OF HIS DEITY?

PHILIPPIANS 2:7

In Charles Wesley's soaring, majestic hymn "And Can It Be?," we sing the following verse:

> He left His Father's throne above,
> So free, so infinite His grace!
> Emptied Himself of all but love,
> And bled for Adam's helpless race![11]

What did Wesley mean by "all but love"? I know some people who won't sing that part because it's vague and potentially misleading. Did Christ give up His deity? His attributes? His throne? But Wesley's poetic rendition was inspired by Philippians 2:7, which says Christ "emptied Himself." And through the centuries this tiny phrase has led to some strange conclusions.

Some have said that this means God the Son gave up His deity and became merely a man. If you find that interpretation in a book or Bible study, throw it away. It's heresy. If you hear it from a pulpit, don't listen. It's blasphemy. Remember, God the Son is *by nature* God—fully, eternally divine. And the Deity cannot change. If He could change, He wouldn't be truly God. Saying that the Son of God voluntarily emptied Himself of His deity is essentially saying He wasn't *truly* God. Others try to soften this by saying He emptied Himself of His attributes of deity. Same thing. The attributes of God are what distinguish God as God. If Christ lost even one attribute in the Incarnation, He never was God to begin with.

The term translated "emptied Himself" is the verb *kenoō* [2758]. Though the term (and its nominal counterpart) can be used literally of physical containers without contents,[12] the vast majority of its uses are figurative. The term is used in Romans 4:14: "If those who are of the Law are heirs, faith is made void." To make faith "void" (*kenoō*) doesn't mean faith is actually destroyed or defeated, but that, in that circumstance, when a person is trying to live by the Law, the effectual power of faith is veiled. Similarly, in 1 Corinthians 1:17, Paul says that preaching the gospel with "words of eloquent wisdom" rather than depending on God to work by His grace could result in the Cross of Christ being "emptied [*kenoō*] of its power" (ESV). Not that the Cross can ever be *objectively* rendered powerless, but in certain situations its inherent power can be clouded, obscured, or veiled—that is, not apparent or evident.

Thus, when Philippians 2:7 says that Christ "emptied Himself," it doesn't mean He gave up His deity or His divine attributes. It means He veiled them. In fact, He gave up the right to use them in situations in which He would have been entirely justified to use them, as He revealed in Matthew 26:53 when He said to Peter, "Do you think that I cannot appeal to My Father, and He will at once put at My disposal more than twelve legions of angels?" Jesus *had* the authority of His divinity; but He voluntarily chose not to use it, in submission to the plan and purpose of the Father.

Theologian Scott Horrell puts it this way:

> The kenosis (or "emptying") of Christ, then, likely refers to the Son of God's voluntary humiliation involved in *adding* a fully human (and therefore finite) nature to His divine, infinite nature and submitting to the suffering and death inherent in that act. This ultimate humility is figuratively called His "self-emptying." We mere mortals are to follow suit and empty ourselves for others.[13]

becoming the earthly Sufferer. In His voluntary descent from heavenly glory to earthly agony, Christ's humility doesn't even stop in the face of the most excruciating form of torture and execution in the ancient world. Consider the steps that Jesus took to share our humanity and die for our sins according to the Father's plan and His own voluntary selfless humility:

1. He emptied Himself (veiling His glorious divine power).
2. He took the form of a bond-servant (becoming fully human).
3. He humbled Himself in obedience unto death (submitting to God's plan).
4. He accepted a most humiliating death: crucifixion (making atonement for sinners).

Many scholars refer to this poetic section of Philippians as the "kenosis hymn" because of the vivid use of the verb *kenoō* [2758] and because it is cast in the ancient form of a hymn to be memorized, recited, or sung. (See explanation of the term "kenosis" in the feature "Did Christ Empty Himself of His Deity?") The "kenosis hymn" can be diagrammed in a V shape, portraying Christ's humiliation and exaltation, from heaven to earth and then from earth to heaven.

The Son of God in glory after leaving earth (2:9-11). God's plan and purpose mandated that God the Son empty Himself by voluntarily, selflessly, and humbly veiling His inherent glory and power in order to take on a humanity like ours (but without sin), subject to pain, suffering,

Kenosis in Philippians 2:6-11

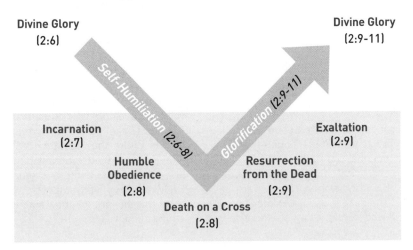

and even death, and to die on the cross for our sins. But once our debt was paid and His mission was accomplished, God raised His Son from the dead, glorified His human body in a miraculous resurrection, and lifted Him again to the position of highest glory and honor.

God not only exalted Jesus to the highest position of authority, but He also bestowed upon the God-man the name of highest significance—the name above every name (2:9). He who willingly bowed to the Father's will in selfless humility is now the recipient of worship, all persons bowing in submission to Him (2:10). Those in heaven will bow—angels and departed saints. Those on the earth will bow, from the most bitter skeptic to the most sincere disciple. And those under the earth will bow—the unsaved, the demonic, and Satan himself—in acknowledgment of the absolute lordship of Christ and His right to rule as God, Judge, and King, "to the glory of God the Father" (2:11).

If Christ, who had every right to remain enthroned on high, selflessly humbled Himself for others, why would any one of us—who have no right to exalt ourselves above anyone—think that we could do otherwise? In this way Christ becomes the perfect example of selfless humility. As Paul said to the Philippians, he says to each of us: "Have this attitude in yourselves which was also in Christ Jesus" (2:5).

APPLICATION: PHILIPPIANS 2:1-11

Beginning Your Descent

Paul's argument in Philippians 2:1-11 is simple: If the God-man, whose right it was to dwell forever in glory, voluntarily and radically surrendered that right *for us*, how could we lowly sinners believe and behave as though selfless humility toward others is beneath us? It's a classic argument from the greater to the lesser. The great question facing each of us today is whether we will follow Christ's example of radical humility by voluntarily and joyfully humbling ourselves, becoming servants of others rather than serving ourselves.

To apply this Christ-centered principle more personally and more specifically, let's go back to the two verses that preceded the Christ hymn. With this example of selfless humility before our eyes (2:5-8), read the following paraphrase of Philippians 2:3-4 and personalize it by filling in the blanks below with the name of someone you are currently struggling to get along with. This person could be a fellow church member, spouse, child, parent, sibling, other relative, friend, boss, employee, or co-worker.

> Following Christ's example and by the Holy Spirit's enablement, I will reject self-seeking glory and vain pride, and I will strive to humbly regard _____ as more important than myself. Rather than constantly looking out for my own interests, I will also look out for the interests of
>
> _____.

Now that you have the *what* and the *who* in place, prayerfully consider the *how*. How will you put this commitment into practice as you perceive the Holy Spirit encouraging you toward greater humility? How will you know if your attitude and actions have really changed toward this person? Don't just wait for opportunities to put this into practice. Find opportunities. Begin this week to live the Christlike life of joyful, selfless humility.

Working Out God's Inner Work
PHILIPPIANS 2:12-18

NASB

12So then, my beloved, just as you have always obeyed, not as in my presence only, but now much more in my absence, work out your salvation with fear and trembling; 13for it is God who is at work in you, both to will and to work for *His* good pleasure.

14Do all things without grumbling or disputing; 15so that you will ªprove yourselves to be blameless and innocent, children of God above reproach in the midst of a crooked and perverse generation, among whom you ᵇappear as ᶜlights in the world, 16holding ªfast the word of life, so that in the day of Christ I will have reason to glory because I did not run in vain nor toil in vain. 17But even if I

NLT

12Dear friends, you always followed my instructions when I was with you. And now that I am away, it is even more important. Work hard to show the results of your salvation, obeying God with deep reverence and fear. 13For God is working in you, giving you the desire and the power to do what pleases him.

14Do everything without complaining and arguing, 15so that no one can criticize you. Live clean, innocent lives as children of God, shining like bright lights in a world full of crooked and perverse people. 16Hold firmly to the word of life; then, on the day of Christ's return, I will be proud that I did not run the race in vain and that my work was not useless. 17But I will rejoice even am being poured out as a drink offering upon the sacrifice and service of your faith, I rejoice and share my joy with you all. [18] You too, *I urge you*, rejoice in the same way and share your joy with me.

2:15 [a] Or *become* [b] Or *shine* [c] Or *luminaries, stars*
2:16 [a] Or *forth*

if I lose my life, pouring it out like a liquid offering to God,* just like your faithful service is an offering to God. And I want all of you to share that joy. [18] Yes, you should rejoice, and I will share your joy.

2:17 Greek *I will rejoice even if I am to be poured out as a liquid offering.*

Examples are wonderful things. People who have gone before us and have lived admirable and exemplary lives are so valuable because they can show us how we ought to live. We can study the lives of great women and men throughout history who have lived inspirational and motivational lives and have set the stage for us to do the same.

We have many examples of good and godly people to imitate, but ultimately, we can look to the radical obedience exemplified in Christ's selfless humility, as described in Philippians 2:6-11. He left the glories of heaven to take on inglorious humanity and live amid suffering, sin, and death. He veiled the brilliance of His divine attributes and willingly accepted the limitations of human life. He ceded angelic adoration and praise to become a victim of torture, and ultimately, of an excruciating death on a cross. And He carried out all of this in perfect obedience. Not one flaw. Not one inconsistency. Not one impatient word. Not one misstep or stray thought contrary to the Father's will.

Mark Twain once wrote, "Few things are harder to put up with than the annoyance of a good example."[14] What about an *impossible* example? I'm not a God-man. Neither are you. Only Jesus, the incarnate Son of God, could embody this kind of supernatural humility and miraculous obedience! How in the world are we expected to follow Paul's exhortation: "Have this attitude in yourselves which was also in Christ Jesus" (2:5)? We can barely follow the good examples of fallen sinners like us!

I've seen a lot of people halfheartedly try to follow Christ's example by faking it in an effort to please others or earn recognition. Like a pop star lip-syncing lyrics on stage while adoring fans look on in ecstasy, some Christ followers put on an outward show when everybody's watching. Then they wipe off the made-up virtues back in their dressing rooms where nobody can see. They focus on *image* rather than *substance*, *doing* rather than *being*.

I've also watched people attempt to live obediently because they think God is some kind of cosmic vending machine that you can pay with good deeds and receive what you want in return. They imitate Christ, fully expecting to experience blessing here and now—usually material riches, physical healing, power, or fame. They want the ecstasy without the agony. They want the glory without the suffering. Perhaps they even want mature obedience, but without the long, buffeting work of patient endurance.

I'm sure neither of these attempts at following Christ's example in Philippians 2:6-11 were what Paul had in mind when he exhorted his audience to conform to the perfect example of Christ. Rather, he wanted them to have a radical new attitude and trajectory. This new trajectory would not lead to earthly perfection, but toward eternal perfection, in a long process of sanctification. It's a life headed in the direction of the perfect obedience of Christ but fully dependent on the inner work of the Holy Spirit to progressively lead in that journey. Philippians 2:12-18 shows us what it looks like to work out that inner working of the Spirit. This passage strikes a perfect balance between our natural condition in which Christlike obedience is impossible and the supernatural inner work of God, which enables us to strive for Christlikeness.

— 2:12-13 —

With a conjunction meaning "therefore" or "for this reason," Paul links 2:12 logically with his previous description of Christ's preeminent example of selfless humility. In light of Christ's example of profound obedience, the Philippians are to build on their own non-hypocritical obedience. At this point, Paul gives them a strange command: "Work out your salvation with fear and trembling" (2:12).

With just a cursory reading of 2:12, we might conclude that Paul is suggesting we need to work hard to earn our salvation! And to make matters worse, we should be shaking in our boots for fear that we might not do enough! If Paul had skipped straight to 2:14, we might be under the impression that Christlikeness is entirely up to us—that God did His part by giving us the example of Christ, and now we're to do the hard work of imitation. But this would be a hasty and false conclusion. Remember that Paul's readers are authentic, born-again believers in Christ. God had already begun a good work in them and would complete it (1:6). So this notion of working out their salvation is not meant to suggest that they are to work *for* their salvation.

We can better understand what Paul means by reminding ourselves of the broader context. What is Paul urging in Philippians 2? He begins

by exhorting his readers to like-minded unity, love, and purposeful-
ness, along with the avoidance of selfishness and conceit (2:2-4) as
Christ demonstrated (2:5-11). In 2:14-15 he again emphasizes how they
are to treat each other in the fellowship of the saints. He urges them to
avoid grumbling and disputing, encouraging them to be "blameless
and innocent" in the midst of a dark and twisted world. So, we can
understand the imperative of 2:12 in this context.[15] The Philippians are
to work out their salvation not in the sense of earning it, but expressing
the reality of their salvation through their practical obedience and selfless humility. The emphasis is on *sanctification* (learning to live more
righteously), not on *justification* (being declared righteous).

But recognizing our inability to practice this kind of Christlike obedience on our own, Paul explains how Christian obedience actually
works. It's like Paul removes the access panel from the Christian life
and we catch a brief glimpse of the inner working that would otherwise
remain unseen. We're able to work out this salvation in real obedience
because God Himself—through His indwelling Spirit—is at work in us
"both to will and to work for His good pleasure" (2:13). As we submit
ourselves to the working of His Spirit, He gives us both the desire and
the power to accomplish His will. He does His invisible work in us by
grace; we simply do what He has commanded.

If we could see the invisible inner working of God with our eyes, it
would take our breath away. He's the One who is striving! He's the One
at work! He's the One empowering us to do the impossible. It's not our
spirit that somehow self-motivates us and perpetuates obedience. The
Spirit of Christ works within us to make us into the people He wants
us to be.

— 2:14-16a —

Next Paul provides a more detailed picture of what working out God's
inner work looks like. It affects our attitude (2:14) and actions (2:15).
We're to do everything "without grumbling or disputing" (2:14). The
word Paul uses for "grumbling" is an onomatopoeia, a word that
sounds like what it is, like "BOOM!" or "CRASH!" or "WHOOSH!" or
"*whisper*." In Greek the word for "grumbling" sounds like a person
mumbling complaints under their breath: *gongusmos* [1112].[16] This is
coupled with "disputing," which refers to complaining and arguing
with others, stirring up dissension and causing strife. These reflect bad
attitudes of discontent and discord—the antitheses of joy.

By checking these joyless attitudes, we demonstrate ourselves to be "blameless and innocent" and "above reproach," as Christ was (2:15; cf. 2:5). Our actions will cause us to shine like brilliant lights in a dark world, or like unbending pillars in a crooked culture. God's goal for His children is not that we retreat from this world into secluded communities. Nor is it His desire that we blend into the world so much that our witness wanes. We are to "[hold] fast the word of life" (2:16), letting nothing slip our grasp as we seek to illumine Christ to all those we encounter.

Jesus said, "You are the light of the world. A city set on a hill cannot be hidden; nor does anyone light a lamp and put it under a basket, but on the lampstand, and it gives light to all who are in the house. Let your light shine before men in such a way that they may see your good works, and glorify your Father who is in heaven" (Matt. 5:14-16). Not only did He say it, but He lived it. And He wants to continue to shine forth through us.

Christians who live with an attitude of joy rather than grumbling and whose pure lives shine like lights in the world will be the talk of the town. They'll transform the morale at the office. They'll become agents of change at school. And if the church as a whole focused on fueling the lights of joyful Christlikeness rather than feeding the fires of mean-spirited conflict, imagine what that could do for our nation or even our world!

— 2:16b-18 —

When the Philippians truly lived out the reality of the inner work of the Spirit in both joyful attitudes and faithful actions (2:14-16a), Paul would be able to see a positive return on his investment of blood, sweat, and tears on their behalf (see 1 Cor. 9:24-27). Paul's lingering concern for all the churches he had planted is that he not be like the runner whose endless hours of training achieved nothing, or like the laborer whose exhausting work produced no results (Phil. 2:16b). Instead, Paul prays that his labor will positively impact the Philippians' ongoing, Christlike, sacrificial service to God.

In 2:17, Paul's tone switches momentarily as he focuses on the grim reality that he could conceivably pour out his very life as a sacrifice for the faith of the Philippians. On the sacrificial imagery Paul uses in this verse, one commentary notes, "In the ancient world, sacrifices, both pagan and Jewish, were usually accompanied and completed by a libation of wine poured out either on top of the sacrifice or at the foot of the altar to honor the deity."[17] Paul felt his life draining away

Toiling in Vain

PHILIPPIANS 2:16

Years ago, a good friend of mine, Dave Roper, was an associate pastor to Ray Stedman at Peninsula Bible Church in Palo Alto, California. I remember Dave telling a story about a time he was ministering on the campus of Stanford University. He had arrived on campus early, before a regular Bible study gathered, and was looking around a courtyard. He noticed an overgrown area and a stonework that was sort of tucked away beneath some vines and overgrown brush.

He made his way over, pulled some vines away, and shoved aside some of the growth to reveal a hand-sculpted birdbath. Completely hidden by overgrowth, the bath was obviously no longer admired, no longer enjoyed even by the little birds that once bathed in its shallow pool.

Dave thought of the hours of work the sculptor had spent on the bath . . . and the labor the landscapers had put into installing it and maintaining it for so many years. Now it was unused. All the toil that had gone into the birdbath had, in a sense, been in vain. In response, Dave sighed and prayed a serious prayer: "Lord, keep me from building birdbaths with my life."

As someone who has been in full-time ministry for more than half a century, I'd hate to look back over my life and wonder whether it was all—or mostly all—for nothing. By the power of the Spirit our human efforts can have heavenly effects.

Photo by Marie-Lan Nguyen/Collection of Charles Hippolyte de Paravey

An image of an ancient libation being poured on an altar

during his long wait for trial, and he was prepared to give his life for the Lord on behalf of the churches he served.

However, throughout his apostolic ministry, Paul had come face-to-face with all sorts of mortal dangers. His imminent trial before Caesar's court was just the latest looming threat that could result in execution. But in classic Pauline style, he balances his somberness with joy. Even if his life were "poured out as a drink offering," he would rejoice, viewing this as a "service" toward the Philippians (2:17). Paul also invited the Philippians to "rejoice in the same way" and share their joy with him (2:18).

William Barclay adds some perspective to this mutual joy:

> Paul was perfectly willing to make his life a sacrifice to God; and, if that happened, to him it would be all joy, and he calls on the Philippians not to mourn at the prospect but rather to rejoice. To him, every call to sacrifice and to toil was a call to his love for Christ, and therefore he met it not with regret and complaint but with joy.[18]

APPLICATION: PHILIPPIANS 2:12-18

Personal Enemy Number One

From Paul's perspective on working out God's inner work in the Christlike life, we recognize that we have one primary enemy who will keep us from walking in step with the Spirit's work: SELF—that is, the sinful self-centeredness inherent in our fallen nature. As soon as we begin to make a little headway, SELF is there to tell us we're pretty special and deserving of praise. That's when true selfless humility flies away and Spirit-empowered obedience comes crashing down.

Even with Christ's example and the Spirit's power, living out our new inner life won't be easy because of SELF. Inside each of us is a rebellious nature that will do everything it can to upset our Christlikeness. It will grouse, dispute, pout, shout, and pull all sorts of shenanigans to convince us to leave God out of our lives and just trust in SELF. Don't let it! Remember Proverbs 16:18: "Pride goes before destruction, and a haughty spirit before stumbling."

Let me share two things to remember as you seek to work out God's inner work by the power of the Spirit in following His perfect example:

1. *Control SELF's urges to take the credit.* Like Paul, make it your goal to exalt Christ, not SELF, in everything. Granted, that won't be easy, but through God's power our hearts and minds can learn to live for Him more than for ourselves. It won't happen overnight. It will require God mercifully and repeatedly picking you up after stumbling. But eventually, with God's enabling grace, SELF can be weakened and begin to lose more battles than it used to win.

2. *Conquer SELF's tendency to take charge.* SELF doesn't like to sit in the backseat or take the passenger side. SELF wants complete control. Don't give in. It is a winnable conflict. But expect a lifelong battle, because SELF will never surrender, never negotiate, and never give in until we die or Christ returns and transforms our sinful SELF into conformity with His glory.

If we depend on our own fallen nature, we'll never work out God's inner work in our lives. Rather, we must lean on Christ to work in us by the power of the Spirit. If we do, He'll help us maintain a Christlike walk, not in constant panic, but with inexplicable joy.

A "Son" and a "Brother"
PHILIPPIANS 2:19-30

NASB

[19] But I hope [a] in the Lord Jesus to send Timothy to you shortly, so that I also may be encouraged when I learn of your condition. [20] For I have no one *else* of kindred spirit who will genuinely be concerned for your welfare. [21] For they all seek after their own interests, not those of Christ Jesus.

NLT

[19] If the Lord Jesus is willing, I hope to send Timothy to you soon for a visit. Then he can cheer me up by telling me how you are getting along. [20] I have no one else like Timothy, who genuinely cares about your welfare. [21] All the others care only for themselves and not for

NASB

22But you know of his proven worth, that he served with me in the furtherance of the gospel like a child *serving* his father. 23Therefore I hope to send him immediately, as soon as I see how things *go* with me; 24and I trust in the Lord that I myself also will be coming shortly. 25But I thought it necessary to send to you Epaphroditus, my brother and fellow worker and fellow soldier, who is also your ᵃmessenger and minister to my need; 26because he was longing ᵃfor you all and was distressed because you had heard that he was sick. 27For indeed he was sick to the point of death, but God had mercy on him, and not on him only but also on me, so that I would not have sorrow upon sorrow. 28Therefore I have sent him all the more eagerly so that when you see him again you may rejoice and I may be less concerned *about you.* 29Receive him then in the Lord with all joy, and hold men like him in high regard; 30because he came close to death ᵃfor the work of Christ, risking his life to complete ᵇwhat was deficient in your service to me.

2:19 ᵃOr *trusting in* **2:25** ᵃLit *apostle* **2:26** ᵃOne early ms reads *to see you all* **2:30** ᵃLit *because of* ᵇLit *your deficiency of service*

NLT

what matters to Jesus Christ. 22But you know how Timothy has proved himself. Like a son with his father, he has served with me in preaching the Good News. 23I hope to send him to you just as soon as I find out what is going to happen to me here. 24And I have confidence from the Lord that I myself will come to see you soon.

25Meanwhile, I thought I should send Epaphroditus back to you. He is a true brother, co-worker, and fellow soldier. And he was your messenger to help me in my need. 26I am sending him because he has been longing to see you, and he was very distressed that you heard he was ill. 27And he certainly was ill; in fact, he almost died. But God had mercy on him—and also on me, so that I would not have one sorrow after another. 28So I am all the more anxious to send him back to you, for I know you will be glad to see him, and then I will not be so worried about you. 29Welcome him in the Lord's love* and with great joy, and give him the honor that people like him deserve. 30For he risked his life for the work of Christ, and he was at the point of death while doing for me what you couldn't do from far away.

2:29 Greek *in the Lord.*

It's impossible to put a price tag on friendship. The relationships we have with some people in our lives are so significant, in fact, that we often liken them to family—"John's an old friend. He's like a father to me." "Sara and I are very close. We're like sisters." "That Dan, he's been at my side like my own son."

Close friends not only help us; they transform us. Just as "bad company corrupts good morals" (1 Cor. 15:33), good company promotes good character: courage, leadership, humility, strength, faithfulness, and joyfulness. Proverbs 17:17 says, "A friend loves at all times, and a brother is born for adversity." Close friends prop us up when we're weak, lift our spirits when we're down, and push us when we peter out. Friends motivate us—sometimes even without words—to be more than we could be without them. As we observe their perseverance, we're prompted to endure hardship. As we hang around a servant leader, seeds of humility are planted into our own lives. As we see a godly saint stare down adversity with a smile, we learn how to have deep-seated joy amid frustrations and challenges.

We shouldn't be surprised, then, that God's Word is filled with references, accounts, and commendations of men and women who were faithful friends—those who remained closer than siblings (see Prov. 18:24). Paul experienced this kind of friendship. Sometimes we are tempted to picture the apostle Paul trudging through forests and swamps, across deserts and over mountains, with someone like Barnabas, Silas, Mark, or Timothy following behind only to help him carry his cloak and scrolls. We may view him as a rugged individualist, a man who didn't really *need* anyone per se, a lone missionary risking all for the sake of the gospel.

But that picture of Paul is completely false. He was a normal man who needed, wanted, and valued friendship. The friends involved, directly or indirectly, in his ministry of evangelism, church planting, teaching, and writing were in the dozens—many names we've heard and others we haven't. From his letters alone the list is massive: over five dozen named men and women supporting, encouraging, or assisting Paul in the work of ministry—and these are just the ones he happens to mention.

In Philippians 2:19-30, Paul focuses his attention on two of his friends who were especially close to him during his time in Rome under house arrest. These men brought him great encouragement, strength, comfort, and joy. One he regards as a "son," the other as a "brother"; both are worth reflection as we consider the faithful friends God has brought into our own lives.

— 2:19-24 —

In all Paul's writings, the friend and ministry companion mentioned more than any other is Timothy. In Philippians 2, Paul informs his readers that he would be sending Timothy to them from Rome in order to bring back personal news of their situation (2:19, 23). He characterized Timothy as having a "kindred spirit" and being someone who had genuine affection for the church in Philippi (2:20). Timothy wasn't simply *told* to go; he wanted to go. Paul says he had "proven worth" (2:22). Since they had been ministering together for over a decade, Paul had been able to observe Timothy in a variety of situations and to see how he handled all sorts of challenges. He was tested and approved. He was, in fact, "like a child serving his father"—a relationship even closer than a friend (2:22).

Who was this young man who figured so prominently in Paul's life and ministry and who appears so frequently in his writings? Paul first encountered Timothy in AD 50, during the first months of his second missionary journey with Silas (Acts 16:1-2). Paul arrived in Lystra, and he heard the Christians speak with glowing praise of the young man. Though Timothy's father had been a Gentile (and presumably an unbeliever), Timothy had been steeped in the Old Testament Scriptures thanks to his Jewish mother, Eunice, and grandmother, Lois (2 Tim. 1:5; 3:14-15). Paul found in Timothy an ideal apprentice. He was an individual much like himself—a scripturally astute, devout follower of Christ with one foot in the Jewish world and the other in the Gentile world. He had a perfect background to join Paul's ministry "to the Jew first and also to the Greek" (Rom. 1:16).

For Timothy to become part of Paul's ministry among the Jews, however, he had to be circumcised (Acts 16:3)—not for spiritual reasons, but for practical ones. While Paul considered himself primarily an apostle to the Gentiles (Eph. 3:1-10), whenever he entered a new city, he first took the gospel to the synagogue (Acts 13:14-15; 17:1-3), and *then* to the marketplace. In order for Timothy to accompany Paul in the Jewish portion of his mission, he had to undergo the rite of access to that community—circumcision. His willingness to do something that was not obligatory for Christians but was expedient for ministry gives us an insight into his passion for the mission.

As the years passed, Paul also found in Timothy a "kindred spirit" (Phil. 2:20). The term translated "kindred spirit" is *isopsychos* [2473], from two Greek words, *isos* [2470], meaning "equal," and *psychē* [5590], meaning "soul" or "mind." Thus it essentially means "being of like mind" or "having much in common."[19] Like Paul, Timothy was studious (2 Tim. 3:14-15), sensitive (2 Tim. 1:3-4), and dedicated (Phil. 2:22).

In time, Paul also came to see Timothy as a reflection of his own ministry priorities and methods, sending his "true child in the faith" (1 Tim. 1:2) to solve problems he normally would have undertaken himself. On his second missionary journey, when Paul worried that the churches in Macedonia—Thessalonica in particular—might have succumbed to Jewish persecution, he sent Timothy to "strengthen and encourage" the members of the church (1 Thes. 3:1-2). During his third missionary journey, he sent Timothy (and Erastus) ahead from Ephesus to prepare the churches in Macedonia and Greece for his visit (Acts 19:21-22). Then, in final preparation for his long-anticipated journey to Spain—not expecting to see most of his pupils again—Paul placed Timothy in charge of the church in Ephesus. This was the most strategically important congregation in Asia and, situated in a center for pagan philosophy, the church most susceptible to corruption.

TIMOTHY IN THE NEW TESTAMENT

The great significance Timothy played in Paul's apostolic ministry is seen in the numerous references to him in the New Testament, including two books written personally to him.

Acts 16:1-3	Philippians 1:1
Acts 17:14-15	Philippians 2:19-24
Acts 18:1-5	Colossians 1:1-2
Acts 19:21-22	1 Thessalonians 1:1-2
Acts 20:1-5	1 Thessalonians 3:1-6
Romans 16:21	2 Thessalonians 1:1
1 Corinthians 4:16-17	The book of 1 Timothy
1 Corinthians 16:10-11	The book of 2 Timothy
2 Corinthians 1:1	Philemon 1:1
2 Corinthians 1:19	Hebrews 13:22-24

— 2:25-30 —

The second close friend Paul mentions appears only in the letter to the Philippians—Epaphroditus (Phil. 2:25-30; 4:18). In this brief snapshot, we still get a clear picture of Paul's friend. To Paul, Epaphroditus is a brother, a fellow worker, a fellow soldier, a messenger, and a minister (2:25). While visiting Paul from Philippi to deliver a financial gift to the apostle from that church (see comments on 4:15-18), Epaphroditus fell ill, even teetering on the brink of death (2:26-27, 30). What I find most remarkable about this is that while deathly sick, Epaphroditus was distressed because of the worry he was causing the Philippians by his illness (2:26). Thankfully, God had mercy on Epaphroditus, restoring him to health and relieving both the Philippians and Paul of their anxiety over him (2:27).

Though having such a faithful friend in Rome would have personally benefited Paul, the apostle decided to send Epaphroditus back to the

TAKING THE ULTIMATE RISK FOR OTHERS

PHILIPPIANS 2:30

When Paul described Epaphroditus as one who had risked his own life for the work of Christ (2:30), he used a Greek word found only here in the New Testament: *paraboleuomai* [3851]. It means to expose oneself to danger and to risk everything.[20] Epaphroditus's example of risking his very life serves as an inspiration for other selfless acts of the saints who risk their lives to minister to others.

Epaphroditus wasn't alone in this self-sacrificial approach to ministry. Either inspired by his example or moved by the same Christlikeness, others throughout history have set aside their own safety and health for the sake of others. A moving description of this kind of risky ministry is found in a description of the ministry of Alexandrian Christians in the face of a plague, recounted by the third-century church father Dionysius of Alexandria:

> The most of our brethren were unsparing in their exceeding love and brotherly kindness. They held fast to each other and visited the sick fearlessly, and ministered to them continually, serving them in Christ. And they died with them most joyfully, taking the affliction of others, and drawing the sickness from their neighbors to themselves and willingly receiving their pains. And many who cared for the sick and gave strength to others died themselves having transferred to themselves their death.[21]

Following these examples, an order of Epaphroditus-like believers known as the Parabolani arose, exhibiting the same kind of life-risking service as their biblical model. One encyclopedia describes the Parabolani as "the members of a brotherhood who in the Early Church voluntarily undertook the care of the sick and the burial of the dead."[22] They were marked by reckless courage, risking their own lives for the sick, dying, and dead, while others turned aside.

church in Philippi, bearing the letter on Paul's behalf. Why didn't Paul keep him around? Likely, Paul wanted to ease the minds of the believers back in Philippi who had been worried about Epaphroditus's physical safety and who were probably wondering whether they had made a mistake in sending him to Paul (2:25-27). Sending Epaphroditus back to his home church would have been a great "thank you" from Paul for the church's own financial contribution to his ministry. Paul knew that Epaphroditus's return home would lead the Philippians to rejoice (2:28-29).

However, it is possible that a few might see the return of Epaphroditus as a failure of his mission and of the purpose of his journey to Paul. Maybe they had expected him not only to deliver financial support, but also to provide physical assistance to Paul for the duration of his imprisonment. Maybe they would have sized him up as a quitter.[23] If so, Paul painted quite a different picture of the man. He expected the church to receive him "in the Lord with all joy" and to hold him "in high regard" (2:29). As a result of his long journey, he had almost lost his life for the cause of Christ and on behalf of the church in Philippi (2:30). Epaphroditus was to be welcomed back, not as a "loser," but as a home-grown hero and an example for them all.

APPLICATION: PHILIPPIANS 2:19-30
Two Orders of Friends

What a friend we have in Jesus,
All our sins and griefs to bear!
What a privilege to carry
Everything to God in prayer![24]

The words of that old hymn "What a Friend We Have in Jesus" remind us that Jesus is not just our God, Savior, and King, but also our close, personal friend. He's available to anyone at any time. He exemplifies selfless humility, sacrificial love, and patience toward people who could never repay His affection.

In the body of Christ we've also been given others who reflect in real, tangible ways the immeasurable friendship of Christ. For Paul, Timothy and Epaphroditus were such friends who exhibited Christlike character. Let's consider the two kinds of friendship encountered in Philippians.

The Order of Timothy. Can you name somebody like Timothy, some individual that you've seen grow into an unselfish adult, perhaps someone in whom you've invested your time, energy, encouragement, and support? There are few things as rewarding as being a mentor for a Timothy, as Paul was. Maybe God is calling you to just that kind of friendship. Maybe you're able to help pay their way through school . . . or support them in a ministry or missions trip . . . or take them under your wing to mentor them or counsel them through hard times. Never underestimate the importance of having a Timothy.

Or maybe you need to be a Timothy to someone else—an older saint involved in ministry who needs support, encouragement, or assistance.

God may be calling you to humbly place yourself in their service, showing genuine concern for their concerns, relieving their stress and burdens, and exhibiting a servant's heart.

The Order of Epaphroditus. This was the man who risked it all for the sake of his call to the service of Christ. Are you willing to join the ranks of Epaphroditus? Truth is, every time you minister to someone in need, you risk something. Every time. You risk being taken advantage of. You risk being misunderstood. You risk being ostracized. In fact, there is no ministry without some kind of risk, great or small. It seems to me that we've become a complacent people, seeking comfort and control over our lives rather than taking even minimal risks for the gospel. Are you willing to start risking for Christ? Have you felt the Spirit nudging you toward certain ministry decisions that might rock your world? Let me tell you, the risk is worth it.

How do you respond to an Epaphroditus in your life? You hold that person in high regard. You don't scold him. You don't despise her. You don't say, "Why are you wasting your time and risking everything for this? Think about your future!" Instead, you lend your prayers, your support, and your encouragement. Of course, when you do that, you step into the Order of Epaphroditus yourself, because inevitably somebody will say to you, "You're a fool to waste your time on somebody as reckless as that!"

The great Roman statesman Cicero said, "He, indeed, who looks into the face of a friend beholds, as it were, a copy of himself."[25] You want to be more Christlike? Befriend those who are of the Order of Timothy and the Order of Epaphroditus—those who exhibit Christlike character that will challenge and transform you.

JOY IN SHARING (PHILIPPIANS 3:1-21)

True joy is a fruit of the Spirit in the life of believers. In fact, it ranks second, after love, in Paul's list in Galatians 5:22-23: "The fruit of the Spirit is love, joy, peace, patience, kindness, goodness, faithfulness, gentleness, self-control; against such things there is no law." Like all manifestations of the Spirit's work in our lives, joy is constantly under attack by the world, the flesh, and the devil.

The deeds of the flesh will try to weaken our joy through things like enmities, strife, jealousy, anger, disputes, dissensions, factions, and envy (Gal. 5:17-21). The world will try to stifle our joy through pain, suffering, tragedies, and stress. And the devil will try to thwart our joy by taking our attention away from Jesus Christ and tempting us to find joy in things that cannot satisfy.

The real threat to the joyful Christian life comes into focus in the third part of Paul's letter to the Philippians. Remember the overarching purpose for Paul's letter to the Christians at Philippi: *to encourage them to find Christ-centered, Spirit-empowered joy in living, serving, sharing, and resting.* Paul reinforces this theme in the opening line of chapter 3: "Rejoice in the Lord." Yet, knowing that there are threats out there, he wants to share with his readers a "safeguard" for their joy (Phil. 3:1). This comes first in the form of a warning about putting confidence in the flesh rather than worshiping God in the Spirit and glorying in Christ (3:2-11). Paul also shares the goal of joyful Christian living—the upward call of God in Christ (3:12-16)—and calls his readers to follow the pattern he has shown them, until the glorious day when their mortal bodies will be transformed to be like Christ's (3:17-21).

KEY TERMS IN PHILIPPIANS 3:1-21

dikaiosynē **(δικαιοσύνη)** [1343] "righteousness," "justice," "fairness"

The term *dikaiosynē* has numerous nuances in the New Testament. At its root is the sense of "uprightness" or "rectitude." In James, the word *righteousness* is used to emphasize the visible manifestation of right actions or moral uprightness (e.g., Jas. 1:20; 2:23). In Revelation 19:11 the term is used to indicate the rightness of Christ's judgment of the world. The apostle Paul, however, typically uses it in more of a legal sense to describe a right standing before God as a result of a declaration of righteousness. In Philippians, as elsewhere in Paul's writings (see Rom. 1:17; 3:22), the "righteousness which is in the Law"—something Paul came to consider impossible—is contrasted with the true "righteousness which comes from God on the basis of faith" (Phil. 3:6, 9).

katatomē **(κατατομή)** [2699] "mutilation"; *peritomē* **(περιτομή)** [4061] "circumcision"

As instituted by God, the rite of circumcision of male Hebrews marked them as "a kingdom of priests and a holy nation" (Exod. 19:6), signifying their role as a people set apart to be a blessing to the nations (Gen. 17:1-14). Jews understood that their circumcision was a sign meant to remind them of their status as God's chosen and elect people. Circumcision was meant to function as an outward symbol to others of God's special favor for the Jewish people. In the early church, there were some Jewish Christians, *Judaizers*, who tried to force Gentile Christians to be circumcised as a requirement to follow Jesus (see Acts 15:1-35; Gal. 2:1-21; 5:1-12). Paul refutes this heresy in Philippians 3 with a blunt play on words. He contrasts the "true circumcision" of the Spirit—believers in Christ who actually fulfill their calling by God's grace to be a light to the nations—with the "false circumcision" of the flesh—hypocritical, self-righteous "evil workers" who put their confidence in the outward, physical expressions of religion. In reference to the latter, Paul uses a slight variation of the term for "circumcision" that means, literally, "cut off" or "mutilated" (3:2).

Human Rubbish versus Divine Righteousness
PHILIPPIANS 3:1-11

NASB

¹Finally, my brethren, rejoice in the Lord. To write the same things *again*

NLT

¹Whatever happens, my dear brothers and sisters,* rejoice in the Lord. I never get tired of telling you these

is no trouble to me, and it is a safeguard for you.

²Beware of the dogs, beware of the evil workers, beware of the ᵃfalse circumcision; ³for we are the *true* ᵃcircumcision, who worship in the Spirit of God and glory in Christ Jesus and put no confidence in the flesh, ⁴although I myself might have confidence even in the flesh. If anyone else has a mind to put confidence in the flesh, I far more: ⁵circumcised the eighth day, of the nation of Israel, of the tribe of Benjamin, a Hebrew of Hebrews; as to the Law, a Pharisee; ⁶as to zeal, a persecutor of the church; as to the righteousness which is in the Law, found blameless.

⁷But whatever things were gain to me, those things I have counted as loss for the sake of Christ. ⁸More than that, I count all things to be loss ᵃin view of the surpassing value of ᵇknowing Christ Jesus my Lord, ᵃfor whom I have suffered the loss of all things, and count them but rubbish so that I may gain Christ, ⁹and may be found in Him, not having a righteousness of my own derived from *the* Law, but that which is through faith in Christ, the righteousness which *comes* from God on the basis of faith, ¹⁰that I may know Him and the power of His resurrection and ᵃthe fellowship of His sufferings, being conformed to His death; ¹¹ᵃin order that I may attain to the resurrection from the dead.

3:2 ᵃLit *mutilation;* Gr *katatome*   3:3 ᵃGr *peritome*
3:8 ᵃLit *because of*   ᵇLit *the knowledge of*
3:10 ᵃOr *participation in*   3:11 ᵃLit *if somehow*

things, and I do it to safeguard your faith.

²Watch out for those dogs, those people who do evil, those mutilators who say you must be circumcised to be saved. ³For we who worship by the Spirit of God* are the ones who are truly circumcised. We rely on what Christ Jesus has done for us. We put no confidence in human effort, ⁴though I could have confidence in my own effort if anyone could. Indeed, if others have reason for confidence in their own efforts, I have even more!

⁵I was circumcised when I was eight days old. I am a pure-blooded citizen of Israel and a member of the tribe of Benjamin—a real Hebrew if there ever was one! I was a member of the Pharisees, who demand the strictest obedience to the Jewish law. ⁶I was so zealous that I harshly persecuted the church. And as for righteousness, I obeyed the law without fault.

⁷I once thought these things were valuable, but now I consider them worthless because of what Christ has done. ⁸Yes, everything else is worthless when compared with the infinite value of knowing Christ Jesus my Lord. For his sake I have discarded everything else, counting it all as garbage, so that I could gain Christ ⁹and become one with him. I no longer count on my own righteousness through obeying the law; rather, I become righteous through faith in Christ.* For God's way of making us right with himself depends on faith. ¹⁰I want to know Christ and experience the mighty power that raised him from the dead. I want to suffer with him, sharing in his death, ¹¹so that one way or another I will experience the resurrection from the dead!

3:1 Greek *brothers;* also in 3:13, 17.   3:3 Some manuscripts read *worship God in spirit;* one early manuscript reads *worship in spirit.*   3:9 Or *through the faithfulness of Christ.*

Our world honors and rewards high achievement. Trophies, medals, plaques, and awards are given to those who stand out among the crowd. Though there's nothing inherently wrong with appreciating and applauding great accomplishments, these accolades can be very deceptive, leading many to believe that their earthly successes and temporal earnings can somehow translate into heavenly merits or eternal rewards.

Among the many worldly messages we're tempted to believe, the one that emphasizes self-promotion—that is, finding confidence in our own pedigrees and achievements—can be the most alluring. In such a world, how desperately we need God's truth! If for no other reason than to counteract society's lies, we need His principles and precepts to guide us aright. Again and again in the Bible we discover a perspective that stands in stark contrast with the rubbish on the street. In our fight-back, get-even world it's so easy to embrace the philosophy espoused there and to adopt its methods.

If anyone ever had the opportunity to boast of their accomplishments, Saul of Tarsus was that person. In fact, that's exactly what he did throughout his adult life—until he met and bowed before Jesus as Lord. That encounter changed everything. From then on he considered all things outside of Christ and His righteousness as mere "rubbish" (3:8).

— 3:1-3 —

Paul opens the third chapter with a unique phrase that appears for the first time here and only again in Philippians 4:4 and 4:10 in the entire New Testament: "Rejoice in the Lord." Yet this refrain sums up what Paul has been accentuating repeatedly with his emphasis on joy and rejoicing (see 1:25; 2:2, 17-18, 28-29). If we recognize Philippians 3:1 as a kind of hinge that transitions Paul from one subject within a broader theme to another, we can better understand the significance of the unique phrase "rejoice in the Lord."

In 3:1 Paul uses an introductory phrase that suggests he is shifting lanes, so to speak—still driving in the same direction, but covering a different line of discussion. He begins with a Greek phrase, *to loipon* [3588 + 3063]. The New American Standard Bible translates the phrase "finally," implying that Paul is concluding his thoughts. However, the New International Version renders it "further," and the New Living Translation uses the expression "whatever happens." In fact, all of these are possible renderings of the enigmatic adverbial phrase.[1] However, I think the translations "furthermore" or "in any case" make the most sense. After all, Paul goes on to write two more meaty chapters!

The imperative "rejoice in the Lord," then, serves not simply to sum up his previous discussion, but to advance it in order to "safeguard" his readers from some imminent harm to their authentic joy. In particular, Paul knew there were legalistic joy stealers, often referred to as Judaizers, on the prowl, hounding the Gentile believers to live by their strict, man-made religious codes. Instead of rejoicing *in the Lord* and the grace of salvation that comes only through His person and work, they were rejoicing in their own accomplishments in fulfilling the Law. This threat was so serious that Paul denounced it with three disparaging descriptions (3:2).

First, in comparing the legalists to "dogs," Paul didn't have in mind polite, pampered, and potty-trained house pets. Instead, picture feral dogs roaming the backstreets in packs—dirty, flea-infested, disease-ridden scavengers with uncertain pedigrees . . . mangy mutts! They were uncontrolled and dangerous to anybody who got too close. So Paul warns the Philippians to stay away! Some self-righteous Jews of the time also used the term "dogs" to refer to unclean Gentiles. Thus it's ironic that Paul turns the insult on these Jewish Christians who were trying to prop up their man-made ways of purity.

Second, he calls them "evil workers." Ironically, the Judaizers were claiming to be the promoters of good works—works so good, in fact, that they could merit a right standing before God. However, Paul says they were actually workers of evil. They sowed a corrupt, twisted non-gospel, teaching that people could be saved only by faith *plus* works of the Law. However, the good news of Jesus Christ is that salvation is by grace alone (it's a gift!), through faith alone (not by works!), in Christ alone (not by any means other than the person and work of Christ!). We are to rejoice *in the Lord* and what He has done for us, not in any human means of trying to gain favor with God.

Third, the false teachers are "the false circumcision." This translation softens the harsh language evident in Paul's original Greek. He uses a Greek term that sounds similar to the word for "circumcision," but he modifies it slightly to render the word for "cutting off," "mutilation," or perhaps, in this specific context, "castration"! This is how Paul describes those who say that men must be circumcised to be saved.

Having fired back at the robbers of Christ-centered joy, Paul concludes his warning by reminding the Philippians that genuine Christians are "the true circumcision" (3:3). He mentions three fundamental differences between the authentic bearers of God's redemption and the pretenders. First, true believers "worship in the Spirit of God," meaning their focus is on the work of the divine Spirit in salvation, not on fleshly means of personal merit. Second, unlike those who bragged about their achievements before God by keeping the Law, Christians "glory in Christ Jesus." And third, authentic Christ followers "put no confidence in the flesh." They rejoice *in the Lord*—not in human works, not in personal piety, not in anything but the person and work of Christ.

— 3:4-6 —

In order to expose the absurdity of those who place confidence in their own achievements, wrought in their own power for the purpose of meriting approval with God, Paul uses himself as an example. Remember, the rabid dogs in Paul's crosshairs were trying to boast about keeping the Law. Now, with one twang of his bow after another, Paul pierces the Judaizers' position by demonstrating that if anybody could boast about their fleshly achievements, it was he himself (3:4). If anybody could have merited favor with God, it would have been this ex-Pharisee whose religious trophies could have lined the walls of a Hall of Fame:

- circumcised on the eighth day as a son of the covenant (3:5)
- born into the nation of Israel, not a converted Gentile (3:5)
- a member of the tribe of Benjamin, an honorable people (3:5)
- a true Hebrew among Hebrews, the best of the best (3:5)
- a Pharisee with respect to observance of the Law (3:5)
- a zealous persecutor of the church in the name of the Law (3:6)
- blameless with regard to external righteousness found in the Law (3:6)

If you were a first-century Jew, you'd be impressed by this list! Paul was the Jew par excellence. He set a high bar for his fellow Jews and an impossible standard for any Gentiles who would hope to fulfill the Law themselves. If the Law were the authentic standard of right standing with God, Paul would have been the paragon of righteousness.

— 3:7-8 —

If you had been able to listen to the Jerusalem rabbis of the day, perhaps you would have heard them name-dropping Saul of Tarsus—that brilliant, passionate rabbinical student who studied under the famous teacher Gamaliel in Jerusalem. When his teachers wanted to scold the less rigorous young men, they may have pointed at Saul and said, "Why can't you be more like him?" And when Saul secured a special commission from the high priest in Jerusalem to help put an end to the Christ followers (Acts 9:1-2), his future as a rising star in Judaism seemed bright.

Until Damascus.

At that point everything changed.

A blazing light from heaven blinded him in an instant, and he heard a voice calling out to him, "Saul, Saul, why are you persecuting Me?" (Acts 9:4).

Traumatized by the sudden encounter with what was clearly a heavenly being—but still completely clueless that he was following the wrong path of devotion—Saul asked, "Who are You, Lord?" (Acts 9:5).

Saul must have stopped breathing and his heart must have sunk when he heard the reply: "I am Jesus whom you are persecuting" (Acts 9:5).

At that moment, the entire checklist of achievements became a pointless scribbling on paper. The trophies of spiritual accomplishments in the display case of his pride turned to dust and blew away. The years and years of torturous labor to distinguish himself "as to the Law . . . as to zeal . . . as to the righteousness which is in the Law" (Phil. 3:5-6)—an utter waste of time, energy, and talent. The words of Isaiah 64:6 became a personal reality for Saul: "All [my] righteous deeds are like a filthy garment."

Having highlighted his accomplishments in Philippians 3:4-6, Paul starts the next statement with a pronounced *BUT!* There are two main words for the contrastive conjunction "but" in Greek: *de* [1161] and *alla* [235]. The softer transitional word *de* is a continuative conjunction, sometimes rendered "but," though also translated "and" or even "now."[2] It could thus imply a very gentle contrast: "Now, whatever things were gain to me . . ." But that's not the word Paul used. Instead, he used *alla*, which implies a much more pronounced contrast: "*But on the contrary*, whatever things were gain to me . . ."[3] The point is clear: Paul is utterly rejecting his former confidence in self-righteousness that was based on his pedigree and prominence in Judaism in favor of "the surpassing value of knowing Christ Jesus my Lord" (3:8).

In making this radical contrast, Paul employs some pretty strong language to drive home his point. In fact, the language he uses increases in rhetorical power, and I imagine the Philippians got the message loud and clear by the time Paul's emphasis shifted to the righteousness that comes through Christ (3:9).

First, Paul begins the pummeling of his past with a vivid image: "Whatever things were gain to me, those things I have counted as loss for the sake of Christ" (3:7). He once regarded his previous religious achievements to be profitable, advantageous, and commendable. But now? These things are recategorized in Paul's mind as "loss." The Greek term used for "loss" is *zēmia* [2209], which is also used in Acts 27:10 for the cargo and lives lost in a shipwreck. Throughout his life, Saul of Tarsus had, as it were, stored up a cargo of what he thought were priceless goods, but that whole cache had been torpedoed by God's saving grace on the road to Damascus. Instead of mourning for the loss, Paul regarded it as a necessary casualty "for the sake of Christ."

Photo by Elie plus at English Wikipedia

Paul considered his former accomplishments in Judaism to be useless, burdensome cargo compared to his new life in Christ.

Next, to avoid any sense that he was regretting the loss of those things he had so highly valued in his former life in Judaism, Paul insists, "More than that, I count all things to be loss in view of the surpassing value of knowing Christ Jesus my Lord" (Phil. 3:8). Everything that had shined so brightly in his life—not just the glory of his former emphases in Judaism—had faded to darkness when placed in the exceedingly brilliant light of the knowledge of Christ's salvation.

Finally, Paul pulls out all the rhetorical stops as he reaches a shocking climax: "For [Christ] I have suffered the loss of all things, and count them but rubbish so that I may gain Christ" (3:8). The term politely translated "rubbish" would have likely raised eyebrows or caused a few gasps when the Philippians first read or heard it. The Greek word Paul chose to compare all earthly treasures and accomplishments to Christ is *skybalon* [4657]. The term literally means "dung, excrement, manure."[4] On this word one commentator notes, "Some scholars are prone to translate this as 'garbage.' It is used for 'dung,' however, and the strongest possible contrast makes best sense of this passage."[5]

— 3:9-11 —

With his ego-laden ship sunk, Paul wasn't mourning his loss but shouting out a jubilant "Good riddance!" What his spiritually blinded eyes had seen as a boatload of treasures, the light of Christ had revealed as a pile of manure! Instead of mourning the loss of those useless things he had hoarded by his own strength, Paul rejoiced *in the Lord* (3:1) for receiving things he could never have earned on his own:

- being found in the Lord Jesus Christ (3:9)
- receiving righteousness from God, not from himself (3:9)
- being justified by faith, not by works of the Law (3:9)
- knowing Christ (3:10)
- experiencing the power of Christ's resurrection (3:10)
- sharing in Christ's sufferings and death (3:10)
- embracing the hope of resurrection from the dead (3:11)

In 3:9 we find a great summary of the doctrine known as *imputation*, a term that refers to crediting something to a person's account. Here's a simple definition of how the word is used theologically: "In salvation, our sin and guilt are credited to Christ, and His righteousness is credited to us."[6] Because Paul was now "in Christ" (see 3:9), everything that Christ had accomplished through His death and resurrection—payment for sin and eternal life—had been credited to Paul's otherwise bankrupt account. Paul had thought that the massive sum in his "righteousness" account had made him rich. What he hadn't realized was that the balance was a negative number! The righteousness that was credited to Paul's account the moment he embraced Christ by faith was the unmeasurable righteousness of the perfect God-man. And Christ's righteousness not only canceled Paul's debt, but it also placed in his account "everything pertaining to life and godliness" (see 2 Pet. 1:3).

The result of this new relationship was that the power of Christ's resurrection became a present reality for Paul, allowing him to rejoice even as he shared in Christ's sufferings (Phil. 3:10). Paul could now see that the sufferings he was enduring for his faith were a means of conforming him to Christ's character of selfless humility. And this new relationship sealed the promise of future hope—attaining to the resurrection from the dead (3:11).

APPLICATION: PHILIPPIANS 3:1-11
An Invitation to High Achievers

To put Paul's accomplishments in Judaism in perspective, let me cast them in a more modern idiom. He had obtained all the honors: Eagle Scout, homecoming king, valedictorian, a full-ride scholarship to an Ivy League school. He had graduated summa cum laude, going on to excel in his field with every possible honor. But then he realized that, in comparison to knowing Christ, everything he had accomplished turned out to be filthy rags. Rubbish. Useless. Dung!

Paul's ancient words hit today's overachievers hard. For those who see high achievement as paramount and seek after rewards and recognition—this passage is for you. Our righteousness, good works, fame, riches, and impressive achievements will not get us one step closer to heaven or one mark higher in God's estimation. In fact, these will drive us further away from depending on Christ alone for salvation. This warning also addresses believers who have received Christ's salvation by grace alone through faith alone, but who nevertheless turn to their own strength and accomplishments to live Christlike lives. That, too, is an impossibility.

A couple very simple reminders grow out of the contrast Paul shares in Philippians 3:1-11. First, *trusting in your own achievements can bring you glory now, but it leaves you spiritually bankrupt later*. The hardest part of getting driven, self-made, "type A" people to understand the gospel is to help them understand that grace is *unmerited* favor. It can't be earned. It can't be bought. It can't be sought and found. It can only be received. This hard truth is painful for go-getters who have come to believe that anything worth having is worth sweating for. The truth is, when it comes to salvation, surrendering our efforts is the only way to gain a restored relationship with God, the result of which is eternal life.

Second, *trusting in Christ's accomplishment on the cross gives Him the glory now and results in our eternal righteousness*. This is what Paul means when he tells the Philippians to "rejoice in the Lord" (3:1). We glory in Him, not in ourselves. We celebrate His accomplishments for us, not our work for Him. We praise and thank Him for who He is and what He has done, forgetting ourselves and our achievements and ignoring our own résumés. We give Him glory now. Paul discovered—and perhaps you will too—that all human efforts to live a life pleasing to God apart from Christ are pointless and fruitless.

Hanging Tough and Looking Up
PHILIPPIANS 3:12-21

NASB

¹²Not that I have already obtained *it* or have already become perfect, but I press on ªso that I may lay hold of that ᵇfor which also I was laid hold of by Christ Jesus. ¹³Brethren, I do not regard myself as having laid hold of *it* yet; but one thing *I do:* forgetting what *lies* behind and reaching forward to what *lies* ahead, ¹⁴I press on toward the goal for the prize of the upward call of God in Christ Jesus. ¹⁵Let us therefore, as many as are ªperfect, have this attitude; and if in anything you have a different attitude, God will reveal that also to you; ¹⁶however, let us keep ªliving by that same *standard* to which we have attained.

¹⁷Brethren, join in following my example, and observe those who walk according to the pattern you have in us. ¹⁸For many walk, of whom I often told you, and now tell you even weeping, *that they are* enemies of the cross of Christ, ¹⁹whose end is destruction, whose god is *their* ªappetite, and *whose* glory is in their shame, who set their minds on earthly things. ²⁰For our ªcitizenship is in heaven, from which also we eagerly wait for a Savior, the Lord Jesus Christ; ²¹who will transform ªthe

NLT

¹²I don't mean to say that I have already achieved these things or that I have already reached perfection. But I press on to possess that perfection for which Christ Jesus first possessed me. ¹³No, dear brothers and sisters, I have not achieved it,* but I focus on this one thing: Forgetting the past and looking forward to what lies ahead, ¹⁴I press on to reach the end of the race and receive the heavenly prize for which God, through Christ Jesus, is calling us.

¹⁵Let all who are spiritually mature agree on these things. If you disagree on some point, I believe God will make it plain to you. ¹⁶But we must hold on to the progress we have already made.

¹⁷Dear brothers and sisters, pattern your lives after mine, and learn from those who follow our example. ¹⁸For I have told you often before, and I say it again with tears in my eyes, that there are many whose conduct shows they are really enemies of the cross of Christ. ¹⁹They are headed for destruction. Their god is their appetite, they brag about shameful things, and they think only about this life here on earth. ²⁰But we are citizens of heaven, where the Lord Jesus Christ lives. And we are eagerly waiting for him to return as our Savior. ²¹He will take our weak

NASB

body of our humble state into conformity with [b]the body of His glory, by the exertion of the power that He has even to subject all things to Himself.

3:12 [a]Lit *if I may even* [b]Or *because also* **3:15** [a]Or *mature* **3:16** [a]Lit *following in line* **3:19** [a]Lit *belly* **3:20** [a]Lit *commonwealth* **3:21** [a]Or *our lowly body* [b]Or *His glorious body*

NLT

mortal bodies and change them into glorious bodies like his own, using the same power with which he will bring everything under his control.

3:13 Some manuscripts read *not yet achieved it.*

In a predominantly humanistic society like ours, it's not uncommon to hear the glories of humanity exalted in exaggerated terms. Our "open-minded" media parade before our eyes immoral living as a virtue. They promise social progress through secular and even anti-Christian means. From politics to education, from spirituality to ethics, our sophisticated, twenty-first-century world functions on the presupposition that people are basically good, society can get better, and the only thing standing in the way is backward-thinking Neanderthals who can't pull their noses out of an ancient, outdated book like the Bible.

The problem with this widely popular narrative is that its foundations are completely false. People are not basically good, the world is not getting better, and our hope is not in humanity.

The truth is, this world is in rough shape. War, not peace, is the norm. Quarrels, conflicts, lawsuits, and family feuds are commonplace. Friendships cool, marriages fracture, partnerships dissolve, personalities collide, and churches split. Why? Because the depravity of humanity has taken an awful toll on this world. Sin abounds. Death, destruction, pain, and chaos are the order of the day.

Yet God has chosen to leave believers on this earth, not to retreat from its pain and suffering, but to engage it—up close and personal. This calling requires us to strap in for a bumpy ride, to hang tough for the long haul. On this rough road between the first and second comings of Christ, we need to keep our heads up, our eyes forward, and our hearts heavenward. The Christian life is a marathon—not through the level, paved streets of a clean and friendly city, but across rocky, toilsome, dangerous terrain filled with pitfalls and predators.

It's comforting to know that we're not the first Christians to make this journey through a wicked, hostile world. Those who have gone before us have cut a path for us to follow. In Philippians 3:12-21 the apostle Paul establishes several markers along the route—important truths to take to heart and practical advice to follow as we hang tough . . . and look up.

— 3:12-16 —

When Saul of Tarsus was confronted by Christ on the road to Damascus (Acts 9:1-6), his whole world was turned upside down—or, rather, right-side up. He had been leaning on his laurels, relying on religion, trusting in tradition, and priding himself on his pedigree. But all of that disintegrated before the glorious, transforming power of the gospel of Jesus Christ. He experienced salvation by grace alone through faith alone in Christ alone. From that moment on, joy entered into his life—true, abiding, deep-seated joy that could keep him singing even during his darkest days and most depressing circumstances (see Acts 16:25).

But this didn't mean Paul had "arrived." His Damascus-road experience didn't pluck him from earth and place him in the foyer of the heavenly Jerusalem. Rather, it turned him from the wrong path and started him on a new journey. A new quest for Christlikeness had commenced. The obstacles on the path and the distractions from the world became even more dangerous, requiring him to "press on" (Phil. 3:12).

In Paul's profound description of the journey of faith in Philippians 3:12-16, we can see a number of vital principles. I find at least five reminders Paul felt were important to share with those who are on that same path.

First, *God's plan is progress . . . not perfection* (3:12). Paul was clear: He had not yet obtained the full outcome of his salvation. As one commentator notes, the "it" in 3:12 probably refers to "the experiential process begun in his salvation. He looked forward to the resurrection from the dead and, secondarily, to the process of conformity to death which would bring it forth."[7] Paul was on the same path as every one of us. He had been *justified* (declared righteous by God) on the basis of the merits of Christ, and like all of us, he was in the process of being *sanctified* as he looked forward to one day being *glorified* through resurrection.

Perfection in this life is not possible. We are frail, fallen, feeble humans; and we will continue in this state until our death. Not only are we imperfect, but so is everyone around us. The best, most moral, most Christlike person who has ever lived is still a wicked sinner saved by grace, unable to be compared to the perfect standard of holiness we see in Christ.

But constant progress toward Christlikeness is possible. I've seen believers get very frustrated with their lack of stunning progress in their pursuit of Christlikeness. I've seen them peter out. I've seen them fail. They get down on themselves for their inability to measure up to an impossible standard in this life. This is precisely when they need to hear that the plan is progress, not perfection. We press on in spite of knowing that in this life we will never fully arrive.

Second, *the past is over . . . so leave it behind* (3:13). We can press on through the long haul when we keep our eyes on the road ahead of us rather than being obsessively fixated on what's behind. To emphasize this point, Paul uses the Greek word *epilanthanomai* [1950], which means "disregard" or "put out of mind."[8] Paul isn't talking about forgetting people in our pasts or vital life lessons or edifying experiences or positive things Christ has done. In this specific context, Paul's talking about the "rubbish" that was strewn in the road when his old life prior to Christ exploded—all his self-righteous striving, and the harm he had done in his pride, arrogance, blasphemy, and heresy (3:4-8; 1 Tim. 1:13, 15). Living in the past—whether basking in old glories or pouting over old defeats—keeps us from advancing boldly into the future.

Think about it. If you drive a car while looking only in the rearview mirror, how far will you get before you drive off the road? You can't dwell on the past if your goal is to move forward. In relation to basking in the past, I find that people who live in the glory of past achievements slacken their efforts for what they might be able to do today. They keep calling to mind the way things were, perhaps even something God did, some great accomplishment He performed. One place this is often seen is in older churches or ministries that obsess over what they once were. We don't want to dishonor our history, but we need to minister in the here and now. We honor the past, we are thankful for the past, and we learn from the past. But we don't worship the past.

With respect to pouting over the past, I'm sure we've all had times when we just couldn't get our minds to stop rerunning scenes of defeat or episodes of disappointment. We all have them—every one of us. These experiences can be great teachers of God's faithfulness in spite of our failures. But to keep projecting that same old reel over and over and over again in our minds will hinder us from engaging in new experiences, making new memories, and learning new lessons.

Third, *the future holds out hope . . . so reach for it* (Phil. 3:13-14). In the same pivotal movement in which Paul consciously lets go of his past, he turns his full attention to the future, pressing on "toward the goal for the prize of the upward call of God in Christ Jesus" (3:14). Here Paul employs language reflecting the intensity of an athlete running a desperate race to the finish line, eager to win first prize. The word translated

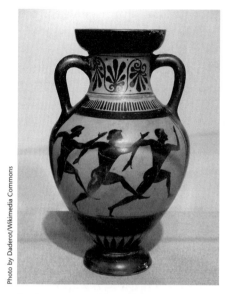

Photo by Daderot/Wikimedia Commons

Paul compares himself to a runner to illustrate the pursuit of progress in the Christian life and the eternal prize.

"reaching forward" (3:13) is *epekteinomai* [1901], a vivid athletic term. One commentator notes, "It means that the athlete throws himself forward in the race with all his energies strained to the very utmost."[9] If earthly athletes give their all for temporal awards, how much more should we who are recipients of a heavenly call push ourselves to receive a heavenly reward?

Fourth, *the secret is a determined attitude ... so maintain it* (3:15). Paul reminds us that it's all about our attitude. The verb translated "have this attitude" (*phroneō* [5426]) means to "set one's mind on" or "be intent on."[10] In light of his personal example of looking forward, not backward, Paul calls his readers to focus all their attention and energy on pressing on in the Christian life.

But why does Paul urge only the "perfect" to have this attitude? Doesn't this sound like a contradiction? How could he say "as many as are perfect" here, but in 3:12 assure the Philippians that he hadn't "become perfect"?

In 3:12, Paul used the Greek verb *teleioō* [5048], meaning "to complete an activity" or "bring to an end."[11] Paul was stating that he hadn't yet reached the end of his journey, which would only occur when he attained his heavenly home and was experiencing glorious, immortal life beyond the resurrection (3:10-11). And this state was certainly not his to be had in the present life. Until then, he would continue to press on toward greater and greater Christlikeness.

In 3:15, Paul uses a similar but distinct term, the adjective *teleios* [5046], to describe the type of person he is addressing with his admonition to press on. This word is best translated not as "perfect" but as "mature."[12] His use of this term here is similar to how he uses it in 1 Corinthians 2:6—"We do speak wisdom among those who are mature." They were not *perfect* in the absolute sense, but mature to the point that they were able to take spiritual things seriously. I like how

Stuart Briscoe paraphrases Paul's thought here: "I am complete in the sense that I have grown as far as I can at the present, and I am ready for the next lesson."[13]

But what about those who aren't mature enough to face the future with the kind of all-out determination and dedication Paul exemplifies? The last part of Philippians 3:15 answers that: "If in anything you have a different attitude, God will reveal that also to you." Paul graciously acknowledges that everybody grows up in Christ at different paces. In the spiritual marathon, some will be nearing the finish line at full speed . . . others will be farther behind . . . some will be trudging along at a snail's pace . . . and a few will be dragged along by others! Paul knew that not everybody was yet in the same condition for running the race at top speed. But he was confident that God would continue to work in them toward the upward call in Christ Jesus.

Finally, the need is to keep a high standard . . . together (3:16). Did you notice that Paul shifted the focus from himself as the example in 3:12-14 to include all believers in the journey in 3:15-16 by saying "let us"? Living the Christian life is a team effort, not a solo mission. As each of us maintains our own level of spiritual maturity, we also encourage others to do the same. We are to lock arms with our brothers and sisters in the family of God. If we see one of our brothers slowing down in the race, we need to take him by the arm and encourage him to press on. When we see a sister out of breath from the exasperating challenges of life, we need to remind her to look up and look forward, to press on toward maturity.

— 3:17-21 —

In the concluding verses of this chapter, Paul's words take on a serious tone . . . but only for a moment. He needs to remind his readers of something he has learned through personal experience: The path before us is not only littered with numerous pitfalls that can slow us down or distract us, but it is also occupied by predators—"enemies of the cross of Christ" (3:18). They sometimes look like us. Often they appear to be trudging along the same trail as we are. In light of this real threat, Paul instructs the Philippians on how to press on. Let me sum up these instructions in three simple statements. I call these "marching orders" for the Christian from a seasoned veteran who has endured countless battles.

First, *we need godly examples to follow* (3:17). To live as salt and light in this dark world, we need mature models in the faith like

Paul—experienced saints who have faced challenges, lived through tragedies, and overcome obstacles. Paul expresses a similar thought in 1 Corinthians 11:1—"Be imitators of me, just as I also am of Christ."

But why doesn't Paul just turn our attention to Jesus? Why point us to himself, a mere human example? Because God has intentionally given to us contemporary models to follow. They, like us, are fallen, frail human beings indwelled by the same Spirit. They, like us, are striving after Christlikeness. They, like us, are seeking to live God-honoring lives in the midst of a twisted, corrupt, sinful world. When we look at Christ, we see the perfection we will one day reflect; but when we look to imperfect men and women growing more like Christ, we see what we are. In this life we will never measure up to the God-man; but we can follow in the steps of godly men and women.

What kind of person makes a good model for us to follow along life's dangerous path? Paul answered that question in a letter he wrote toward the end of his life to Timothy: "Now you followed my teaching, conduct, purpose, faith, patience, love, perseverance, persecutions, and sufferings . . . ; what persecutions I endured, and out of them all the Lord rescued me!" (2 Tim. 3:10-11). At this point someone might think, "Well, Paul was an apostle. I could see why Timothy would want to follow his example. But we don't have any apostles today." But Paul also said, "Observe those who walk according to the pattern you have in us" (Phil. 3:17). He turned their attention not just to himself, but to any examples of Christlike living in a Christless world.

God has given to each of us people who live admirable lives on earth today. There is nothing wrong—in fact, there is everything right—about following their examples. The only warning is that we don't idolize them or put them on a pedestal. If they're genuine examples of Christlikeness, they wouldn't want to be on a pedestal anyway! So choose your spiritual heroes carefully, study their lives, and follow only those who truly sought or are seeking to be like Christ.

Second, *we live among many enemies of the cross* (3:18-19). In these verses, Paul sets up a basic contrast. After urging the Philippians to follow the pattern of godly believers (3:17), he gives the reason: "For many walk, of whom I often told you, and now tell you even weeping, [as] enemies of the cross of Christ" (3:18). Paul then describes these opponents in 3:18-19. Their negative characteristics were so destructive that they made Paul weep, and they can give us an idea of the kind of positive examples we need in our lives to counter the numerous purveyors of evil.

If bad examples are like this:	Then good examples should be like this:
Enemies of the cross	Embracers of the cross
On a path to destruction	On a path to salvation
Idolize their appetite	Subdue their appetite
Glory in their shame	Mourn over their shame
Set their minds on worldly things	Shun worldly things

Destined for eternal hopelessness, driven by sensual appetites, and dedicated to material things, these men and women who have rejected Christ's person and work are lost, wandering souls. We bump up against them every day. They don't need our condemnation and judgment, nor our agreement and affirmation. They need to be reconciled to Christ, becoming allies—not enemies—of His cross. As we travel along our path, following the good examples of godliness, we can't forget why God left us in this world among the lost. Our mission is to call them to believe in the One they reject, to submit to His kingdom, and to enter with us into heavenly citizenship.

This leads to the third statement: *We belong among those who are bound for heaven* (3:20-21). Paul dwells on the unbelieving evildoers for only a moment (3:18-19). He needed to warn the Philippians and contrast the way of the "enemies" with the path of believers, but he quickly turns again to the positive: our future hope as heavenbound citizens of Christ's kingdom. Remember, the lost "set their minds on earthly things" (3:19); but as believers, we're to set our minds on the things above (see Col. 3:2). We do this by always looking forward and upward, eagerly awaiting the coming of Jesus Christ, our Savior (Phil. 3:20).

The Greek word Paul uses for "citizenship" is *politeuma* [4175], which means "commonwealth" or "state."[14] Paul uses it to convey the idea that our homeland isn't here; our place of residence is in another realm entirely. That makes us expatriates—"a colony of foreigners."[15] But we don't need to see ourselves as helpless refugees huddled in an overcrowded camp. We're more like ambassadors, emissaries, and representatives of the next world as we live in the present one. Yes, one day our King will come. He'll "transform the body of our humble state into conformity with the body of His glory" (3:21) and escort us to our heavenly home. As Paul wrote to the Thessalonians,

> The Lord Himself will descend from heaven with a shout, with the voice of the archangel and with the trumpet of God, and the dead in Christ will rise first. Then we who are alive and remain

will be caught up together with them in the clouds to meet the Lord in the air, and so we shall always be with the Lord. Therefore comfort one another with these words. (1 Thes. 4:16-18)

One day, we will be home in heaven. The long, arduous, painful journey—whether it's a sprint toward the finish line or a limp along the path—will end. We'll stand together victorious, clothed in glory, and basking in the brilliance of our Savior. Finally, we will be free from the pain and sorrow of this world, reunited with those beloved saints who have gone before us, and rejoicing eternally in Christ our King.

APPLICATION: PHILIPPIANS 3:12-21

Standing Firm without Standing Still

Throughout Paul's letter to the Philippians there is a focus on the Lord as the source of our ability to stand firm with confidence, joy, and strength. However, we must never confuse standing firm with standing still. A lot of things in this messed-up world can cause us to stall. God didn't put us here to huddle in a corner, hide in a crevice, or hurry ourselves to heaven. He has called us to make a difference where we are—to be insulated from the wickedness of our times but not isolated from the world itself.

To help us stand firm without standing still, let me ask you some probing—maybe even meddling—questions that arise from Philippians 3:12-21. Don't just rush through these questions, but ponder them. Mull them over. Talk to others about them. Let them urge you to think through areas of your spiritual walk you need to address.

First, *are you dwelling on the past, letting it control your attitudes and actions?* Or are you letting go of those things that happened long ago, setting your mind on the things above and continuing to take steps forward toward maturity? I strongly suggest you memorize those epic words of Paul in Philippians 3:13-14.

Second, *are you following good examples?* Do you have a Paul to look up to, a Timothy to imitate, an Epaphroditus to follow, a godly hero to learn from? Do the people you look up to, spend time with, and learn from live up to the qualities Christ wants to see formed in you? Or do you need to seek out a mentor more like what Paul had in mind?

Finally, *are you eagerly anticipating the coming of Christ?* Do you live today by the principles of your true heavenly home? Would the enemies of the cross know that this world is not your home? Or do you blend in, compromise, and hide your true identity in Christ? Are there people in your life today—family, friends, neighbors, co-workers—who need to hear a word of testimony, encouragement, or warning from you as a heavenly ambassador? Are there areas in your life that have a negative impact on others? What do you need to do to change that? Start now!

JOY IN RESTING
(PHILIPPIANS 4:1-23)

Earlier I noted that from the first word to the last, Paul's letter to the Philippians is saturated with the theme of joy. Admittedly, some parts of Philippians 3 seemed more like frightening warnings than joyful encouragement. But Paul had to share a vision of the world as it really is in order for us to appreciate the inexplicable joy that comes from Christ in the midst of the mess and madness of our earthly realm.

In Philippians 4, Paul puts the finishing touches on his symphonic "ode to joy" with a soaring, moving, inspiring conclusion. Some of the most quoted, best-loved passages of Scripture are found in Philippians 4—as are a few obscure lines. We also get a sneak peek into the lives of some Philippian Christians and their real-life conflict. In this final chapter Paul argues that there is *joy in resting*. He includes perhaps the finest passage on contentment in all the Scriptures, and this contentment is the essence of joyful living in the midst of a restless world. Whether the cause of our unrest is disunity (4:1-3), anxiety (4:4-7), lack of peace (4:8-9), discontent (4:10-13), or need (4:14-19), Paul encourages believers to find Christ-centered, Spirit-empowered joy in resting in God, and God alone.

KEY TERMS IN PHILIPPIANS 4:1-23

merimnaō (μεριμνάω) [3309] "to worry," "to be anxious," "to be apprehensive"

The opposite of being at peace and rejoicing, *merimnaō* refers to a disproportionate, excessive concern, usually over things beyond our control (see Matt. 6:25-34). It stems from an emotionally agitated preoccupation with distressing burdens and fears. Here, it doesn't refer to wise and prudent foresight, thoughtful concern for others, or taking reasonable responsibility. Rather, in Paul's discussion in Philippians 4:6, the emphasis is on being "unduly" concerned.[1]

---

eirēnē (εἰρήνη) [1515] "peace," "harmony," "concord"

Eirēnē is the antithesis of conflict, anger, and anxiety. From this Greek term we get our English word *irenic*, which describes calm, gentle interaction. In Philippians 4, God's "peace" is probably related to the Old Testament concept of *shalom* [H7965], which connotes more than merely the absence of conflict or anxiety. It involves wholeness, harmony, and delight.[2]

The Cure for Anger and Anxiety
PHILIPPIANS 4:1-9

NASB

¹Therefore, my beloved brethren ᵃwhom I long *to see,* my joy and crown, in this way stand firm in the Lord, my beloved.

²I urge Euodia and I urge Syntyche to ᵃlive in harmony in the Lord. ³Indeed, true companion, I ask you also to help these women who have shared my struggle in *the cause of* the gospel, together with Clement also and the rest of my fellow workers, whose names are in the book of life.

⁴Rejoice in the Lord always; again I will say, rejoice! ⁵Let your gentle *spirit* be known to all men. The Lord is ᵃnear. ⁶Be anxious for nothing, but in everything by prayer and supplication with thanksgiving let your requests be made known to God. ⁷And the peace of God, which surpasses all ᵃcomprehension, will guard your hearts and your minds in Christ Jesus.

⁸Finally, brethren, whatever is true, whatever is honorable, whatever is right, whatever is pure, whatever is ᵃlovely, whatever is of good repute, if there is any excellence and if anything worthy of praise,

NLT

¹Therefore, my dear brothers and sisters,* stay true to the Lord. I love you and long to see you, dear friends, for you are my joy and the crown I receive for my work.

²Now I appeal to Euodia and Syntyche. Please, because you belong to the Lord, settle your disagreement. ³And I ask you, my true partner,* to help these two women, for they worked hard with me in telling others the Good News. They worked along with Clement and the rest of my co-workers, whose names are written in the Book of Life.

⁴Always be full of joy in the Lord. I say it again—rejoice! ⁵Let everyone see that you are considerate in all you do. Remember, the Lord is coming soon.*

⁶Don't worry about anything; instead, pray about everything. Tell God what you need, and thank him for all he has done. ⁷Then you will experience God's peace, which exceeds anything we can understand. His peace will guard your hearts and minds as you live in Christ Jesus.

⁸And now, dear brothers and sisters, one final thing. Fix your thoughts on what is true, and honorable, and right, and pure, and lovely, and admirable. Think about things that are excellent and worthy of

ᵇdwell on these things. ⁹The things you have learned and received and heard and seen in me, practice these things, and the God of peace will be with you.

4:1 ᵃLit *and longed for* **4:2** ᵃOr *be of the same mind* **4:5** ᵃOr *at hand* **4:7** ᵃLit *mind* **4:8** ᵃOr *lovable and gracious* ᵇLit *ponder these things*

praise. ⁹Keep putting into practice all you learned and received from me—everything you heard from me and saw me doing. Then the God of peace will be with you.

4:1 Greek *brothers;* also in 4:8. **4:3** Or *loyal Syzygus.* **4:5** Greek *the Lord is near.*

"Stand firm in the Lord!"

With this command Paul begins to wrap up his letter to the Philippians. But what does it look like to "stand firm"? We might picture a righteous man or woman who is "like a tree firmly planted by streams of water" (Ps. 1:3)—fruitful and unshakable, even by the strongest storms. Or we may imagine a believer clad in the spiritual armor of God, standing firmly against the "schemes of the devil" (Eph. 6:11, 13), dodging and deflecting his fiery arrows of temptation.

In Philippians 4, though, Paul unexpectedly applies the notion of "standing firm" in relation to the experiences of anger and anxiety. The former causes outward conflict and division, while the latter leads to inward turmoil and despair. I can't imagine two subjects more relevant and practical to deal with than anger and anxiety. In a world of constant infighting and hand-wringing, anger and anxiety have pervaded even our churches, which should be flagships of both relational harmony and inner peace.

Paul tackles these problems head-on in Philippians 4:1-9, revealing how we can "stand firm in the Lord" against anger and anxiety.

— 4:1-3 —

Standing firm in the Lord precedes relating well in the family of God. This isn't the first time Paul mentions this crucial principle. In 1:27 he wrote, "Conduct yourselves in a manner worthy of the gospel of Christ, so that whether I come and see you or remain absent, I will hear of you that you are standing firm in one spirit, with one mind striving together for the faith of the gospel."

This is a foundational concept for Paul. Standing firm includes following the Lord's commands, believing His Word, embracing His priorities, loving His people, and following His example. Believers who are committed to standing firm in the Lord have less difficulty when it comes to relating well to fellow believers who are united "in the Lord." Those who stand firm in the Lord have Christ as their unshakable

OTHER PAULINE USES OF "STANDING FIRM"

"Be on the alert, stand firm in the faith, act like men, be strong." (1 Cor. 16:13)

"It was for freedom that Christ set us free; therefore keep standing firm and do not be subject again to a yoke of slavery." (Gal. 5:1)

"For now we really live, if you stand firm in the Lord." (1 Thes. 3:8)

"So then, brethren, stand firm and hold to the traditions which you were taught, whether by word of mouth or by letter from us." (2 Thes. 2:15)

common ground. His big picture and overarching plan become the shared narrative of our lives together—narrow-minded opinions and personal preferences become silly things in light of the unity that comes through standing together in the Lord. Harry Ironside once wrote, "It is always the effort of Satan to hinder the people of God from steadfastly clinging together, and presenting a united front to the enemy. Alas, that his efforts to introduce dissension so readily succeed because of the flesh in us."[3]

In 4:1 Paul says, "*In this way* stand firm in the Lord" (emphasis added). In what way? Paul probably had in mind what he was about to say to Euodia and Syntyche—two women in the church at Philippi who had an unresolved dispute. By dissolving the dissension, these two women would apply the principle of standing firm in the Lord. To underscore this, Paul repeats the phrase "in the Lord" in his exhortation to the two women: "Live in harmony *in the Lord*" (4:2; emphasis added). In other words, they would apply the general principle of standing firm in the Lord (4:1) by living in harmony in the Lord (4:2).

Though Paul mentions Euodia and Syntyche only briefly, we can still draw a few reasonable conclusions about them based on our observation of these verses. First, they are both members of the same church in Philippi. We don't know what their specific relationship is. Perhaps they are sisters, in-laws, or ministry partners—maybe even a mother and daughter. In any case, they are sisters "in the Lord" and members of the same body of Christ.

Second, they are in the midst of a disagreement that's causing strife and disunity. Paul urges them both, literally, to "think the same thing" (4:2). He uses the same phrase in Romans 15:5 ("Be of the same mind with one another according to Christ Jesus") and in 2 Corinthians 13:11 ("Be like-minded, live in peace"). This doesn't mean that we cease holding our own opinions about things, but it does mean that we don't hold our opinions on certain issues over our value for other people. We don't know what the particular issue was that was causing a dispute between Euodia and Syntyche, but we do know that it cannot have been a major doctrinal dispute like the truth of the Resurrection or the deity of Christ or whether we're saved by faith. When significant doctrinal issues like that arise, Paul tackles them head-on. Here he doesn't even mention the issue in dispute, suggesting it is not worth correcting. However, we do know that these two women have made a pit out of a pothole. They've taken a small matter and turned it into a big matter. How do we know that? Because Paul sees a need to call them out by name in a letter written to the whole church. In other words, they have caused a ruckus over something minor, and it is starting to affect the church.

Third, Paul expects both of them to respond positively to his exhortation. This implies that both are at fault in the dispute and each needs to take steps toward reconciliation. Notice the verb Paul uses—and that he uses it twice: "I *urge* Euodia and I *urge* Syntyche" (Phil. 4:2; emphasis added). Both are responsible for the conflict and both need to retune their harsh tones to sing again in harmony. Paul obviously knows them well—they have shared in his struggle for the gospel (4:3)—and he seems confident they will respond to his exhortation. He doesn't rebuke, lecture, threaten, or plead with them. He simply "urges" reconciliation.

Finally, Paul calls on others to help in the reconciliation. Yes, Euodia and Syntyche are responsible for humbling themselves and restoring unity. But sometimes a division is so deep and a dispute so long-standing that it requires accountability from someone else, an objective third party who can serve as an arbitrator. In this case, Paul requests that his "true companion . . . help these women" (4:3). We don't know who the "true companion" was. Perhaps it was Timothy or Epaphroditus, or some other authority figure in the church at Philippi. Regardless, this person was well known, well respected, and obviously well qualified to serve as a mediator to help bring about reconciliation.

Having begun this section on a positive note—"I long to see [you], my joy and crown" (4:1)—Paul also ends with an encouraging word. Not only had Euodia and Syntyche shared in Paul's quest to further the gospel of Jesus Christ, but so had a man named Clement (mentioned only here in the New Testament), along with many other co-laborers "whose names are in the book of life." Paul no doubt encouraged a speedy reconciliation by reminding the disputing parties that they were one "in the Lord"—with a common hope of eternal life—and were part of a community of co-workers focused on a common goal. ·

THE BOOK OF LIFE

PHILIPPIANS 4:3

For Paul's original audience, the image of the "book of life" (4:3) probably brought to mind a rolled scroll rather than a bound volume with pages like a modern book. Paul didn't have in mind a physical, written record, like a church membership roll or a list of baptized believers in Philippi. Even if such a written record did exist for each church, Paul was drawing both on the Old Testament and on Greco-Roman concepts when he referred to the "book of life."

Scrolls, like the one pictured here, were the most common apparatus for writing in Paul's day.

With regard to the secular realm, Paul may have been making a connection to a concept he had developed earlier in this letter: citizenship (3:20). One commentator notes,

> The citizens of the Roman colony of Philippi who have their names recorded in a civic register of citizens know that they have a duty to live in harmony and peace with one another. The citizens of the colony of heaven in the Roman colony of Philippi who have their names written in the book of life in heaven are called by their Lord above all powers to live in peace with one another.[4]

But this image would have brought to mind some important biblical themes as well. The idea of a "book of life" has deep roots in the Old Testament (see Exod. 32:32-33; Ps. 69:28; Dan. 12:1-2; Mal. 3:16). Believers during Old Testament times were saved by grace through faith as they trusted in God's promises in anticipation of the coming

Savior predicted in the Prophets and portrayed in types and images in the Law. When Jesus initiated the new covenant, He told His disciples, "Rejoice that your names are recorded in heaven" (Luke 10:20). The book of Hebrews also declares that the church comprises those "who are enrolled in heaven" (Heb. 12:23).

Importantly, having one's name recorded in the register of heavenly citizenship provides security. Christ promises in the book of Revelation that God will never erase the believer's name from the book of life. If a person is clothed with eternal righteousness, make no mistake—they have an eternally secure future. Obviously, God has no need of a literal book to remind Him of our standing before Him. The book of life is a memorable symbol of permanent security. Our future blessings are certain, as if God has written our names in a great registry of the citizens of heaven.

— 4:4-7 —

In Philippians 4:1-3, we saw how standing firm in the Lord precedes relating well in the family of God. Now, in 4:4-7, Paul explains how standing firm in the Lord relieves our anxiety.

I think we've come to a point in our society when "worry" has become an epidemic, if not an outright plague. Strangely, some seem to treat anxiety like a close friend they don't want to lose: They excuse it, make room for it, accommodate it, and coddle it. They treat it like a destructive, codependent relationship, and it eats away at their joy day after day. Think about what worry really is and does. When we worry, we're preoccupied with distressing fears—burdened by the past, nervous about the present, and tormented by the future. We live in the realm of "what-ifs." That kind of mental and emotional agitation can't be healthy.

No wonder Jesus took worldly worry head-on in His Sermon on the Mount (see Matt. 6:25-34). Five times in that famous passage the Greek term meaning "to worry," *merimnaō* [3309], appears:

> "For this reason I say to you, do not be worried about your life." (Matt. 6:25)
> "Who of you by being worried can add a single hour to his life?" (Matt. 6:27)
> "And why are you worried about clothing?" (Matt. 6:28)
> "Do not worry then." (Matt. 6:31)
> "Do not worry about tomorrow; for tomorrow will care for itself." (Matt. 6:34)

Those who engage in incessant worry find their entire lives off-kilter, teetering on the brink of breakdown. To combat this dangerous trajectory, Paul recenters our focus in Philippians 4:4: "Rejoice in the Lord always; again I will say, rejoice!" In a letter in which joy has been a constant theme, it's no surprise that Paul reiterates that theme now, as he is about to discuss the threat of anxiety. By refocusing on the joy we have "in the Lord," we already begin to pour water on the flames of worry.

In 4:5, Paul relays two more dimensions of the joyful life in the Lord, both of which can help to combat anxiety. First, when we let our "gentle spirit" shine through in our words, attitudes, and actions, it will have a transformative effect on our hearts and minds. The idea here is having an easygoing temperament. Instead of worrying about every jot and tittle of our lives—and the lives of others—we need to relax. Let things go. Yield to others. Extend a hand of grace to brothers and sisters in Christ. Let insignificant things slide. Accept differences. This kind of "gentle spirit" will rain on the uncontrolled fires of anxiety.

Second, we need to always bear in mind that "the Lord is near" (4:5). The fact that Christ could step into this world at any moment to take us to be with Him forever can give us hope and peace in every moment. In another letter, Paul described Christ's coming, in which He would resurrect and rescue believers at His return (1 Thes. 4:16-17). Paul concluded that passage, "Therefore comfort one another with these words" (1 Thes. 4:18). Comfort in Christ's promised return smothers the smoldering anxiety fed by fears of the future.

Another cure for worry is to bring our concerns to God in prayer. Instead of living uptight, tense, uneasy lives, we need to bring everything to God "by prayer and supplication with thanksgiving" (Phil. 4:6). And "everything" means *everything*. This is key. Worry about nothing; pray about everything. If you feel agitated, pray about it. If you're scared, lift it to the Lord. If you're burdened by a past that threatens to come back and haunt you, go to God and ask Him to take it from you. If you can't get through a minute of the day without stressing about your loved ones, spend that time interceding on their behalf instead of mentally and emotionally running through fruitless "what-if" scenarios.

When you do these things—rejoice in the Lord, exhibit gentleness, expect Christ's return, and reach out to God in prayer—then God's Spirit will quench the flames of anxiety in your heart and mind. In 4:7 Paul describes this relief in terms of "the peace of God." Paul probably had in mind the Jewish concept of shalom. Theologian Barry Jones brings out the fullness of the concept of shalom in his description:

Shalom is often translated in our English Bibles as the word "peace." But it means much more than our common conceptions of that word convey. Shalom is more than the absence of hostility or an inner sense of personal well-being. The nuances contained in this single Hebrew word require a cluster of English terms to adequately represent it: wholeness, harmony, flourishing, delight, fulfillment. . . . Shalom is the dream of God for a world set right.[5]

No wonder Paul says that God's peace "surpasses all comprehension" and is able to "guard" our hearts and minds in Christ! This is no mere absence of anxiety, but a positive presence of God's Spirit of comfort and joy. This kind of peace doesn't simply extinguish the flames of anxiety—God's shalom replaces the dry, parched conditions that ignite worry with the cool, clear, nourishing streams of the river of life!

— 4:8-9 —

Thus far Paul has discussed how standing firm in the Lord (4:1) cures divisive anger (4:2-3) and anxiety (4:4-6). In place of both interpersonal conflicts and inner discontent, God sends His peace (4:7). In 4:8-9, Paul concludes this section with some very simple, practical ways to continue to experience the presence of "the God of peace" (4:9).

First, we need to clean up our thinking by feeding our minds positive thoughts (4:8). Regardless of our difficulties, disappointments, and heartaches, focusing our minds on things of beauty and virtue will quench the flames of anger and anxiety that would otherwise fuel the fire. A change in our patterns of thinking in these areas will result in greater peace with others and deeper peace in our own hearts.

Second, we need to focus our attention on excellent models (4:9). Whenever the Philippians needed their faith, love, and hope encouraged, they could look to Paul's example. He provided a course to follow—one focused on the person and work of Christ and empowered by the Holy Spirit. Though we don't have Paul around today, God always places in our lives observable examples who can spur us on to growth and help us experience "the dream of God" as our minds are fixed on Christ.

Anger and anxiety steal our joy and rob us of peace. They force us to focus on the wrong things, drawing us away from a Christlike life. When we turn our attention to things that are excellent and worthy of praise (4:8) and follow the godly examples before us (4:9), we will truly know and experience what it means to "stand firm in the Lord" (4:1) and will encounter God's peace.

APPLICATION: PHILIPPIANS 4:1-9

Fighting for Peace

Chances are good that you find yourself resonating with one of the roles played in Paul's discussion of how to stand firm in the Lord. Maybe you can relate to Euodia and Syntyche: You're in the midst of a long-standing conflict with somebody in the church, at home, at work, or perhaps in your neighborhood. Or maybe you're stuck in the awkward position of Paul or the "true companion"—somebody in a position to help others resolve their conflicts. Perhaps you're struggling with nagging worry or uncontrollable anxiety, either caused by real sources of stress or by your own obsession over things outside of your control.

Whatever your present situation—external conflict or internal unrest—Paul gives you some practical principles to begin fighting for peace in your life. Let me share with you three specific things you can begin doing in your life to help you overcome anger and anxiety, enabling you to restore peace in your relationships and in your heart.

First, *rejoice*. Trade in your old upside-down grin and put a smile back on your face. Teach your heart to rejoice again. Laugh more freely. Live lightheartedly. Cultivate a good sense of humor. Take God seriously and take others seriously, but don't take yourself so seriously. Proverbs 17:22 says, "A joyful heart is good medicine." In my years on earth, I've seen very few joyful people able to remain in conflict with each other. And rarely do rejoicing and fretting dwell for long in the same heart and mind. So rejoice!

Second, *relax*. We need a healthy dose of gentleness and forbearance. To put it another way, we need to *chill out*. We don't have to respond nastily to every nasty comment somebody makes. It's all right to just let things slide sometimes. We can be easy on people, rather than being hard on them. Relax in your relationships—with your spouse, with your children, with your friends, even with total strangers. If Euodia and Syntyche would have just relaxed a little, they probably could have smoothed over their differences. And if we learn to relax in the midst of stressful circumstances, we can enjoy the peace of God that surpasses all comprehension.

Third, *rest*. This doesn't mean doing nothing. It means ceasing the mind-racing, heart-pounding, stomach-churning activities that keep us in a constant state of anxiety and edginess. Do you ever notice how dysfunctional our relationships are when we're stressed out? Paul's concept of rest is to fix the heart and mind on positive things. Take a good look at Paul's sampling of things worth dwelling on in Philippians 4:8, and consider their alternatives:

- whatever is true . . . not false, untrustworthy, or imagined
- whatever is honorable . . . not shameful, twisted, or foolish
- whatever is right . . . not wrong, sinful, or rebellious
- whatever is pure . . . not tainted, coarse, or immoral
- whatever is lovely . . . not distorted, ugly, or offensive
- whatever is of good repute . . . not gossipy, slanderous, or sarcastic
- whatever is excellent . . . not inferior, wasteful, or flawed
- whatever is worthy of praise . . . not objectionable, insulting, or evil

Rejoice. Relax. Rest. When these principles become practices, and the practices become patterns, then "the peace of God, which surpasses all comprehension, will guard your hearts and your minds in Christ Jesus" (4:7). God's dream will become your reality.

Living beyond Our Needs
PHILIPPIANS 4:10-23

NASB

10 But I rejoiced in the Lord greatly, that now at last you have revived your concern for me; indeed, you were concerned *before,* but you lacked opportunity. 11 Not that I speak ᵃfrom want, for I have learned to be ᵇcontent in whatever circumstances I am. 12 I know how to get along with humble means, and I also know how to live in prosperity; in any and every circumstance I have learned the secret of being filled and going hungry, both of having abundance and suffering need. 13 I can do all things ᵃthrough Him who strengthens me. 14 Nevertheless, you have done well to share *with me* in my affliction.
15 You yourselves also know,

NLT

10 How I praise the Lord that you are concerned about me again. I know you have always been concerned for me, but you didn't have the chance to help me. 11 Not that I was ever in need, for I have learned how to be content with whatever I have. 12 I know how to live on almost nothing or with everything. I have learned the secret of living in every situation, whether it is with a full stomach or empty, with plenty or little. 13 For I can do everything through Christ,* who gives me strength. 14 Even so, you have done well to share with me in my present difficulty.
15 As you know, you Philippians were the only ones who gave me

Philippians, that at the [a]first preaching of the gospel, after I left Macedonia, no church shared with me in the matter of giving and receiving but you alone; [16]for even in Thessalonica you sent *a gift* more than once for my needs. [17]Not that I seek the gift itself, but I seek for the [a]profit which increases to your account. [18]But I have received everything in full and have an abundance; I am [a]amply supplied, having received from Epaphroditus [b]what you have sent, [c]a fragrant aroma, an acceptable sacrifice, well-pleasing to God. [19]And my God will supply [a]all your needs according to His riches in glory in Christ Jesus. [20]Now to our God and Father *be* the glory [a]forever and ever. Amen.

[21]Greet every [a]saint in Christ Jesus. The brethren who are with me greet you. [22]All the [a]saints greet you, especially those of Caesar's household.

[23]The grace of the Lord Jesus Christ be with your spirit.

4:11 [a]Lit *according to* [b]Or *self-sufficient* 4:13 [a]Lit in 4:15 [a]Lit *beginning of* 4:17 [a]Lit *fruit* 4:18 [a]Lit *made full* [b]Lit *the things from you* [c]Lit *an odor of fragrance* 4:19 [a]Or *every need of yours* 4:20 [a]Lit *to the ages of the ages* 4:21 [a]Or *holy one* 4:22 [a]V 21, note 1

financial help when I first brought you the Good News and then traveled on from Macedonia. No other church did this. [16]Even when I was in Thessalonica you sent help more than once. [17]I don't say this because I want a gift from you. Rather, I want you to receive a reward for your kindness.

[18]At the moment I have all I need—and more! I am generously supplied with the gifts you sent me with Epaphroditus. They are a sweet-smelling sacrifice that is acceptable and pleasing to God. [19]And this same God who takes care of me will supply all your needs from his glorious riches, which have been given to us in Christ Jesus.

[20]Now all glory to God our Father forever and ever! Amen.

[21]Give my greetings to each of God's holy people—all who belong to Christ Jesus. The brothers who are with me send you their greetings. [22]And all the rest of God's people send you greetings, too, especially those in Caesar's household.

[23]May the grace of the Lord Jesus Christ be with your spirit.*

4:13 Greek *through the one.* 4:23 Some manuscripts add *Amen.*

Remember the purpose of Philippians? *To encourage believers to find Christ-centered, Spirit-empowered joy in living, serving, sharing, and resting.* The theme is summed up with a word Paul repeats throughout the letter: "Rejoice!" We can have a contagious, deep-seated joy when we have confidence that Christ is in full control—not just of the big things, but of the little things as well.

As we have discovered in the first part of Philippians 4, such joy can be applied to strained relationships as well as to difficult circumstances, leaving us worry-free. As we fix our minds on things that are positive, uplifting, virtuous, and excellent, we become transformed individuals, enveloped in God's wonderful peace. What a way to live!

As Paul begins to wrap up this great letter to the Philippians, he explores another realm that could use a healthy dose of authentic joy: contentment. In 4:10-13, Paul again presents himself as a model for his readers to follow. Then, in 4:14-19, we see the fruit of contentment: generosity. Finally, in 4:20-23, Paul concludes his letter with a joyful, grace-filled farewell.

— 4:10-13 —

Ten years had passed since Paul founded the church at Philippi (Acts 16:11-40). He had made a subsequent return visit en route home from his travels (Acts 20:6), but that was the only time he had seen the Philippians in that decadelong period. However, when word reached the Philippians that Paul had been imprisoned in Rome as he faced the uncertainty of a trial before Caesar's court, they hastened to send Epaphroditus with a financial gift to help him with his expenses (Phil. 4:18).

This act of unexpected and unrequested benevolence caused Paul to rejoice "in the Lord greatly" (4:10). That monetary gift was more than just a means to pay the bills. It was a tangible expression of the church's self-sacrificial love. It was a token of their concern for him and of their willingness to continue to partner with him in the ministry. Paul also recognized that even before this specific chance to send a financial gift, they had been concerned about his welfare but had "lacked opportunity" to put that concern into action (4:10).

Lest they think he was putting a guilt trip on them or fishing for even more cash, Paul assured them that he had learned to be content in any circumstance (4:11). The Greek word Paul used for "content" is *autarkēs* [842], which could be rendered "self-sufficient."[6] Some Greek philosophers took this to mean not only being "independent of circumstances" but also finding the source of contentment in ourselves.[7] However, this secular sense was the farthest thing from Paul's mind. Paul wasn't promoting self-sufficiency but Christ-sufficiency. He rested in Christ's provision and timing, not his own ability to exert energy and improve his circumstances and outlook.

I find it fascinating that Paul wrote these words while he was under house arrest for an indefinite period of time. He was likely chained to a Roman soldier, paying for his own rented house and enduring a total lack of privacy and freedom. However, he had learned contentment through the years, enduring such extreme circumstances that his present condition under house arrest was much easier to face.

Paul describes some of the conditions he had faced over the years— the roller-coaster-like ups and downs. He had learned contentment by experiencing various—often intense—circumstances (4:12). If we were to chart this verse, it would look something like this:

Paul's Contentment in All Circumstances

Through it all Paul learned how to get along in whatever circumstances life gave him. He didn't lose faith when he slept on hard ground with an empty stomach. And when he was hosted in a comfortable home, receiving hot meals every day and a warm bed each night, he didn't forget that God alone is the source of all things. He learned how to handle both extremes, and everything in between.

This led to his ability to face whatever challenges awaited him with both flexibility and confidence. Paul summarizes this approach to life with one of the most quoted, but also most misinterpreted, verses in the Bible: "I can do all things through Him who strengthens me" (4:13). This doesn't mean that Paul could accomplish all his personal goals, fulfill all his dreams, or acquire fame and fortune. The "all things" refers to surviving the extremes of life. To paraphrase: "Whatever ups and downs life sends my way, I can handle whatever comes, not through my own strength, but by the power of Christ." Nothing else suffices but Christ. He alone gives the strength we need to endure. Not education, not money, not political clout, not positive thinking, not self-assertiveness.

— 4:14-19 —

Since we can do all things—that is, be content in all circumstances—through Christ, does this mean that we don't need anybody else? Do we stop making our needs known, cease asking for help from others, and just pray for God to provide for all our needs? Paul goes on in 4:14-19 to show how God provides for us through others who fulfill our needs. While all things come from God the Father, through Christ, by the power of the Spirit, the triune God delights in using believers to accomplish His purposes.

Paul begins this section by commending the Philippians because they had shared in his affliction (4:14). How? By never forgetting about Paul, even at the low points. After he left Philippi, they willingly and generously contributed to his ministry needs as he continued to travel on his missionary journeys. In fact, Paul recalled a time when no other church from Macedonia had contributed financially to the cause (4:15). The Philippians demonstrated in tangible ways their commitment to him and to the preaching of the gospel—not just with a one-time farewell gift, but several gifts over the up-and-down course of his ministry (4:16).

Why does Paul point out that "even in Thessalonica" they had sent a gift on several occasions? What's so significant about that? It emphasizes the fact that the Philippians had begun donating to the cause *immediately* . . . and continued to donate *repeatedly*. Their partnership with Paul was both *early* and *enduring*. Their generosity overflowed.

Note also that Paul was genuinely concerned about how the Philippians' commitment to giving would be a blessing to them, not just to himself (4:17). Yes, he needed the gifts to continue in order to carry out the ministry, but there was something more important involved in the Philippians' commitment. Paul was encouraged by the maturity developed among the Philippians as they gave freely to support the cause. Their self-sacrificial giving was a clear example of Christlike love shown toward Paul and toward those among whom Paul was ministering.

Through their compassion and sacrificial generosity, Paul had all he needed—and then some! Not only was his account full, but he had "an abundance" (4:18). Epaphroditus had delivered to Paul in Rome an ample offering of funds. These he received as an act of worship and devotion from the Philippians. In fact, he uses language often employed with respect to temple sacrifices to draw attention to the holy nature of their gifts: "a fragrant aroma, an acceptable sacrifice, well-pleasing to God" (4:18).

Because of their worshipful, sacrificial, Christlike contribution to the ministry, Paul was confident that the Lord would continue to bless them financially: "My God will supply all your needs according to His riches in glory in Christ Jesus" (4:19). Like 4:13, this verse is often misquoted and misapplied by Christians. Some people imagine a massive treasure house in heaven, full of health, wealth, and happiness, just waiting for believers to unlock it with faith and thus receive riches to their hearts' content. I know certain health-and-wealth preachers who like to claim that sending them your cash will open the floodgates of heaven, allowing you to experience "the good life." But that's a very different scenario from what Paul was envisioning. Rather, the idea seems to be that as we serve as faithful conduits of generosity toward those who, like Paul, have genuine needs, God will continue to supply what we need—so we can continue to bless others! And as many have rightly observed, Philippians 4:19 says that God will provide for all our *needs*, not all our *greeds*.

— 4:20-23 —

Paul began this letter with a prayer (1:3-5; 9-11); now he brings it to a close with a doxology: "Now to our God and Father be the glory forever and ever. Amen" (4:20). In the gospel ministry, Paul had his role to play as apostle to the Gentiles, and the Philippians contributed through their prayers and financial support. Co-laborers like Timothy and Epaphroditus served with diligence and determination. But none of these could take ultimate credit or praise for the distinct parts they played in the mission of God. God alone—who supplies all things—deserves all the praise and all the glory.

Paul concludes with a standard blessing (4:23); but before doing so, he exchanges a couple of greetings. Paul begins by offering his own personal greeting to the "saints" in Philippi (see 4:21). Without mentioning each by name, he encourages every believer, reminding them of their status as being set apart (the root meaning of *saint*) for the service and worship of God.

After his personal greeting, Paul extends a farewell from "the brethren" (4:21), probably referring to his co-laborers, including Timothy, Epaphroditus, and others. Beyond this circle are "all the saints," including believers from Caesar's household staff (4:22). This likely would have included many of the names referred to in Romans 16, like Andronicus and Junias (Rom. 16:7), Aristobulus (Rom. 16:10), Narcissus (Rom. 16:11), and many others. By referring to these believers as "saints," Paul thus reminded the Philippians that they, too, were part of something much bigger than themselves. Though separated by space, one day they would be gathered into the same kingdom under the same Lord for all eternity.

What an occasion for Christ-centered, Spirit-empowered joy!

SAINTS IN CAESAR'S HOUSEHOLD

PHILIPPIANS 4:22

In his closing greetings to the Philippian church, Paul refers to "all the saints . . . especially those of Caesar's household." This line has led to much speculation about just how deeply into social and political circles the gospel had penetrated. Did this mean that the emperor's family had been converted? His wife? His children? Were they working behind the scenes to help Paul get released?

Probably not. There's no evidence that anyone in the emperor's immediate family had accepted Christ as Savior—not at this early date. Centuries later, however, the gospel would penetrate the very home of the emperor. Most notably, Helena, the Christian mother of Emperor Constantine, who ruled in the fourth century, would become a great influence on her son and encourage in him a favorable disposition toward Christians. But in the first century, the emperor Nero and his family had no interest in what looked like a quirky Jewish sect.

But we do know that a number of slaves and freemen associated with the imperial palace called Jesus Christ Lord.[8] We must recall that the term *household* didn't necessarily refer to a nuclear family. It could also refer to all those employed by a family to carry out the work in the home, including slaves. The gospel had apparently spread among these men and women, setting the stage for a more extensive and favorable reception of Christianity by all levels of society in generations to come.

APPLICATION: PHILIPPIANS 4:10-23

Looking within, Looking around, Looking up

Both Paul and the Philippians exhibited a high level of spiritual maturity in their Christlike character, as expressed through contentment and generosity. How do we follow their example? How can we develop the marks of maturity evidenced by Paul and the Philippians? Let me suggest three places to look in your life that will enable you to grow up in your joyful resting in the Lord.

First, *look within . . . and release.* Is there something in your heart that's stunting your growth? Something that's holding you down and keeping you from experiencing true contentment and joyful generosity? Perhaps it's a need for comfort rather than contentment or a desire for luxury rather than generosity. Maybe it's an unquestioned sense of entitlement instead of self-sacrificial benevolence. Do a little internal diagnostic test right now. Ask yourself, "What's keeping me from experiencing the kind of contentment Paul describes in Philippians 4?" Or, "What's keeping me from giving more time and money to the cause of Christ than I do now?"

Look within . . . and release those things.

Second, *look around . . . and respond.* Sometimes we don't give our time, energy, or financial resources because we're too busy to see the needs. The Philippians saw Paul's needs from many miles away and responded immediately, continually, and faithfully. They sent not only money but also personal help—Epaphroditus. They didn't wait for another church to act first. They saw the need and met it. Why don't you try it? There's no need to start with something extreme like a long-term commitment to a jungle tribe in South America. But you could find a missionary who's working there and start supporting him or her financially. Or you could find a place to serve at your church. Or you could reach out to help a family in the neighborhood that is struggling, perhaps one with a single parent. Many different kinds of people need your help and would welcome it.

Look around . . . and respond.

Third, *look up . . . and rejoice.* Never forget to take time to look up and survey all that God has done in the past, is doing in the present, and promises to do in the future. Don't forget to praise Him and thank Him for what He has done specifically in your own life. Rejoice in the many good things He has given to you and done for you, remembering that every good gift comes from Him (Jas. 1:17). As Paul did with the Philippians, rejoice over the good things God accomplishes daily in the lives of others, and thank Him. God loves to hear our words of gratitude and our expressions of praise.

Look up . . . and rejoice!

INSIGHTS ON COLOSSIANS

Anyone who digs deeply into Paul's brief but powerful letter to the Colossians soon realizes that while it addressed specific problems of first-century Christians, its relevance easily bridges twenty centuries of history. Paul's ancient words still describe what we face today. The heresies of his day are still flourishing in our own. His exhortations to the wayward believers of Colossae still speak directly to us living in the towns and cities of the modern world.

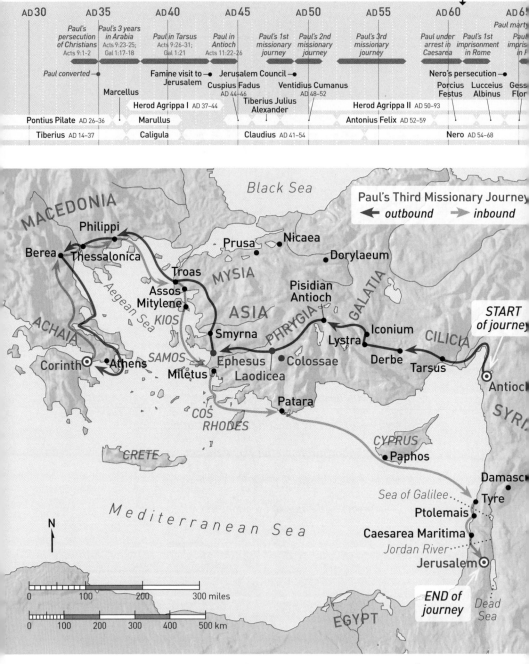

Paul's Third Missionary Journey. Colossae was located in Asia Minor (modern-day Turkey), not far from Laodicea to the north. Paul visited the churches of Ephesus, Laodicea, and Colossae on his third missionary journey.

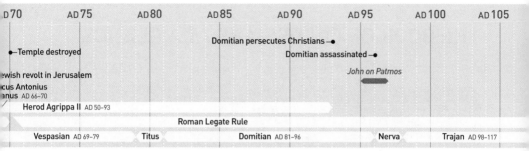

D 70   AD 75   AD 80   AD 85   AD 90   AD 95   AD 100   AD 105

Domitian persecutes Christians —•

•—Temple destroyed   Domitian assassinated —•

ewish revolt in Jerusalem   John on Patmos

cus Antonius

anus AD 66–70

Herod Agrippa II   AD 50–93

Roman Legate Rule

Vespasian AD 69–79   Titus   Domitian AD 81–96   Nerva   Trajan AD 98–117

COLOSSIANS

INTRODUCTION

A dense fog of religious pluralism has rolled in, clouding the church's spiritual discernment and muddling the clarity of the gospel of Jesus Christ. The ever-shifting winds of vain philosophies blow anchorless believers farther from the safe harbors of the faith. Some face this spiritual crisis with a rigid legalism, resorting to dos and don'ts with no basis in Scripture. Others retreat into a quasi-magical mysticism that tends toward superstition. Drifting, aimless believers are slowly sinking into the murky waters of spiritual concession and moral compromise, heading dangerously toward a shipwreck of their faith.

And the ever-present lighthouse of biblical truth? Ignored.

These words describe the prevailing conditions of the first-century Colossian church in the heart of Asia Minor. But these images of a Christian church suffering from cultural capitulation and spiritual surrender could also describe many twenty-first-century churches that have drunk too deeply from their surrounding culture.

Anyone who digs deeply into Paul's brief but powerful letter to the Colossians soon realizes that while it addressed specific problems of first-century Christians, its relevance easily bridges twenty centuries of history. Paul's ancient words still describe what we face today. The heresies of his day are still flourishing in our own. His exhortations to the wayward believers of Colossae still speak directly to us living in the towns and cities of the modern world. Those who deceive others with self-centered philosophies, self-promoting legalism, and self-serving asceticism live on to this day. Deceivers still gain an audience with their well-crafted arguments that seek to diminish the gospel of Jesus Christ.

The Colossians of the first century—like many believers today— needed a drastic course correction before their vessels splintered on the

THE BOOK OF COLOSSIANS AT A GLANCE

SECTION	JESUS CHRIST, OUR LORD	
PASSAGE	1:1–2:23	
THEMES	Doctrinal and Corrective	
	Instructions	Warnings
	Paul's personal introduction Paul's gratitude Paul's prayers Paul's praise Paul's calling	Because Christ is Lord: "Don't let anyone . . ." "Don't submit to . . ."
KEY TERMS	Faith, hope, love	
	To have first place Fullness	

JESUS CHRIST, OUR LIFE	JESUS CHRIST, OUR LEADER
3:1–4:1	4:2-18

Practical and Reassuring	
Challenges	Reminders
Christ-centered thinking Christ-centered living Christ's peace in your heart Christ's control in your home	Devotion to prayer Wise words for the lost Relationships with friends Personal conclusion

Wisdom, philosophy	
Renew Life	Bond-servant Fellow laborer

jagged rocks of heresies. As it did among the first generation of Christians, Paul's letter to the Colossians can serve today as an immovable lighthouse. Its bright light can pierce the thick fog of false teaching and guide wandering vessels into the safe harbor of the sufficiency of Christ.

All we need to do is look up and follow Him home.

THE AUTHOR, AUDIENCE, AND OCCASION OF COLOSSIANS

In the closing words of the book of Acts, Luke ends his sweeping account of the birth and growth of the church with the apostle Paul in legal limbo under house arrest in Rome (Acts 28:30-31). For two years, between about AD 61 and AD 63, Paul was forced to remain in a holding pattern that would have driven most missionaries mad. But Paul wasn't languishing in a prison, isolated from the outside world. Though under the constant, watchful eye of a soldier (Acts 28:16), Paul had considerable freedom to carry on his ministry while awaiting a hearing before the court of Caesar.

The rental where Paul stayed at his own expense was spacious enough to host a large number of visitors at once (Acts 28:23), and apparently, the Roman soldier guarding him had no problem allowing visitors. Clearly Paul didn't interpret his two-year hiatus as a tragic setback to his ministry. Paul didn't sit around staring at a sundial or twiddling his thumbs. During that forced furlough from the mission field, the apostle Paul was able to devote time to a few writing projects that must have been on his mind for some time, including the handful of writings scholars call the "Prison Epistles."[1] These include Ephesians, Colossians, Philippians, and Philemon. No, Paul didn't lament his immobility or fret over his confined circumstances. Instead, he took the opportunity to build up the body of Christ through a ministry of teaching and writing.

But why a letter to the Colossians? Whereas Paul had a close, personal relationship with the churches of Philippi (Acts 16:12; 20:6) and Ephesus (Acts 19–20), the city of Colossae isn't even mentioned in the book of Acts. In fact, it was one of Paul's fellow missionaries, Epaphras,

COLOSSAE IN THE FIRST CENTURY

COLOSSIANS 1:2

Today the site of the ancient city of Colossae is nothing more than an elevated green bump on a wooded countryside. About 120 miles to its west, tour buses continually load and unload Christian pilgrims at the well-excavated ruins of Ephesus. But the burial site of the city of Colossae has barely been scratched by the tools of archaeologists. It's not an exaggeration to say that if Paul hadn't written his letter to the church in Colossae, nobody but historians and residents of the nearby city of Honaz would remember that once-bustling city.[2]

Near the time Paul was under house arrest (between AD 61 and AD 63), the town of Colossae was shaken to its core by a massive earthquake that left it and neighboring larger cities devastated. However, its favorable location in the Lycus River valley and its proximity to the larger sister cities Laodicea and Hierapolis eventually motivated its rebuilding.[3] Already a town that had waned in significance in the first century, Colossae declined even further with the later rise of Islam and the conquering of the region by the Turks in the Middle Ages. Eventually its population abandoned the city.[4]

© Barry Beitzel

The once-prosperous ancient city of Colossae, now only an unexcavated mound, was located along the Lycus River in the central region of Phrygia in Asia Minor.

In its heyday prior to the Roman era, Colossae was well known for its textile industry, especially its purple-dyed wool.[5] But the ancient city, situated in a region settled by a variety of ethnic communities, would have also traded in diverse religious and cultural ideas.[6] The first-century Jewish historian Josephus mentions that Antiochus III resettled two thousand Jewish families from Babylon to the region of Phrygia around the late third or early second century BC.[7] By Paul's day some two centuries later, this Jewish presence would have had ample time to establish roots in Colossae, which was known for great religious diversity.

The swirl of cultural and religious ideas seems to have had a significant impact on the newly founded Christian community in the small town of Colossae. They would have faced the threat of syncretism with Judaism and pagan religions. Like the purple-dyed wool for which Colossae was famous, the Colossian Christians were beginning to take on the mixed hue of the world around them rather than the solid purity of the gospel of Christ.

who had planted the church in Colossae (Col. 1:7), possibly with the help of another friend of Paul's, Philemon, who was serving as a leader in that new church (Phlm. 1:1-2). Although he was unacquainted with the church in Colossae, Paul had heard good reports about the congregation (Col. 1:4, 8). And as he learned of the gospel spreading eastward beyond Ephesus into the cities of Laodicea, Colossae, and Hierapolis (4:13), he felt burdened to write a letter that could be easily circulated among those newly established churches (4:15-16).

It is likely that upon visiting Paul in Rome, Epaphras had shared some specific concerns he had for the fledgling church in Colossae. Indeed, Paul remarked that Epaphras was constantly praying for the Colossian church that they would "stand perfect and fully assured in all the will of God" (4:12). In response to Epaphras's concerns, Paul did what he could to help strengthen the church in their faith. Throughout this letter we discern that the sprouts of false teaching had made their way into the congregation. Paul was determined to nip these in the bud before they grew deep roots. So through both positive encouragement and clear warnings, Paul sought to strengthen the churches in Colossae and the surrounding cities.

Paul sent his letter to the Colossians through Tychicus—also the carrier of Ephesians and Philemon—who was accompanied by Onesimus (4:7-9; see also Eph. 6:21; Phlm. 1:10-12). Tychicus was one of Paul's coworkers, who would not only serve as the courier for the letter, but also as a trustworthy messenger to help the Colossians understand Paul's teachings. He would then bring back news to Paul of the church's spiritual condition.

THE SUFFICIENCY OF CHRIST IN COLOSSIANS

The theme of Colossians is that *Jesus Christ is sufficient as our Lord, our Life, and our Leader.* The young believers at Colossae still lacked the deep-rooted, mature faith in the sufficiency of the person and work of Christ that would enable them to withstand the onslaught of worldly philosophies and man-made religions. The letter to the Colossians, with its Christ-centered focus, came in the nick of time. The immature Christians at Colossae were under attack from false teachers who were downgrading Christ's identity as God the Son, degrading the sufficiency of His saving work, and denigrating His absolute authority as heir and ruler over all creation.

Though Paul had never visited the church in Colossae, he knew how to address these issues head-on: by centering their attention on the complete sufficiency of the person and work of Christ. The nature of Jesus Christ as Creator and Redeemer was nonnegotiable. Without this clear understanding that He was their heavenly Lord, their Source of life, and their exalted Leader, the Colossians would be continually tempted to seek revelations from other heavenly lords, to seek eternal life through rites, rituals, and religiosity, and to follow the lead of false teachers who had compelling messages and persuasive personalities. It was imperative for Paul to turn the Colossians' attention away from those deceptive works and ways . . . and to center their hearts and minds fully on the greatness and glory of Jesus Christ.

In the first section of Colossians, which I am calling "Jesus Christ, Our Lord" (1:1–2:23), Paul expresses genuine thanks to God that the Colossians had come to faith in Jesus Christ (1:1-8). But he prays that they will have greater knowledge, wisdom, and understanding to be able to serve their Savior and Lord according to His will (1:9-14). The doctrinally rich "Christ hymn" in 1:15-20 emphasizes the supreme lordship of Jesus Christ, who occupies the first place in all things. Christ alone is both fully human and fully divine, and He is the Reconciler of heaven and earth (1:21-23). Thus, Christ is sufficient for salvation and for life (1:24-29). In light of the Colossians' newfound faith in Christ, they must take care not to be led astray by worthless deceptions (2:1-8). Through the unparalleled person and work of Christ, the Colossians were made complete—forgiven, cleansed, and empowered to live a life worthy of their Lord (2:9-15). As such, man-made regulations and religion are of no use for true spiritual growth, for which the Lord Jesus Christ alone is sufficient (2:16-23).

In the second section, labeled here as "Jesus Christ, Our Life"

FALSE TEACHING AT COLOSSAE

- Deluding persuasive arguments (2:4)
- Godless philosophy and empty deception (2:8)
- Traditions of worldly men (2:8)
- Legalistic ritualism (2:16, 20-21)
- Mystical speculations and experiences (2:18)
- Fleshly attitudes of pride (2:18)
- Rejection of Christ's sufficiency (2:8, 17)
- Harsh asceticism (2:23)

(3:1–4:1), the focus shifts upward and forward to eternal life—to the believer's heavenly calling and a yearning for the return of Christ (3:1-4). In light of the reality of eternal life with Christ, Paul urges the Colossians to live new lives after the pattern of Jesus (3:5-17). This new life in Christ should affect all relationships, including those of husbands and wives, parents and children, and masters and slaves (3:18–4:1). The supreme person of Christ and His complete work are sufficient for every aspect of our lives—personal, moral, and social.

In the final section, which I refer to as "Jesus Christ, Our Leader" (4:2-18), Paul unpacks the implications of the fact that Christ is the believer's "Master in heaven" (4:1). As our Leader, He directs our paths, providing both opportunities and challenges (4:2-6). Faithful workers in the ministry are but bond-servants and fellow laborers of Christ, who uses numerous people to carry out His work (4:7-18). No individual can do the work alone; every believer needs the entire body, which draws its sufficiency from Christ alone, who is the only Leader to whom we owe absolute allegiance and obedience.

Colossians, then, is all about the Lord Jesus Christ. In this letter, the apostle Paul describes Jesus with some of the loftiest language in all the New Testament, focusing on Christ's preeminence and sufficiency in all things. Paul presents Christ as the center of the universe, not only as the active Creator but also as the Heir of creation. Christ is the visible image of the invisible God, containing within Himself the fullness of deity (2:9). Because of His divine nature, Jesus is sovereign over all things, having an authority given to Him by the Father. He is also Head over the church, having reconciled all things to Himself through His death on the cross, thus making believers alive to God and setting them on the path to right living. This proper view of Christ serves as the antidote for the Colossian heresies and as a foundation for Christian life and doctrine.

In short, *Jesus Christ is sufficient as our Lord, our Life, and our Leader.*

KEY TERMS IN COLOSSIANS

pistis; agapē; elpis (πίστις; ἀγάπη; ἐλπίς) [4102; 26; 1680]
"faith"; "love"; "hope"

Commonly called the "theological virtues," this trio forms the foundation of the Christian life in Paul's writings. In 1 Corinthians 13:13 Paul notes, "Three things will last forever—faith, hope, and love" (NLT). They play a foundational role in Paul's prayer for the Colossians (Col. 1:4-5). In Paul's writings, *pistis* refers to faith, confidence, reliance, or trust—the starting point and foundation of the Christian life (Eph. 2:8). Paul's concept of love (*agapē*) relates not only to God's unconditional love for us (Rom. 8:38-39) but also to the love believers should have for one another (1 Cor. 13:1-3). Finally, hope (*elpis*), which has an upward, heavenly orientation, turns our attention to things yet unseen or future (1 Thes. 1:3; 2:19; 4:13; 5:8).

sophia (σοφία) [4678] "wisdom," "higher knowledge";
philosophia (φιλοσοφία) [5385] "philosophy," "sophistry"

The Greek term *sophia* means "the capacity to understand and function accordingly."[8] It's not a theoretical term, but a practical term related to skillful living rather than to clever reasoning. The term is used six times in Colossians, five of which are used positively for true "spiritual" wisdom that comes through Christ (Col. 1:9, 28; 2:3; 3:16; 4:5). Only once does *sophia* refer negatively to worldly wisdom (2:23). This "wisdom" is associated with the false, groundless, worldly, man-made "sophistry" that Paul calls "philosophy" (*philosophia*), concocted to lead believers away from authentic spiritual wisdom (2:8).

JESUS CHRIST, OUR LORD (COLOSSIANS 1:1–2:23)

The overarching theme of Paul's letter to the Colossians is that *Jesus Christ is sufficient as our Lord, our Life, and our Leader.* In Colossians 1:1–2:23, "Jesus Christ, Our Lord," Paul takes a close look at the implications of the sufficiency of Christ's supreme person and work in all areas of our lives. He begins by expressing his deep gratitude for the Colossian believers; his authentic care and concern is evident in his prayer for them (1:3-8). With a thankful heart, he prays for the indispensable spiritual virtues of knowledge, wisdom, and understanding—each of which points to the will of Jesus Christ, our Lord (1:9-14).

We also encounter one of the most profound and powerful articulations of the deity and humanity of Christ and His absolute lordship over all things. Probably an early hymn about the supremacy and sufficiency of Christ, Colossians 1:15-20 reminds us that He alone is preeminent over everything. He is fully human and fully divine, the Source of and Ruler over all creation, and the One who reconciles heaven and earth. Paul uses this magnificent hymn to encourage and challenge the Colossians to continue in their faith in Jesus as Lord, explaining that authentic ministry derives from that faith and from the hope they received from the proclamation of the gospel (1:21-29).

However, many forces of wickedness in both the heavenly and earthly spheres resist the lordship of Christ and try to lead others astray. The Colossians were being tempted—through vain philosophies, worldly religious traditions, and works righteousness—to compromise their confidence in the sufficiency of Christ and to exchange His lordship for a lie (2:1-23). Paul's exaltation of Christ in Colossians 1 and 2 makes an irrefutable case for His absolute sufficiency as Lord.

KEY TERMS IN COLOSSIANS 1:1–2:23

prōteuō (πρωτεύω) [4409] "to hold the highest rank," "to have the preeminent/first place"

Though this term only occurs once in this section (1:18), *prōteuō* epitomizes in one word the image of Christ's person and work projected by the "Christ hymn" of Colossians 1:15-20. In fact, this term is so unique that it occurs nowhere else in the New Testament. It's related to the adjective *prōtos*, which refers to something that is first in priority or place.[1] *Prōteuō* emphasizes Christ's absolute superiority over all things.

plērōma (πλήρωμα) [4138] "fullness," "completion"

Both occurrences of this word in Colossians refer to Jesus Christ as possessing the fullness of the Godhead. The first use refers to the fullness of His authority, priority, and power (1:19); the second refers to the completeness of His deity within a bodily form (2:9). These uses of the term translated "fullness" underscore the absolute sufficiency of Christ in all things. If He is the fullness of God's nature and character, power and preeminence, there is no need to turn to anything or anyone else besides Him for all our needs.

Praying for Knowledge of the Truth
COLOSSIANS 1:1-14

NASB

¹Paul, an apostle of Jesus Christ ᵃby the will of God, and Timothy ᵇour brother,

²To the ᵃsaints and faithful brethren in Christ *who are* at Colossae: Grace to you and peace from God our Father.

³We give thanks to God, the Father of our Lord Jesus Christ, praying always for you, ⁴since we heard of your faith in Christ Jesus and the love which you have ᵃfor all the ᵇsaints; ⁵because of the hope laid up for you in ᵃheaven, of which you previously heard in the word of

NLT

¹This letter is from Paul, chosen by the will of God to be an apostle of Christ Jesus, and from our brother Timothy.

²We are writing to God's holy people in the city of Colosse, who are faithful brothers and sisters* in Christ.

May God our Father give you grace and peace.

³We always pray for you, and we give thanks to God, the Father of our Lord Jesus Christ. ⁴For we have heard of your faith in Christ Jesus and your love for all of God's people, ⁵which come from your confident hope of what God has reserved for you in heaven. You have had this expectation ever since you first heard the truth of the Good News.

NASB

truth, ᵇthe gospel ⁶which has come to you, just as ªin all the world also it is constantly bearing fruit and ᵇincreasing, even as *it has been doing* in you also since the day you heard *of it* and ᶜunderstood the grace of God in truth; ⁷just as you learned *it* from Epaphras, our beloved fellow bondservant, who is a faithful servant of Christ on our behalf, ⁸and he also informed us of your love in the Spirit.

⁹For this reason also, since the day we heard *of it,* we have not ceased to pray for you and to ask that you may be filled with the ªknowledge of His will in all spiritual wisdom and understanding, ¹⁰so that you will walk in a manner worthy of the Lord, ªto please *Him* in all respects, bearing fruit in every good work and ᵇincreasing in the ᶜknowledge of God; ¹¹strengthened with all power, according to ªHis glorious might, ᵇfor the attaining of all steadfastness and ᶜpatience; joyously ¹²giving thanks to the Father, who has qualified us ªto share in the inheritance of the ᵇsaints in Light.

¹³ªFor He rescued us from the ᵇdomain of darkness, and transferred us to the kingdom of ᶜHis beloved Son, ¹⁴in whom we have redemption, the forgiveness of sins.

1:1 ªLit *through* ᵇLit *the* 1:2 ªOr *holy ones* 1:4 ªOr *toward* ᵇOr *holy ones* 1:5 ªLit *the heavens* ᵇOr *of the gospel* 1:6 ªOr *it is in the world* ᵇOr *spreading abroad* ᶜOr *came really to know* 1:9 ªOr *real knowledge* 1:10 ªLit *unto all pleasing* ᵇOr *growing by the knowledge* ᶜOr *real knowledge* 1:11 ªLit *the might of His glory* ᵇLit *unto all* ᶜOr *patience with joy* 1:12 ªLit *unto the portion of* ᵇOr *holy ones* 1:13 ªLit *Who rescued* ᵇLit *authority* ᶜLit *the Son of His love*

NLT

⁶This same Good News that came to you is going out all over the world. It is bearing fruit everywhere by changing lives, just as it changed your lives from the day you first heard and understood the truth about God's wonderful grace.

⁷You learned about the Good News from Epaphras, our beloved co-worker. He is Christ's faithful servant, and he is helping us on your behalf.* ⁸He has told us about the love for others that the Holy Spirit has given you.

⁹So we have not stopped praying for you since we first heard about you. We ask God to give you complete knowledge of his will and to give you spiritual wisdom and understanding. ¹⁰Then the way you live will always honor and please the Lord, and your lives will produce every kind of good fruit. All the while, you will grow as you learn to know God better and better.

¹¹We also pray that you will be strengthened with all his glorious power so you will have all the endurance and patience you need. May you be filled with joy,* ¹²always thanking the Father. He has enabled you to share in the inheritance that belongs to his people, who live in the light. ¹³For he has rescued us from the kingdom of darkness and transferred us into the Kingdom of his dear Son, ¹⁴who purchased our freedom* and forgave our sins.

1:2 Greek *faithful brothers.* 1:7 Or *he is ministering on your behalf;* some manuscripts read *he is ministering on our behalf.* 1:11 Or *all the patience and endurance you need with joy.* 1:14 Some manuscripts add *with his blood.*

I've noticed throughout my life of ministry that false teachers tend to target new believers or those who haven't properly matured in their faith. They rarely go after the well-trained Christians, the pastors, the teachers, or the theological thinkers in the church. I guess that makes sense. If false teachers had solid biblical evidence and strong doctrinal

arguments, they'd find ready ears among the more biblically and theologically astute. Instead, like ravenous predators, false teachers prowl
around the edges of the flock, scoping out the stragglers, the newborns,
the spiritually weak and sick—easy victims of deception and confusion.

Why is that?

First, false teachers know that those who are well grounded in Scripture and mature in their theology will be centered on the truth; they
won't be easily led astray. True knowledge that comes from God's Word
strengthens and stabilizes believers. Second, false teachers know that
those with a growing knowledge of God will have a greater awareness
of doctrinal lies. These often know heresies by name. Third, mature believers have had experience in discerning the difference between truth
and falsehood, between good and evil, and between light and darkness.

In the small, newly established church in Colossae, false teachers
were trying to take advantage of the believers' spiritual youth and ig-
norance. Whatever the spiritual disease brought by these teachers—
worldly philosophy, pagan mysticism, Jewish legalism, or pious
asceticism—the cure was the same: knowledge of the truth of Jesus
Christ and acceptance of His sufficiency for all things.

— 1:1-2 —

Paul begins this letter in his customary fashion: the identification of the
author and audience. Though the letter is from Paul, he also mentions
"Timothy our brother" (1:1). At the time Colossians was written, about
a decade had passed since Paul had invited young Timothy—a convert
from Lystra in Asia Minor—to participate in his missionary work (Acts
16:1-3). For more than a decade Timothy had accompanied Paul through
some very exciting and dangerous adventures—including the establish-
ment of churches in Philippi, Thessalonica, Athens, and Corinth (Acts
17–19). Timothy had also assisted Paul throughout his third missionary
journey, which climaxed with Paul's arrest and eventual imprisonment
in Rome (Acts 21:27–28:31).

We can't be certain whether this mention of Timothy indicates that
the epistle was in some sense coauthored by him or that Timothy served
as Paul's amanuensis (scribe or secretary).[2] Parts of the letter are written in the first-person plural ("we"), suggesting that Paul and Timothy
both expressed those sentiments (see Col. 1:3-12). However, the letter
abruptly switches in 1:23 when Paul says, "I, Paul." From that point on,
when employing the first person, the letter primarily uses the singular
form (see 1:23-29; 2:1-5; 4:7-18). Regardless of Timothy's involvement in

the writing and sending of this epistle, clearly the primary authority behind it was the apostle Paul.

The recipients of the letter were "the saints and faithful brethren in Christ who are at Colossae" (1:2). Though they were almost one thousand miles away as the crow flies, the bond they enjoyed through the Holy Spirit made Paul and the Colossians members of the same spiritual family. They shared the same Father and were brothers and sisters in Christ. As such, Paul felt obligated to aid their spiritual well-being. How easy it would have been for him to think, "Colossae? Never even been there! If they're having problems, it's not my responsibility. That's Epaphras's and Philemon's baby! They need to deal with it." Instead, he went out of his way to intervene for the spiritual health of people he knew only by proxy.

The phrase "grace to you and peace" (1:2), though it was Paul's standard salutation, was particularly appropriate. The grace he was extending to the Colossians by his letter and his desire for their peace made this not merely a meaningless formula, like a flippant "God bless you" after somebody sneezes. Paul genuinely desired grace and peace for his readers, even though he hadn't met them face-to-face.

— 1:3-8 —

Paul's authentic care and concern for the Colossians is clearly seen in the prayer of thanksgiving in 1:3-8. Paul hadn't even met the people for whom he was praying, but he was thankful for them because of what he had heard. By the next chapter Paul would sharpen his tone, pointing out some areas of grave concern and calling the Colossians to get back to the straight and narrow path. But he expresses his gratitude and praise for them up front and sets a positive tone. For an audience that knows him only as "the apostle," his prayer of heartfelt thanksgiving for them is intended to disarm them with grace.

Though Paul didn't know the Colossians personally, he knew what all believers need: growth and strength in what theologians often call the "theological virtues" of faith, love, and hope. These three pillars of the Christian life are fundamental, and Paul expresses his thankfulness to God that the Colossians are not lacking in these essentials. Faith is mentioned first in the trio because the Christian life begins with faith (Eph. 2:8-9), and without it, it is impossible to please God (Heb. 11:6).

From the fountainhead of faith flows love.

Once the Holy Spirit enters our hearts, love wells up—love for God and for others. In fact, in Paul's list of the fruit of the Spirit in Galatians

5:22, love comes first. Paul notes that he had heard of the Colossians' "love . . . for all the saints" (Col. 1:4). These believers were demonstrating a God-given capacity for unconditional love.

Then Paul mentions hope (1:5). Though this is a future, heavenly hope, it doesn't distract believers from trusting God and loving others in the here and now. Quite the opposite! Our assurance of heavenly reward inspires us to greater faith and love.

Faith looks back to the anchor of salvation—Jesus Christ's person and work. Love looks around, building up the body of Christ through selfless service toward one another by the power of the Spirit. Hope looks ahead to the unalterable promise of God the Father, that He will one day usher us into His presence. These inseparable theological virtues form the bedrock upon which everything else in the Christian life rests. When our lives are anchored by faith in Jesus Christ, a love for God and others comes naturally, resulting in harmony and unity. Both faith and love point to and are strengthened by a confident hope that will get us through the recurring trials and struggles of life.

Continuing his prayer of thanksgiving for the Colossians, Paul expands on the subject of the gospel, which they had given a notable reception. First, he says the gospel "has come to you" (1:6). As stated in Colossians 1:7, Epaphras—a co-worker of Paul and fellow servant of Christ—was the one who brought the saving message to the Colossians. This underscores an obvious but important point: Nobody is born knowing the good news. People don't discover it on their own. They need somebody to tell them. The gospel comes to us through a messenger. In Romans 10:14, Paul puts it this way: "How then will they call on Him in whom they have not believed? How will they believe in Him whom they have not heard? And how will they hear without a preacher?"

Second, Paul says the gospel is bearing fruit and increasing throughout the world (Col. 1:6). The ministry of Epaphras to the Colossians was just one example of many missionary efforts by which men and women were sharing their faith with a lost world. A closer look at this verse suggests that the Colossians themselves may have been involved in passing on the faith to those around them. The phrase "even as it has been doing in you" refers to the gospel bearing fruit and increasing in the world. The phrase translated "in you" could mean "among you," emphasizing the fruitfulness of the gospel's work in transforming the Colossians' lives. But it can also be translated "by you," highlighting the Colossian believers' involvement in spreading the gospel throughout the world. If this latter sense is intended, then Paul was commending the Colossians for not bottling up the good news they had received; rather, they were proclaiming it to those around them.

Third, Paul indicates that the gospel was transforming their lives (1:6, 8). The gospel was not simply received and passed on. From the moment they "understood the grace of God in truth" (1:6), the Spirit began working in the lives of the Colossians to produce love (1:8). The word for "love" (*agapē* [26]) is not simply about warm feelings or kind regard for others. It refers to self-sacrificial, generous love. Paul had learned of the magnitude of the Colossians' love from Epaphras, who was apparently so impressed by the transforming work of the gospel in their lives that it was a highlight of his report to Paul.

— 1:9-14 —

Seeing the threat of deceptive false teaching and anticipating a more direct refutation of its deficient claims (Col. 2), Paul's prayer for the Colossian Christians in 1:9-14 pays particular attention to knowledge (1:9-10). In this prayer he draws their attention from false spiritual knowledge to the intimate and experiential knowledge of Christian faith, love, and hope. Our understanding of how Paul is using the term *knowledge* in his letter to the Colossians can be illuminated by how he discusses this concept in his other letters. In 1 Corinthians 8:1 Paul makes an important observation about unbridled knowledge: "Knowledge makes arrogant, but love edifies." The Greek word Paul uses there for "knowledge" is *gnōsis* [1108], a general term for intellectual content. It often refers to spiritual insight (e.g., Rom. 11:33; 1 Cor. 12:8) or to accurate knowledge of God (e.g., 2 Cor. 2:14). As we will see, some false teachers had begun to promote a kind of deeper *gnōsis* that went beyond the saving knowledge of Christ as proclaimed through the gospel. In another letter, Paul may be referring to this kind of teaching when he alludes to "what is falsely called 'knowledge'" (1 Tim. 6:20).

False teachers often promise knowledge that "goes deeper" or provides an alternative to the "simple" or "unrefined" knowledge of the masses. They frequently appeal to a person's ego, offering to present people with a higher knowledge reserved only for a special elite, who can then look down on the average believer who has a simple, supposedly naive faith in "mere Christianity." But what these false teachers provide isn't a true knowledge of God, His wisdom, or His will. They proffer a newfangled doctrine, cobbling together Scripture in unconventional ways—taking various bits out of context—as they hammer out their false teachings. And they use words with which Christians are familiar, but do

so in unfamiliar ways. Warren Wiersbe puts it well: "Satan is so deceptive! He likes to borrow Christian vocabulary, but he does not use the
Christian dictionary!"[3] The false teachers in Colossae were twisting the
meaning of perfectly good Christian terms like *knowledge, wisdom,* and
understanding. The knowledge they were promoting wasn't based on
theological truth but on philosophical meanderings.

In response, Paul prays earnestly and continually for the believers
in Colossae, that they would be filled with true knowledge, wisdom,
and understanding (Col. 1:9). It's interesting to note that the word Paul
uses here for the "knowledge" of God's will is not mere intellectual
or speculative knowledge. He uses the modified term *epignōsis* [1922],
which some commentators interpret as an intensification of the word
gnōsis. We might translate *epignōsis* as "full knowledge" or "complete
knowledge" (as in the NLT).[4] Paul prays that they will be "filled with the
knowledge of His will" (1:9) and "increasing in the knowledge of God"
(1:10). I can't help but think that Paul's use of this term so prominently
here was meant to rescue the Christian concept of knowledge away
from the know-it-all false teachers who were trying to twist the term
for their own purposes.

The full knowledge of God's will for which Paul prayed was not just
information but "all spiritual wisdom and understanding" (1:9). This
finds its source in God through Jesus Christ, who is sufficient for all
things. And it is given to believers not simply to *inform* them, but to
transform them.

In 1:10 Paul outlines three results of receiving this knowledge of
God's will. First, the way we live will honor and please the Lord: "You
will walk in a manner worthy of the Lord." Everything we think, say,
and do will be in pursuit of His glory.

A second result of true knowledge, wisdom, and understanding is
that our lives will produce healthy fruit: "bearing fruit in every good
work." Again, we should think of the theological virtues of faith, love,
and hope (1:4-5) and the fruit of the Spirit in Galatians 5:22-23 (see also
2 Pet. 1:5-8).

A third result is that we will continue to grow deeper in our knowledge of God. Because Christians enjoy a personal relationship with
God, our potential knowledge of Him is infinitely deep. We can never
cease growing in our knowledge of and relationship with Him.

Having prayed for their complete knowledge, Paul next prays for
the Colossians' spiritual strength (Col. 1:11-12). He has just mentioned
honoring and pleasing the Lord through lives marked by spiritual fruit

ROOTS OF GNOSTICISM IN THE FIRST CENTURY

COLOSSIANS 1:9-10

The diverse sects that church historians commonly call "Gnosticism" may have their roots in the syncretistic and esoteric teachings of the followers of Simon the Magician in the late first century. Mentioned in Acts 8:9-24 first as a practitioner of magic, and then later as having an insufficient faith, he was rebuked by Peter (Acts 8:20-23). Early Christian history tells us that Simon began claiming that he was a great god who had come down from heaven and that his accompanying prostitute, Helena, was his first creation.[5] Simon was in Rome during the reign of Claudius, the emperor preceding Nero. According to some accounts, Simon had made such an impact by his demon-inspired magical arts that the Romans made a statue of him that bore the inscription: "TO SIMON THE HOLY GOD."[6] The great infamy of Simon may explain why Luke chose to include his false conversion when he wrote the book of Acts in the 60s. Simon's so-called conversion probably happened sometime in the mid-30s, so by the time Luke was writing, his crooked activities could have been influential among false teachers from Samaria to Rome.

We can't be sure that Simon's teachings had made their way to Colossae by the 60s, but it is certainly possible. Regardless, the teaching of Simon was not the only one of its kind at the time of Paul's ministry. Other teachers and splinter groups had been trying to mix pagan religion, Eastern mysticism, and a dualistic worldview with Christianity. These are the basic ingredients of Gnosticism. Gnostics generally taught that Christ was only one of many spirit-beings and that he sprang forth from an unknown god to bring salvation by special, esoteric knowledge (*gnōsis*) to the spiritually elite. Many Gnostics either wrote their own false scriptures to compete with the writings of the apostles, or they reinterpreted Scripture in a highly allegorical or spiritual sense to support their strange, speculative theologies.

Regardless of its various manifestations, Gnostic teaching tended to have a few key features. First, Gnostics shared the idea that there was a divine spark in all humans. This spark had fallen from the heavenly realm into this world and needed to be awakened and reintegrated into the divine. Second, they believed that the creation of this evil, physical world was not the work of the one true God but rather the work of an inferior, devolved being. Third, the Gnostics taught that salvation was by illumination or esoteric knowledge, whereby the "knower" came to recognize the spiritual/divine component within, leading to a return to the heavenly, spiritual realm.[7]

and deeper spiritual growth (1:10). Now he reminds his readers that God is the source of the true spiritual power that fosters that growth. We depend on Him alone for everything. God's "glorious might," not our paltry efforts, results in "steadfastness and patience" (1:11).

The word *hypomonē* [5281], translated "steadfastness," refers to "the capacity to hold out or bear up in the face of difficulty."[8] It emphasizes persevering strength exhibited through triumphing in adverse situations. The word rendered "patience," *makrothymia* [3115], suggests inner resolve or mental and emotional fortitude, the "state of remaining tranquil while awaiting an outcome."[9] Anybody who has faced challenges against all odds or encountered people who are impossible to please knows how desperately we need these God-given strengths. Paul knew that the Colossians needed this kind of heavenly strength in order to be shielded from the flurry of false teachings that were challenging their faith in the sufficiency of Christ.

When God gives this kind of miraculous inner resolve and persevering strength, the result is joyful thanksgiving—not for the pain, suffering, trials, and tribulations we are enduring, but for the firm hope that God has "qualified us to share in the inheritance of the saints in Light" (1:12).

This hope of future glory is firm because in Christ it's already accomplished! Note that in 1:13-14 Paul connects our future deliverance to the past and present. He doesn't say that one day, in the sweet by and by, we may find ourselves in God's kingdom. He says we were "rescued" (past tense) from the dark domain of depravity and death in which we were born and "transferred" (past tense) into the kingdom of His Son, Jesus Christ (1:13). This transference of citizenship is a *done deal*. Because of that, we "have redemption" (present tense), which Paul defines as "the forgiveness of sins" (1:14).

In this opening prayer in Colossians, we see a fascinating relationship between past, present, and future. Because of what He has done in His death and resurrection, the price has been paid to redeem us and forgive us of our sins. Each of us who has trusted in Christ alone for salvation has received this deliverance and transference from darkness to light, from the kingdom of this world to the kingdom of Christ. Thus, our heavenly citizenship has been fully conferred on us, though currently we reside as aliens during this temporary age. In Philippians 3:20, Paul underscores this relationship between our present state and future hope: "For our citizenship is in heaven, from which also we eagerly wait for a Savior, the Lord Jesus Christ."

APPLICATION: COLOSSIANS 1:1-14

Let Us Pray

Paul didn't know the Colossians personally, but that didn't stop him from praying for them faithfully and specifically. I suggest that Paul's prayer for those brothers and sisters in Christ in that small town of Colossae, with whom he was not yet acquainted, provides a model for us to remember and emulate. Even when we know people well and are deeply familiar with their struggles and needs, we should keep in mind the lofty things for which Paul dropped to his knees on behalf of the Colossians.

Like Paul, *let's be faithful in our prayers*. We should lift up one another continually. Let's not wait around for a text message, e-mail, or Sunday school announcement listing a person's conflicts, anxieties, needs, or pains. We can pray for people we know or don't know even if we have no knowledge of their every struggle. In other words, we don't need to wait to learn about every ache and pain to be faithful in prayer. We don't need to have a detailed description of every financial hardship or relational difficulty to intercede on behalf of fellow brothers and sisters in Christ. We can pray faithfully and continually for anyone.

And like Paul, *we should be specific in our prayers for others*. This may seem like a contradiction of the first point. If we don't wait for a list of prayer requests, how can we pray for specifics? What I mean is this: We should pray specifically for things Scripture itself emphasizes as needs that are common to all believers. We can do more than bow our heads, close our eyes, and say, "God, be with Joanne and Bob. And help Mary and Joe." "Being with" and "helping" can be pretty vague. The prayer of Colossians 1 shows that we can be specific even for people we don't know. It gives us insight into some very specific things everybody needs.

1. Pray for *knowledge,* specifically praying that they would discern His will, that they would stay faithful to the truth, and that they would have critical minds to handle deceptive false teachings. Also, ask the Lord to grant them deeper wisdom and spiritual understanding to handle skillfully whatever tests and challenges come their way.

2. Pray for *God-honoring lives,* specifically praying that they would know and do what pleases Him. Ask that they would yield to

the Spirit's inner work to produce quality spiritual fruit, and that they would continually grow in faith, love, and hope.

3. Pray for *strength*, specifically praying that they would have an attitude of inner patience and would exhibit endurance. Pray that the Lord would grant them joyful fortitude and the ability to hold up under trying circumstances and rejoice even in the most frustrating adversity.

Now to drive this application home, think about a person you know at church, at work, at school, or in your extended family. Whether he or she is a believer or unbeliever, pray for that person. Spend time going through the things I've mentioned—the essentials of spiritual victory drawn from Colossians 1:1-14. Intercede for that person daily over the next several weeks. As you do, know that you are praying according to God's will and that God delights in imparting things that can only come from Him: true knowledge, real holiness, and abiding strength.

Crowning Christ as Lord of All
COLOSSIANS 1:15-23

NASB

15aHe is the image of the invisible God, the firstborn of all creation. 16For aby Him all things were created, *both* in the heavens and on earth, visible and invisible, whether thrones or dominions or rulers or authorities—all things have been created through Him and for Him. 17He ais before all things, and in Him all things bhold together. 18He is also head of the body, the church; and

NLT

15 Christ is the visible image of the invisible God.
He existed before anything was created and is supreme over all creation,*
16 for through him God created everything
in the heavenly realms and on earth.
He made the things we can see and the things we can't see—
such as thrones, kingdoms, rulers, and authorities in the unseen world.
Everything was created through him and for him.
17 He existed before anything else, and he holds all creation together.
18 Christ is also the head of the church,
which is his body.

NASB

He is the beginning, the firstborn from the dead, so that He Himself will come to have first place in everything. [19]For [a]it was the *Father's* good pleasure for all the [b]fullness to dwell in Him, [20]and through Him to reconcile all things to Himself, having made peace through the blood of His cross; through Him, *I say,* whether things on earth or things in [a]heaven.

[21]And although you were formerly alienated and hostile in mind, *engaged* in evil deeds, [22]yet He has now reconciled you in His fleshly body through death, in order to present you before Him holy and blameless and beyond reproach— [23]if indeed you continue in [a]the faith firmly established and steadfast, and not moved away from the hope of the gospel that you have heard, which was proclaimed in all creation under heaven, and of which I, Paul, [b]was made a [c]minister.

1:15 [a]Lit *Who is* 1:16 [a]Or *in* 1:17 [a]Or *has existed prior to* [b]Or *endure* 1:19 [a]Or *all the fullness was pleased to dwell* [b]I.e. fullness of deity 1:20 [a]Lit *the heavens* 1:23 [a]Or *in faith* [b]Lit *became* [c]Or *servant*

NLT

He is the beginning,
  supreme over all who rise from
    the dead.*
So he is first in everything.
[19] For God in all his fullness
  was pleased to live in
    Christ,
[20] and through him God reconciled
  everything to himself.
He made peace with everything
  in heaven and on earth
  by means of Christ's blood on
    the cross.

[21]This includes you who were once far away from God. You were his enemies, separated from him by your evil thoughts and actions. [22]Yet now he has reconciled you to himself through the death of Christ in his physical body. As a result, he has brought you into his own presence, and you are holy and blameless as you stand before him without a single fault.

[23]But you must continue to believe this truth and stand firmly in it. Don't drift away from the assurance you received when you heard the Good News. The Good News has been preached all over the world, and I, Paul, have been appointed as God's servant to proclaim it.

1:15 Or *He is the firstborn of all creation.*
1:18 Or *the firstborn from the dead.*

The official hymn of Dallas Theological Seminary, where I not only had the privilege of studying and graduating but where I've also been honored by God's grace to serve as both president and chancellor, is "All Hail the Power of Jesus' Name." We call it "The Diadem," named after the particular arrangement by James Ellor that has become the version we know and love. We sing it at official ceremonies (like commencement) and alumni gatherings, and sometimes we sing it just to kick off a new school year. I get goose bumps every time I hear the voices of men and women, young and old, belting out those glorious lyrics in harmony:

> All hail the power of Jesus' name!
> Let angels prostrate fall.
> Bring forth the royal diadem,
> and crown him Lord of all.
> Bring forth the royal diadem,
> and crown him Lord of all![10]

The writing of such God-exalting hymns has gone on for millennia. Throughout the Old Testament we find songs composed to praise and thank the Lord for His great works (see Exod. 15:1-18; Deut. 31:30–32:43; Judg. 5:1-31). The book of Psalms is an entire inspired collection of ancient hymns that many churches still set to music and sing in worship services. And for two thousand years gifted Christian songwriters and composers have been writing psalms, hymns, and spiritual songs for worshiping the Lord through music (see Eph. 5:19; Col. 3:16).

As we turn our attention to Colossians 1:15-20, we find embedded in this little letter one of the earliest distinctly Christian hymns written in praise of Christ. Like "The Diadem," its purpose was to "hail the power of Jesus' name" and to "crown Him Lord of all." Its words are packed with deep reverence for Christ and profound theological truth. It focuses on His unique person and work, underscoring the absolute sufficiency of Christ as Lord.

— 1:15-20 —

Most scholars today agree that Colossians 1:15-20 contains a first-century hymn to Christ. In fact, many Bibles structure these verses in the form of poetry, with indentation of separate stanzas. This hymn was either written by Paul or, more likely, adapted by Paul from a hymn previously written by another apostle, prophet, or early church leader.[11]

Like most great hymns of the faith, Paul's hymn in Colossians 1 centers on the person and work of the Lord Jesus Christ. This passage is one of the single greatest statements in all of Scripture regarding the authority, supremacy, headship, and sufficiency of Jesus Christ. For a church struggling with forms of false teaching that were shifting the attention from the central truths of the gospel of Christ toward mythical, mystical, and mysterious speculations, Paul used this memorable hymn to refocus all eyes on Jesus. Take the next few moments to read through these six verses and note how often Paul uses the pronouns "He," "Him," and "Himself." Christ is the center and source of everything.

HISTORIC HYMNS IN THE NEW TESTAMENT

COLOSSIANS 1:15-20

Around the year AD 111, the Roman governor Pliny the Younger wrote a letter to the emperor Trajan describing the results of his investigation into the "error" of Christians. He reported, "They had met regularly before dawn on a fixed day to chant verses alternately among themselves in honour of Christ as if to a god."[12]

Already in the New Testament we find evidence of such hymns exalting Christ and emphasizing His unique person and work as the incarnate God-man who died and rose again. According to Pliny, such early Christological hymns were sung or recited in worship. Clearly, creative hymn writing thrived in the earliest days of the church.

The following passages are regarded by many scholars as examples of early Christian hymns in the New Testament:[13]

- John 1:1-5
- Philippians 2:6-11
- Ephesians 2:14-16
- Colossians 1:15-20
- 1 Timothy 3:16
- 2 Timothy 2:11-13
- Hebrews 1:3
- 1 Peter 3:18-22

In this hymn I see six realms in which Christ is absolutely supreme. To see what Paul is asserting regarding Christ, I'll treat these topically rather than moving through the passage in strict order.

First, *Christ is supreme in eternity* (1:15, 17). Paul establishes Christ's eternal relationship with the Father, affirming that God the Son is "the image of the invisible God" (1:15). God, who is by nature utterly transcendent and unable to be looked at by finite mortals, has made known His attributes, character, power, will, and works through His Son. Hebrews 1:3 conveys a parallel idea: "He is the radiance of His glory and the exact representation of His nature." The word translated "exact representation" in Hebrews expresses a figurative use of the noun *charaktēr* [5481], a term used in reference to "an engraved character or impress made by a die or seal," like the minted impression on coins.[14] The term used in Colossians is "image" (*eikōn* [1504]). This term doesn't mean Christ is a lesser being, but the contrary: He is equal to the Father. The point for Paul's original readers—and for us—is clear: To truly know God, we must focus attention on God the Son, through whom the transcendent Godhead has been revealed.

Christ is also "before all things" (Col. 1:17). Before planets, before galaxies, before matter and energy, before time and space—as far back as our finite minds can hope to imagine—God the Son was already there. Theologians call this the "coeternality" of the Son with the Father. Although not addressed in this Christ hymn, the Holy Spirit, too, is coeternal with the Father and Son. Never was the eternal Father without His eternal Son and eternal Spirit. All things visible and invisible originate from the Father, through the Son, and by the Holy Spirit.

Second, *Christ is supreme in creation* (1:15-17). Not only is Christ the "image of the invisible God," but He is "supreme over all creation" (1:15, NLT). Some translations render this last phrase "firstborn of all creation" (as in the NASB), which has sometimes been misinterpreted as teaching that Christ is the first being created by God. This snag comes from the term *firstborn*. Theologian Scott Horrell explains,

> This term can mean either a parent's eldest child—as in, Jesus was Mary's firstborn (Luke 2:7, first in order of time)—or the chief heir of a father's legacy, preeminent in rank (Ps. 88 [LXX]; cf. Deut. 21:15-17). Both meanings were standard fare in both Jewish and Gentile culture. The context here, however, requires that we understand the Son as the 'firstborn' heir over all creation.[15]

Thus, Christ is the "firstborn over all creation" (NIV) in the same sense in which King David in the Old Testament was God's "firstborn, the highest of the kings of the earth" (Ps. 89:27). This figurative use of "first-born" emphasizes Christ's place as supreme authority *over* creation, not the first creature *within* creation.[16]

This understanding of "firstborn" as "supreme over all creation" is confirmed by the logic of the following verse. Paul explains, "For by Him all things were created" (1:16). If "firstborn" in Colossians 1:15 meant "first created," it would make no logical sense to say that the reason He is the first created is because all things were created by Him. However, if "firstborn" means "supreme authority," then Paul's logic holds: Christ is supreme over all things because "by Him all things were created."

By "all things" Paul really means *all things*. To avoid any confusion, Paul notes that this comprises things in heaven and on earth, things visible and invisible, and he also includes "thrones or dominions or rulers or authorities," which are references to angelic beings.[17] In short, nothing—from subatomic particles to massive galaxies—exists apart from His creative power. This thought is similar to a statement in the opening lines of the Gospel of John: "All things came into being through Him, and apart from Him nothing came into being that has come into being" (John 1:3).

For this reason, Paul is able to sum up this notion by saying, "All things have been created through Him and for Him" (Col. 1:16). He then adds, "and in Him all things hold together" (1:17). This latter statement is true both literally and figuratively. Literally, all things in heaven and earth are held together by Christ's supreme authority over all creation. The author of Hebrews puts it this way: "He . . . upholds all things by the word of His power" (Heb. 1:3). Figuratively, all things hold together as a meaningful whole because of Christ. That is, they find their ultimate meaning and purpose in Him, because all things were created not only "by Him" and "through Him" but also "for Him."

Remember that the Gnostics viewed Christ as merely one of many emanations from the supreme God. As the rays of the sun diminish in their potency the farther they get from the source, so Gnosticism's "Christ," as an emanation from the Father, would necessarily have less power and authority. He would necessarily have a derived existence, having come into being later than the Father. Paul dispenses with such philosophical nonsense with just a few strokes of the stylus—Christ is not a creature, but the Creator. He isn't a mere beam from a light source, but the Source itself. He isn't a cog in the universe, but the One who holds it all together and gives it meaning and purpose.

Third, *Christ is supreme in the church* (Col. 1:18). Having presented a clear picture of Christ's absolute supremacy over time and space (1:15-17), Paul brings the cosmic and abstract down to an area more tangible for his readers. Remember, believers have been rescued "from the domain of darkness" and transferred into "the kingdom of [God's] beloved Son" (1:13). We are no longer subject to sin and the evil forces of the world. We who are in the church are now under one head, Jesus Christ (1:18).

Although Paul doesn't elaborate on the image of the "body of Christ" here, he does so in other writings, especially in letters to the Corinthians and the Ephesians. In Ephesians, the portrayal of the headship of Christ over the body emphasizes not only His sole authority over the church but also the unity of the members with one another (see Eph. 1:22-23; 4:15-16; 5:23). The unity of the body of Christ isn't comparable to the unity of a man-made society like a club or organization. Rather, the Holy Spirit baptizes each individual believer into spiritual union with

Christ (1 Cor. 12:13), joining them all into one spiritual body, united to Christ as the head. Note that Christ—and Christ alone—is the head of the church. Not a pastor or a pope. Not a council or a congregation. Not elders or deacons or bishops. Not an archbishop or a monarch. Though Christ has established undershepherds to carry out His earthly ministry (Eph. 4:11-12; 1 Pet. 5:1-3), He is the "Chief Shepherd" (1 Pet. 5:4). The church must never surrender the headship of the church to anyone but Christ alone.

Fourth, *Christ is supreme in resurrection* (Col. 1:18). Paul doesn't mean that Christ was the first one to experience a restoration to bodily life after dying. In the Old Testament, the prophet Elisha prayed to the Lord to restore life to a child who had died (2 Kgs. 4:32-37). And during His earthly ministry, Jesus also raised the dead as a sign of the coming kingdom (Matt. 11:5; Mark 5:35-43; Luke 7:11-17; John 11:41-44). However, in each of these cases, those restored to mortal bodies were again subject to death. Their resurrections were temporary resuscitations.

The resurrection of Christ, however, was the first of its kind. He was raised in a glorious, incorruptible body that could never again suffer death. As such, Christ is "the first fruits of those who are asleep" (1 Cor. 15:20). Later in 1 Corinthians 15, Paul compares the present body with the future resurrection body, demonstrating the qualitative difference between the two: "It is sown a perishable body, it is raised an imperishable body; it is sown in dishonor, it is raised in glory; it is sown in weakness, it is raised in power" (1 Cor. 15:42-43).

Because Christ's resurrection is superior to death, death has lost its sting (1 Cor. 15:55). Because He is our head, we are united with Him in all things, including the experience of our own glorious resurrection. In Philippians 3:21 Paul says, "[He] will transform the body of our humble state into conformity with the body of His glory, by the exertion of the power that He has even to subject all things to Himself." This means we should no longer fear death. If we are in Christ—united to Him by the Holy Spirit through faith—we have absolute confidence in our own resurrection. Because of the supremacy of Christ in resurrection, we, too, have victory over death.

Fifth, *Christ is supreme in redemption* (Col. 1:19-20). In these last two verses of the Christ hymn, Paul describes in two statements the person of Christ in relation to His work of redemption. First, the "fullness" dwells in Christ (1:19). Gnostic teachers speculated about the existence of a great *plērōma* [4138] or "fullness" of divinity diffused throughout a pantheon of lesser emanated beings, of which Christ was merely one among many. Paul counters that the entire fullness of divine power and authority—all the attributes of God—are in Christ.

Second, because of who He is—fully divine and fully human—Christ is able to fully accomplish the reconciliation between heaven and earth. Here Paul shifts from the person of Christ to the work of Christ, from His supremacy over all to His sufficiency for all. Through Christ's atoning work on the cross, He has reconciled all things, "whether things on earth or things in heaven" (1:20).

The Gnostics were wrong in their speculation that only spiritual, invisible, heavenly things could be saved. Just as both heavenly and earthly things were originally created by Christ (1:16), so also heavenly and earthly things would be reconciled by Christ (1:20). Since the fall of Adam, all of humanity has been in disharmony with God. However, because of Christ's substitutionary death in our place—the righteous for the unrighteous—we have been reconciled with God (see 2 Cor. 5:18-21). In our helpless, hopeless state, God took the initiative to make "peace through the blood of His cross" (Col. 1:20). Our whole being—body and soul—is saved by the work of Christ.

Sixth, *Christ is supreme in everything* (1:18). At the heart of the Christ hymn Paul makes the ultimate statement for Christ's all-supremacy: "He Himself will come to have first place in everything." Because of who Christ is and what He has done, we can surrender everything to Him. Over little things and big things, over the past, present, and future, and over things seen and unseen—Jesus Christ is Lord. He is to have first place in everything.

— 1:21-23 —

The resounding chorus of the Christ hymn reached its climax in 1:20. With the profound lyrics still echoing in the air, Paul picks up the theme of Christ's work of reconciliation and turns it into a personal challenge for his readers. The hymn of Colossians 1:15-20 has spoken generally of "all things," "the church," and "the dead." Now Paul moves from the general to the particular, from the universal to the personal, with one little pronoun: *you.*

All of us, being sinful by nature and by choice, need reconciliation. It isn't enough to think that Christ has abstractly reconciled heaven and earth through His incarnation, death, and resurrection. This reconciliation must be made personal and practical. The Colossians experienced this when they received reconciliation with God by grace alone through faith alone in Christ alone. They had been "alienated and hostile" toward God, which manifested in wickedness (1:21). Paul didn't have to make a list of their sins; they knew the evil deeds from which they had been saved. But when the reconciliation Christ accomplished became theirs through His sacrificial death for them, their transformation from sinful to holy had begun. The purpose of their salvation was not only forgiveness of sins (1:14) but also a life that is "holy and blameless and beyond reproach" (1:22).

Whatever the specific danger threatening some among the Colossian church, Paul saw the need to add a sobering warning to this positive statement. He says that they were reconciled to God "if indeed" they would continue in the faith and hope of the gospel (1:23). At first glance, this conditional phrase seems to suggest that if they failed to continue steadfastly in faith and hope, then they would lose their salvation and forfeit their reconciliation with God, once again becoming alienated and hostile toward the One who had redeemed them. Does this mean that our salvation is ultimately based on our own faithfulness?

It is true that an "if" phrase can sometimes indicate that kind of conditional relationship, as in the statement every child dreads: "If you eat your vegetables, then you can have ice cream." The implication is clear: If you don't eat the green food, no dessert for you! However, an "if" phrase can also be used to demonstrate the genuineness of something, as in the declaration, "If you can play this rhapsody by Franz Liszt, then you're a real pianist." Playing the music doesn't make you a pianist; being a true pianist is evidenced by playing the difficult piece. This is how Paul is using the "if" phrase here. He's saying that if the Colossians persevere in their original faith and hope, it will prove that they are truly members of the body of Christ.

Of course, Paul knew that not all those who claimed to experience conversion by faith in Christ were the real deal. And the report that some of the Colossian converts had been abandoning the true faith for false, Gnostic teachings would have given him reason for concern. Perhaps the true gospel of the supreme person and work of Christ hadn't been properly understood. Perhaps the simplicity and clarity of the gospel preached by Epaphras was being corrupted by fanciful myths and speculations by Gnostic know-it-alls.

Whatever the specific threat, Paul set the record straight with the Christ hymn in 1:15-20 and a personal application in 1:21-23. Jesus Christ was sufficient as their supreme Lord.

APPLICATION: COLOSSIANS 1:15-23

Stand Firm in the Faith

After proclaiming the absolute superiority of Christ over everything (1:15-20), Paul places a burden on his readers to "continue in the faith firmly established and steadfast, and not [be] moved away from the hope of the gospel" (1:23). As we are reminded in Jude 1:24, God is ultimately responsible for preserving us: He is referred to as "Him who is able to keep you from stumbling, and to make you stand in the presence of His glory blameless with great joy." However, He has also called us to faithfulness and perseverance in order that we might receive the abundant blessings of the Christian life.

Both of these aspects of perseverance are needed. We rest in the security of our salvation by grace through faith, and we take responsibility to walk with integrity before God by the power of the Spirit, knowing that God is working His power in and through us. But what specifically should we do to stand firm in the faith, according to Paul's message in Colossians 1:15-23? Let me suggest a couple of practical instructions that true believers in Christ can adhere to in their desire to continue steadfastly in faith and hope.

First, *make Christ first in everything.* Think of how it would completely revolutionize our lives if we began each day not with the words "I'm worried about . . ." but with the words "Christ is supreme over . . ." If the significance of this reality isn't sinking in, let me give you some specific examples of the "everything" over which Christ is to take the first place:

- our plans and decisions
- our words and actions
- our thoughts and emotions
- our food and drink
- our homes and families
- our careers and pastimes
- our churches and ministries
- our schedules and disruptions
- our priorities and passions
- our hardships and struggles
- our victories and successes

Christ has this world under control—every moment of every day. Remind yourself of that truth. If you've come to Christ by grace through faith, trusting in Him alone as Savior, why wouldn't you submit to Him alone as Lord of every aspect of your life?

Second, *refocus your attention on Christ.* Note that the center of the hymn in Colossians 1:15-20 is not us, but Him. It isn't God's creatures, but the Creator. It isn't salvation, but the Savior. Christ and Christ alone should be the focus of our attention in worship.

In Colossians 1:21-23, the emphasis is on "the faith" and "the hope of the gospel." This isn't a general faith or a subjective trust in ourselves, but *the* faith—the truth about the person and work of Jesus Christ. It's what Jude called "the faith which was once for all handed down to the saints" (Jude 1:3). And this isn't vague hope, blind optimism, or wishful thinking, but *the* hope—the promise of salvation through the person and work of Christ. He must be the focus of our attention.

How easy it is for us to become inward focused, concerned about our own wants, needs, and desires! And how often we become distracted by things around us that attract our attention and command our allegiance! Even in our churches we can buy into ministry models that focus on pastors, musicians, programs, or productions that draw attention to themselves rather than point to the faith and hope of Jesus Christ.

When we make Christ first in everything and refocus our attention on Him, we can stand firm in the faith and be presented holy, blameless, and beyond reproach before Him (Col. 1:22).

A Precise Explanation of Ministry
COLOSSIANS 1:24-29

NASB

24 Now I rejoice in my sufferings for your sake, and in my flesh I ᵃdo my share on behalf of His body, which is the church, in filling up what is lacking ᵇin Christ's afflictions. 25 Of *this church* I ᵃwas made a minister according to the stewardship from God bestowed on me for your benefit, so that I might ᵇfully carry out the *preaching of* the word of God, 26 *that*

NLT

24 I am glad when I suffer for you in my body, for I am participating in the sufferings of Christ that continue for his body, the church. 25 God has given me the responsibility of serving his church by proclaiming his entire message to you. 26 This message was kept secret for centuries

NASB

is, the mystery which has been hidden from the *past* ages and generations, but has now been manifested to His ªsaints, ²⁷to whom God willed to make known what is the riches of the glory of this mystery among the Gentiles, which is Christ in you, the hope of glory. ²⁸We proclaim Him, admonishing every man and teaching every man ªwith all wisdom, so that we may present every man ᵇcomplete in Christ. ²⁹For this purpose also I labor, striving according to His ªpower, which ᵇmightily works within me.

1:24 ªOr *representatively...fill up* ᵇLit *of* 1:25 ªLit *became* ᵇLit *make full the word of God* 1:26 ªOr *holy ones* 1:28 ªLit *in* ᵇOr *perfect* 1:29 ªLit *working* ᵇLit *in power*

NLT

and generations past, but now it has been revealed to God's people. ²⁷For God wanted them to know that the riches and glory of Christ are for you Gentiles, too. And this is the secret: Christ lives in you. This gives you assurance of sharing his glory.

²⁸So we tell others about Christ, warning everyone and teaching everyone with all the wisdom God has given us. We want to present them to God, perfect* in their relationship to Christ. ²⁹That's why I work and struggle so hard, depending on Christ's mighty power that works within me.

1:28 Or *mature.*

If used occasionally, a knife remains sharp and continues to cut with precision. However, when we use a knife regularly, it begins to lose its edge. Words are like that. Certain words are used so frequently that they begin to lose their edge. Their real meanings become blunted by clichés, dulled by familiarity, and rendered ineffective by diminished precision.

This is especially true of the word *ministry*, a word that is tossed around in churches and other Christian contexts. Because of its overuse, the term now conveys a wide variety of meanings, many of which have little if anything to do with actual ministry. The same could be said of those who serve as "ministers." What exactly does it mean to be a "minister"? And what is involved in having a "ministry" in the lives of others?

It's interesting to me that when we think about ministry, we're often better at pointing out what it's not supposed to be than explaining what it should be. For example, we know it's not supposed to be a commercial enterprise that involves the sale of goods and services. We know it's not supposed to be an entertainment industry that sells tickets to an eager audience, hoping to get great reviews and to boost ratings. And we know it's not supposed to be an educational institution that charges tuition, offers degrees, or provides on-the-job training to further a person's career. A ministry is not supposed to be a country club, a manufacturing plant, or a war room. We know that much.

But how do we define an authentic, healthy ministry? Paul understood his role as God's servant. He was first and foremost under the authority of the Lord, to whom he had to give an account. Though he was to serve on behalf of the flock, it was not to the flock that he was to be subject but to the Lord Jesus Christ (see 1 Pet. 5:1-4). And as a minister of God, he was sworn to a single task: to proclaim the gospel of Jesus Christ (Col. 1:23). Paul had a clear understanding of the calling, character, responsibility, and task of the minister. But what about ministry itself?

In the remainder of Colossians 1, Paul provides insight into authentic ministry. Through his candid appraisal, we're able to discern some things that make a healthy ministry. A careful reading of these final verses reveals that Paul has in mind three essential aspects of authentic ministry, which are pertinent for every generation: suffering for Christ (1:24), proclaiming Christ (1:25-28), and depending on Christ (1:29).

— 1:24 —

Let's start with a little exercise in word association. What's the first thing that comes to mind when you hear the word *suffering*?

Like most people, you probably thought about pain, misery, sadness, or something similar. If you're in a more theological frame of mind, maybe you thought of the suffering of Christ on the cross. Chances are, the first word that popped into your mind wasn't *rejoicing*. But this is exactly how Paul describes suffering as he begins to discuss his own ministry: "I rejoice in my sufferings" (1:24).

Now, before we begin to think that Paul had lost his mind, we need to understand why he would rejoice in his sufferings. As an authentic minister of the gospel of Christ, Paul knew that his suffering was for the sake of others: "My sufferings [are] for your sake" (1:24). This is the first essential aspect of authentic ministry: *suffering for Christ and His people*. What kinds of sufferings had Paul endured? In 2 Corinthians, he recounts the hardships he had faced. As a genuine servant of Christ, he had endured the following:

> labors, . . . imprisonments, [being] beaten times without number, often in danger of death. Five times I received from the Jews thirty-nine lashes. Three times I was beaten with rods, once I was stoned, three times I was shipwrecked, a night and a day I have spent in the deep. I have been on frequent journeys, in dangers from rivers, dangers from robbers, dangers from my countrymen, dangers from the Gentiles, dangers in the city, dangers in the wilderness, dangers on the sea, dangers among false brethren; I

have been in labor and hardship, through many sleepless nights, in hunger and thirst, often without food, in cold and exposure. Apart from such external things, there is the daily pressure on me of concern for all the churches. (2 Cor. 11:23-28)

In all these sufferings for the sake of the ministry of the gospel, there isn't a hint of self-pity. Rather, Paul expresses real, deep-seated joy in doing his share "on behalf of His body, which is the church" (Col. 1:24). He knew that what he suffered had purpose. Yes, Paul experienced the grace and power of God by suffering like Christ suffered (see Phil. 3:10-11). And there is special honor given to those who suffer for Christ (Rom. 8:17-18). But in Colossians, Paul is much more concerned about fulfilling his ministry of suffering on behalf of others for the strengthening of the church.

This suffering, Paul says, is "filling up what is lacking in Christ's afflictions" (Col. 1:24). At first blush this may sound like there was something lacking in Christ's once-for-all suffering and death on the cross. If this was the case, then Paul's suffering was necessary to continue to pay for residual sins that Christ's suffering somehow didn't cover. But what did Paul mean by this expression?

Numerous interpretations have been proposed for this difficult phrase,[18] but I like how New Testament scholar Douglas Moo explains it: "Because Paul's apostolic ministry is an 'extension' of Christ's work in the world, Paul identifies his own sufferings very closely with Christ's. These sufferings have no redemptive benefit for the church, but they are the inevitable accompaniment of Paul's 'commission' to proclaim the end-time revelation of God's mystery."[19] It may be that Paul has in mind the idea of Christ's close association with His body, the church, so that when one persecutes the body, they are in a sense persecuting Christ. This notion is seen in Acts 9:3-5. When Paul (still called Saul at that point) was persecuting the church prior to his conversion, he was confronted by the resurrected Lord on his way to Damascus. Jesus said to him, "Saul, Saul, why are you persecuting Me?" Saul responded, "Who are You, Lord?" Jesus answered, "I am Jesus whom you are persecuting."

Now, years later, Paul himself has suffered great persecution on behalf of the church at the hands of the enemies of Christ. Paul is, in a sense, filling up the fixed amount of suffering that the church must endure until the second coming of Christ and the end of all persecution and suffering.

In short, authentic ministry is characterized by those who are willing to suffer for the sake of Christ, for the church, and for the gospel proclamation. In our world of indulged comfort, where we recoil at any thought of hardship or mistreatment, this concept of fulfilling our calling to suffer for Christ seems foreign. In many places around the world, though, this is a common expectation for ministers of Christ, who suffer regularly at the hands of unbelievers. Eugene Peterson puts it this way:

> Among other things pastoral work is a decision to deal, on the most personal and intimate terms, with suffering. It does not try to find ways to minimize suffering or ways to avoid it. It is not particularly interested in finding explanations for it. It is not a search after the cure for suffering. Pastoral work *engages* suffering. It is a conscious, deliberate plunge into the experience of suffering.[20]

Even in places where Christ can be freely proclaimed and embraced, authentic ministry requires ministers to enter into the suffering of their flock, instead of fleeing from it.

One of my tasks as a minister is to help people live through their pain and suffering—in fact, to survive and thrive in the midst of it. Ministers who are too busy to do that are too busy for authentic ministry. People who enter into the lives of others invest time. They listen. They care. They weep and grieve. A ministry is not healthy if those who minister refuse to enter into suffering on behalf of others.

— 1:25-28 —

The second essential aspect of authentic ministry is *proclaiming Christ*. Paul states that it's his God-given stewardship to "fully carry out the preaching of the word of God" (Col. 1:25). The content of this message from God was once stored in His unrevealed plans, but with the coming of Christ it has been unveiled and made manifest to believers (1:26). What's this great secret that has been entrusted to Paul and his fellow ministers? It's that Christ now dwells among and within the Gentiles—"Christ in you, the hope of glory" (1:27). The revealed mystery is Christ Himself (2:2).

God's saving mercy, once openly proclaimed only among the Jews through their prophets and in their Holy Scriptures, was now being proclaimed far and wide among Jews and Gentiles alike through the person and work of Jesus Christ! The Gentiles could now experience all the benefits of being children of God:

- They were now included in the glory and the riches of God's grace.
- They had received redemption, reconciliation, and forgiveness of sins.
- Christ lived in them by the Spirit, filling them with inner hope.

This was absolutely revolutionary. Not only would the Gentiles have difficulty believing this message, but the Jews would resent it and reject it. Think about what this message of salvation by grace alone through faith alone in Christ alone must have meant to those Gentiles who never dreamed that such salvation would come to them!

In Colossians 1:28 Paul reveals the main content of his proclamation: "We proclaim Him." Christ alone was the focus of Paul's preaching. As he had written to the Corinthians, "I determined to know nothing among you except Jesus Christ, and Him crucified" (1 Cor. 2:2). A ministry that drifts from the proclamation of the saving work of Christ is a ministry that has strayed from authenticity. No gospel message is complete and no ministry is healthy if it doesn't point people to the Name above every name, Jesus Christ.

The passionate proclamation of the person and work of Jesus Christ—and what He expects from those who have been saved by His grace—involves both "admonishing" and "teaching" (Col. 1:28). "Admonishing" represents what might be called the negative ministry of the Word. The Greek word *noutheteō* [3560], translated "admonish," means "to counsel about avoidance or cessation of an improper course of conduct."[21] Any ministry that neglects or deliberately leaves out admonition is an unreliable and inauthentic ministry. This is why Paul solemnly charged his understudy Timothy to "preach the word; be ready in season and out of season; reprove, rebuke, exhort, with great patience and instruction" (2 Tim. 4:2).

The second aspect of proclamation is teaching. This represents the positive ministry of the Word. While admonishing warns people about what *not* to believe or do, teaching instructs them in how to think and live as followers of Jesus Christ. In a healthy ministry, both of these sides of authentic proclamation go hand in hand. Just as some ministries can get off-kilter by neglecting admonition, other ministries can go awry by overemphasizing the negative.

Authentic proclamation needs both teaching and admonition. How useful would road signs be if all they told us was where the roads were *not* going? We need to know where they *can* take us or we won't get anywhere. Or how many accidents would we encounter on our daily commute if there were no yellow warning signs, speed limits, or prospects of getting pulled over? People need some constraints to keep them from danger.

How do ministers know how much admonition and how much teaching to apply for each person's particular circumstance? It takes God-given wisdom and a clear understanding of where it is we're trying to lead people. This is why Paul writes that ministers are to admonish and instruct every person "with all wisdom, so that we may present every man complete in Christ" (Col. 1:28). The word "complete" refers to maturity—the result of ongoing spiritual growth through the effective application of God's Word. A ministry is unhealthy if those who minister fail to proclaim Christ by wisely admonishing and instructing others toward maturity in Him.

— 1:29 —

The third essential aspect of authentic ministry is *depending on Christ*. Anybody who has spent any length of time in ministry knows that it's agonizing work. Paul uses strong language to communicate this fact to readers who may have no idea about the struggles involved in authentic ministry. The two verbs Paul uses to describe the work of the ministry are *kopiaō* [2872], meaning "to labor," and *agōnizomai* [75], meaning "to strive." The first term means "to exert oneself physically, mentally, or spiritually."[22] It's also used to describe the all-night toiling of fishermen (Luke 5:5). The second term is the source of our English word *agonize*. It refers to fighting or struggling to accomplish a difficult task.[23] Clearly, sloth is an enemy of authentic ministry.

But Paul doesn't leave his description at "labor and strive." Had he done so, we'd have the impression that God assigns a nearly impossible task and says, "It's all your responsibility now. Have at it! See you on the other side . . . if you even make it!" Not at all! Rather, Paul says, "I labor, striving *according to His power*, which mightily works within me" (1:29, emphasis mine). The key to laboring effectively in the agonizing struggle of ministry is dependence on the power of Christ. He is the Lord of the church and the Lord of its ministry. He empowers His ministers to suffer, to proclaim the good news, and to endure hardship and labor until the end. A ministry is not healthy if those who minister fail to depend on Christ for the power to labor and strive for the sake of the call.

APPLICATION: COLOSSIANS 1:24-29

Our Common Calling

We don't need a Damascus-road conversion or a personal Shore-of-Galilee summons to be called into ministry. Every one of us who has personally accepted Christ as Savior and seeks to serve Him as Lord has a calling to minister to others and has been gifted by the Spirit. It's not just the evangelists, pastors, and teachers who are called to ministry. In fact, their God-given task is "the equipping of the saints for the work of service" (Eph. 4:12). That includes all those in the body of Christ, which means that if you're reading this and you claim the name of Christ, you share a common calling with all other believers. Since we're all called to minister in the body of Christ, let me offer four important reminders about healthy, authentic ministry that directly relate to all of us.

First, *we're appointed as servants, not hired to hold a job*. Yes, some of us who have been trained, ordained, and called into full-time service get compensated for our labor (see 1 Tim. 5:17-18). But even then, those paid workers are to be servants of Christ and ministers in His body. They take their cues from Him and follow His example of shepherding. (For a great reminder of what this shepherding involves, see 1 Peter 5:1-4.)

Second, *we should be joyful in suffering, not resentful of it*. It's vital that a minister doesn't try to circumvent the difficult road of hardship and the painful path of struggle. As we endure our own trials and tribulations, we learn how to empathize with others who are going through the same kinds of struggles. (For additional perspective on the role of suffering in ministry, meditate on 2 Corinthians 1:3-7.)

Third, *we should loudly proclaim the mystery of Christ, not keep it to ourselves*. Everyone needs to hear the good news of reconciliation, redemption, and eternal salvation through Jesus Christ. It isn't a burden to share the message, but a privilege. Because the gospel came to Jews and Gentiles, slaves and free, men and women, we shouldn't discriminate in our ministries along racial, ethnic, socioeconomic, or religious lines. It is our joy to share the good news with all. (To this end, reflect on the principles of James 2:1-9.)

Fourth, *we should give ministry our all, not slack off or hold back*. When we reach the end of our lives—whenever that will be—we'll never regret the time we spent serving others for the sake of Christ. We'll never wish we'd played more golf rather than teach our children the fear of the Lord. We won't shed tears over missed naps when we spent Sunday afternoons meeting the needs of brothers and sisters in Christ. We won't regret spending our time and money on evangelism and missions rather than on a remodeled bathroom or a European vacation. (Read 1 Corinthians 3:5-15, reflecting on the quality of your contribution in building up your own local church.)

Counsel from a Concerned Apostle
COLOSSIANS 2:1-10

NASB

¹For I want you to know how great a struggle I have on your behalf and for those who are at Laodicea, and for all those who have not ªpersonally seen my face, ²that their hearts may be encouraged, having been knit together in love, and *attaining* to all the wealth ªthat comes from the full assurance of understanding, *resulting* in a true knowledge of God's mystery, *that is,* Christ *Himself,* ³in whom are hidden all the treasures of wisdom and knowledge. ⁴I say this so that no one will delude you with persuasive argument. ⁵For even though I am absent in body, nevertheless I am with you in spirit, rejoicing ªto see ᵇyour good discipline and the stability of your faith in Christ.

⁶Therefore as you have received Christ Jesus the Lord, *so* ªwalk in Him, ⁷having been firmly rooted *and now* being built up in Him and established ªin your faith, just as you were instructed, *and* overflowing ᵇwith gratitude.

⁸See to it that no one takes you captive through philosophy and empty deception, according to the tradition of men, according to the elementary principles of the world, ªrather than according to Christ. ⁹For in Him all

NLT

¹I want you to know how much I have agonized for you and for the church at Laodicea, and for many other believers who have never met me personally. ²I want them to be encouraged and knit together by strong ties of love. I want them to have complete confidence that they understand God's mysterious plan, which is Christ himself. ³In him lie hidden all the treasures of wisdom and knowledge.

⁴I am telling you this so no one will deceive you with well-crafted arguments. ⁵For though I am far away from you, my heart is with you. And I rejoice that you are living as you should and that your faith in Christ is strong.

⁶And now, just as you accepted Christ Jesus as your Lord, you must continue to follow him. ⁷Let your roots grow down into him, and let your lives be built on him. Then your faith will grow strong in the truth you were taught, and you will overflow with thankfulness.

⁸Don't let anyone capture you with empty philosophies and high-sounding nonsense that come from human thinking and from the spiritual powers* of this world, rather than from Christ. ⁹For in Christ lives all the

NASB

the fullness of Deity dwells in bodily form, [10] and in Him you have been made [a]complete, and He is the head [b]over all rule and authority;

2:1 [a]Lit *in the flesh*   **2:2** [a]Lit *of the full assurance*   **2:5** [a]Lit *and seeing*   [b]Or *your good order*   **2:6** [a]Or *lead your life*   **2:7** [a]Or *by*   [b]One early ms reads *in it with*   **2:8** [a]Lit *and not*   **2:10** [a]Lit *full*   [b]Lit *of*

NLT

fullness of God in a human body.* [10]So you also are complete through your union with Christ, who is the head over every ruler and authority.

2:8 Or *the spiritual principles;* also in 2:20.
2:9 Or *in him dwells all the completeness of the Godhead bodily.*

There was a period of time during my Christian "adolescence" when I went through an unhealthy phase of spiritual independence. I thought I didn't need anybody but God or anything but the Bible. I knew Christ. I had the Holy Spirit. I was able to read God's Word. I was engaged in my own daily study of Scripture. My parents had played their part in raising me and sending me on a wholesome spiritual trajectory. My wife was there to provide encouragement and companionship. I was plowing forward with a go-it-alone attitude and a pioneering spirit.

How wrong I was! As I grew spiritually through the years, one of the greatest things I learned was that we need others. Not occasionally but continually. And not just our families and close friends. We need all of our brothers and sisters in Christ, both in our local churches and in the universal body of Christ.

This is one of the most difficult truths to convince believers of. We talk about accepting Christ as our "personal Savior" and having a "personal relationship with God." We emphasize the "priesthood of each believer." These biblical truths are often misinterpreted through the distorted lens of an unaccountable individualism. Yes, each of us must personally accept Christ as Savior, but we are all baptized into one body, the church. We each have a personal relationship with God, but that relationship is a Father-child relationship with many siblings. And each of us has the freedom by the power of the Spirit to approach the throne of God without any mediator but the Lord Jesus Christ, but we are called to pray and intercede for our fellow believers, serving as one another's priests. A lone-ranger mentality isn't biblically supported.

Sometimes I fear that, though we rightly emphasize the importance of personal Bible study, we neglect the equally important aspects of Christian community and accountability. What an unbalanced and unhealthy way to live the Christian life! It should jolt us out of our privatized Christianity to realize that the great apostle Paul, who labored on the frontier of missions, surrounded himself with people. His letters are filled with the names of fellow workers, companions, and colleagues.

Some of them are familiar to us; others are not. But all were very familiar to Paul because they were his friends and supporters.

When we get to Colossians 2, we find Paul writing words of love, understanding, and compassion to people he had never even met, though they shared a mutual friendship with fellow ministry workers Epaphras and Philemon. But even though Paul and the Colossian believers didn't know each other personally, they needed each other. As members of the same body of Christ, they were connected, whether they were aware of it or not. In this section Paul shares with his fellow believers in Colossae personal encouragement (2:1-5), foundational truth (2:6-7), and doctrinal warnings (2:8-10).

— 2:1-5 —

The chapter breaks and verse numbers in our Bible translations are not inspired by God. They were added later to help people find passages of Scripture more easily. In the original text penned by the apostle Paul, the material of chapter 1 flowed right into that of chapter 2, perhaps written without Paul even lifting the stylus. Regardless, the thoughts from Colossians 1:29 flow right into 2:1. Paul had mentioned that in his God-given ministry as an apostle, he was determined to labor, striving according to the power of Christ working in him (1:29). In the next statement, Paul makes this striving personal: "I want you to know how great a struggle I have on your behalf" (2:1). Here Paul uses a noun form related to the verb meaning "to strive," which he had used in 1:29 to refer to the great struggle he endured in ministry.

Not only was he striving on their behalf, but his arduous labor in the ministry also benefited their neighbors to the north in Laodicea, and in fact, all those churches who had not met Paul face-to-face (2:1). Though these believers did not have a direct relationship with him, Paul desired that they would be encouraged by having their hearts "knit together in love" (2:2). The Greek word translated "knit together" is *symbibazō* [4822]. This same word is used in Ephesians to describe how the body of Christ is "fitted and held together by what every joint supplies," as each part works together to build up the whole body "in love" (Eph. 4:16).

This spiritual growth of the body that occurs as the members are fitted together in love results in "all the wealth that comes from the full assurance of understanding" (Col. 2:2). Paul had already emphasized this point in his prayer that the Colossians would be filled with "all spiritual wisdom and understanding" (1:9). This full assurance of understanding would result in "a true knowledge of God's mystery" (2:2).

Remember that the Gnostic false teachers emphasized seeking mysterious knowledge (*gnōsis* [1108]), but as something beyond Jesus Christ. The *true* knowledge of God's mystery, Paul says, is "Christ Himself, in whom are hidden all the treasures of wisdom and knowledge" (2:2-3). This could be a bold, blunt, and direct refutation of budding Gnostic heresies.[24] The fact that Paul had in mind a specific kind of false teaching is confirmed in his statement "I say this so that no one will delude you with persuasive argument" (2:4).

I'm sure the speculations of the false teachers were fascinating and their rhetoric tantalizing. No doubt they wowed their hearers with sophisticated "facts" and intricate logic. But every step of their mesmerizing methodology steered their listeners farther away from Christ. So it always is with false teachers. They demote, decentralize, or downplay the person and work of Jesus Christ. Cults have always done this and always will. Because Jesus alone is the treasure trove of wisdom and knowledge (2:3), the only way false teachers can persuade people to buy their fool's-gold philosophies is to turn attention away from Christ and toward their fabulous fabrications.

These false teachers posed a real danger, but instead of dwelling on the dark clouds of potential threats, Paul follows his warning with bright rays of affirmation. Though he and the Colossians were separated by distance, Paul assured them that he was with them "in spirit" (2:5). This isn't just a cliché phrase meaning "I've got your back." In reality Paul and the believers in Colossae were united by the bond of the Holy Spirit, who brings together in spiritual unity members of the body of Christ who are separated physically. In the context of this spiritual camaraderie, Paul's thoughts and emotions were with them as he expressed genuine interest and concern for them. He commended them for their good discipline and the stability of their faith in Christ. He rejoiced that they were living as they should and that they had a firm footing in the truth of the Christian faith.

Yet, Christians can always use more exhortation to continue to grow in the faith. And the Colossians, under the lingering threat of false teachers, needed an extra boost of foundational truth to keep them strong.

— 2:6-7 —

To strengthen them in their faith, Paul adds to his affirmation in 2:5 an exhortation to follow the way of Christ (2:6-7). The essence of the Christian life is packed into these two simple verses. We would do well

Rooting for Growth

COLOSSIANS 2:7

Years ago there was a tree in my front yard that gave me fits several times a year. It leaned. No, it never broke or stopped growing. It just leaned. It was an attractive, deep-green, nicely shaped tree that annually bore fragrant blossoms. But as soon as a good, healthy gust gave it a shove, over it leaned, like it was taking a bow after a performance.

One day it tilted at about a forty-five-degree angle toward the north. Stake and all, over it went. It seemed such a shame that my good-looking, charming tree couldn't hold its own. If I took away its support ropes, it was only a matter of time before it humbled itself and bowed its branches all the way to the ground.

Why did it lean like this? Well, in layman's terms, it was top-heavy. It had a lot of leafy branches and heavy foliage above ground, but under the earth it had weak, shallow roots. It had thin, little shoots here and there, reaching out for water and nutrients, but they were insufficient for supporting the fast-growing green above. And the tree didn't have sense enough to hold off on the new leaves until the roots caught up!

If nothing else, that overgrown, ornery tree has provided me with an object lesson I will never forget: Strong roots stabilize growth. What's true of trees is certainly true of Christians. Roots strengthen and support us against the prevailing winds of persuasion. When the mind-bending gales attack without warning, it's our network of solid roots that holds us firm and keeps us straight. Beautiful branches and delicate leaves, no matter how attractive, fail to fortify us as the velocity increases. It takes roots—thick, deep, powerful roots—to keep us standing strong.

That explains why the apostle Paul wanted the Ephesians to be "rooted and grounded in love" (Eph. 3:17) and why he echoed a

(continued on next page)

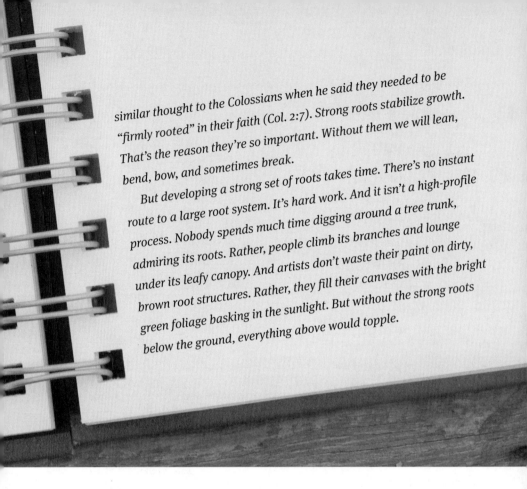

similar thought to the Colossians when he said they needed to be "firmly rooted" in their faith (Col. 2:7). Strong roots stabilize growth. That's the reason they're so important. Without them we will lean, bend, bow, and sometimes break.

But developing a strong set of roots takes time. There's no instant route to a large root system. It's hard work. And it isn't a high-profile process. Nobody spends much time digging around a tree trunk, admiring its roots. Rather, people climb its branches and lounge under its leafy canopy. And artists don't waste their paint on dirty, brown root structures. Rather, they fill their canvases with the bright green foliage basking in the sunlight. But without the strong roots below the ground, everything above would topple.

to meditate on them or even memorize them. I see four foundational truths here worth examining.

First, *the Christian life starts with new birth.* We "received Christ Jesus the Lord" (2:6). The word translated "received" is *paralambanō* [3880], which Paul uses in 1 Corinthians 15:1-5 in reference to receiving the gospel of Jesus Christ by faith:

> Now I make known to you, brethren, the gospel which I preached to you, which also you received, in which also you stand, by which also you are saved, if you hold fast the word which I preached to you, unless you believed in vain. For I delivered to you as of first importance what I also received, that Christ died for our sins according to the Scriptures, and that He was buried, and that He was raised on the third day according to the Scriptures, and that He appeared to Cephas, then to the twelve.

Second, *the Christian life continues when we "walk in Him"* (Col. 2:6). Like newborn babies, we grow slowly at first. Later, we learn to put one foot in front of the other as we begin to learn the meaning of Christian language and grasp basic truths about the faith. We learn what is expected of followers of Christ: how to pray, how to read His Word, how to deal with sin and resist temptation. As we stay close to Him and keep our focus on Him, we continue to walk in the right direction toward spiritual maturity. All this takes time.

In Colossians 2:7, Paul uses the image of a tree "firmly rooted" to illustrate the kind of deep faith needed to stand strong.

Third, *as the Christian walk continues, stability and growth occur* (2:7). Contrary to modern literary standards, Paul switches metaphors twice in this verse. He begins in 2:6 with the image of walking. Then, in 2:7, he uses the image of a tree being "firmly rooted" in the ground and follows this immediately with a structural metaphor ("being built up in Him"). Through these mixed metaphors, however, we see a consistent picture. As we grow, we become more stable; and with this stability comes greater maturity and the outworking of our spiritual growth, resulting in even greater stability.

Fourth, *as the Christian walk matures, it's marked by overflowing gratitude* (2:7). The mature believer knows that his or her spiritual growth comes from God, who, by the Holy Spirit, provides what is needed to conform Christians to the image of His Son (see 1 Cor. 3:6). The appropriate response to God's provision of growth and strength is not pride or self-confidence but thanksgiving.

Walking, Growing, and Bearing Fruit

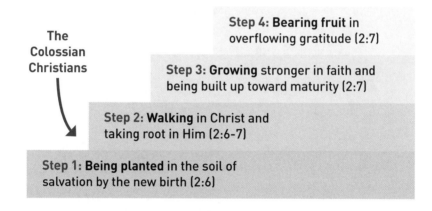

The Colossian Christians

Step 4: **Bearing fruit** in overflowing gratitude (2:7)

Step 3: **Growing** stronger in faith and being built up toward maturity (2:7)

Step 2: **Walking** in Christ and taking root in Him (2:6-7)

Step 1: **Being planted** in the soil of salvation by the new birth (2:6)

— 2:8-10 —

Paul knew that, in terms of the four steps outlined above, the Colossian Christians were standing between steps one and two in their growth in the Christian faith. They had been truly converted, were becoming stable in their faith, and were beginning to live the Christian life. But they were like freshmen in the lifelong curriculum of spiritual growth. Thus the Colossians were prime targets for spiritual deception from false teachers, who prefer to target the newly converted. So Paul transitions to stern doctrinal warnings in Colossians 2:8-10.

Earlier Paul warned his readers about being deluded by "persuasive argument" (2:4). Now he expands on this warning. And he doesn't merely caution against smooth talk by slick charlatans. Rather, he addresses deeper, darker levels of false teaching, by which the victims are taken captive (2:8). This image is not of people falling into a trap, but of being snatched and dragged off, as in the kidnapping of a child.[25] It's a violent and sobering image, intended to shock the Colossians to attention. How did those false teachers capture and carry their victims away from the truth?

First, *the false teachers sought to capture them through "philosophy and empty deception*" (2:8). Paul isn't condemning all philosophy or science, but false, baseless, worldly philosophy concocted to confuse and deceive Christians.[26] It's important to note that the burgeoning Gnosticism that likely threatened the baby Christians in Colossae was probably some sort of amalgam of selected Christian teachings and pagan mysticism, held together with a heavy dose of Platonic philosophy, and all of it badly twisted and distorted. In other words, the false teachers in Colossae were not only bad theologians and questionable scholars, but they were also terrible philosophers!

Second, *the false teachers followed the traditions of men and demons* (2:8). The phrase "elementary principles of the world" may refer to wicked spirits believed to control the events of heaven and earth.[27] If so, what a fitting rebuff this would be against a Gnostic system that proposed a pantheon of quasi-divine emanations that filled up the cosmos and controlled people's fates! Whether through the influence of wretched people or wicked spirits, these false teachers were drawing people away from Jesus Christ. Elsewhere Paul expressed similar concern for the Corinthians. He feared that "as the serpent deceived Eve by his craftiness," the believers would be "led astray from the simplicity and purity of devotion to Christ" by a false teacher proffering "another Jesus" instead of the true Lord Jesus Christ or imparting "a different spirit" from the Holy Spirit or proclaiming "a different gospel" from the one that centers on the person and work of Jesus Christ (2 Cor. 11:3-4).

As a defense against this two-pronged attack by the malicious false teachers, Paul again turns the focus to Jesus Christ. In a powerful theological statement concerning the person of Christ, Paul affirms, "In Him all the fullness of Deity dwells in bodily form" (Col. 2:9). This means that Jesus Christ is God incarnate (see John 1:1-3, 14). He is fully divine and fully human. He is undiminished Deity—including all the attributes, power, glory, honor, and authority of Deity—united with perfect humanity. A single dose of the doctrine of the Incarnation would instantly cure the disease of Christ-denying heresy.

Paul's use of the word *plērōma* [4138] ("fullness") was intentional. The term *plērōma* had special significance in Gnosticism. One scholar provides this description of its Gnostic usage:

> What then is the pleroma? It is the fullness, the totality, the completeness of all things. From it all good has come, to it all good will return and be taken up completely in it. That what has come

from it are the aeons and the "spiritual" seed in some of humanity. Indirectly, all evil has come from it also.[28]

By declaring that the fullness of Deity dwells in Christ in bodily form (Col. 2:9), Paul both refutes the mythical, speculative notion of *plērōma* in Gnosticism and counters the dualistic nature of their false religion. The Gnostics despised the body, the physical world, and all things material. They believed the physical world—especially the fleshly body—to be inherently evil. To confess that the fully divine Son of God could dwell in bodily form would have been anathema to those heretics.

Because of who Christ is—the God-man—He is able to fully accomplish His saving and sanctifying work. In 2:10 Paul strongly affirms the total sufficiency of Christ: "In Him you have been made complete." There's no need to seek so-called fullness anywhere else and no need to find additional saving wisdom, insight, knowledge, understanding, or truth from any other philosophy. In Christ we have everything necessary. In fact, even the angelic spiritual realm that so fascinated Gnostics was under His authority: "He is the head over all rule and authority" (2:10).

Jesus Christ is sufficient as Lord.

APPLICATION: COLOSSIANS 2:1-10

Watering Our Roots

No matter where we are in our process of spiritual growth, we need to keep our spiritual roots healthy, deep, and strong. But how do we do this? What can we do to remain firmly rooted in our faith? Let me suggest three things we can do to apply Paul's teaching in Colossians 2:1-10.

First, *once every week, affirm and encourage another believer.* Just as Paul went out of his way to exhort, encourage, warn, and teach other believers, you can do the same. You'll find that this love and concern for others, being with them "in spirit" (2:5), not only helps to strengthen their roots but will also grow your own. You could do this through a personal meeting, a phone call, a card, an e-mail, or even a brief text message. Make yourself available, demonstrating that those brothers and sisters in Christ are not alone. And before you know it, you'll find that you're the recipient of others' notes of encouragement.

Second, *once a day, think of something for which you're grateful and tell the Lord, "Thank You."* Thank Him for the food He provides and the friends He has brought into your life. Thank Him for health, for deliverance from various temptations, and for perseverance through trials. Thank Him for salvation in Jesus Christ and the hope of eternal life. Thank Him for big things and little things. Don't let a day go by without expressing your gratitude to the Lord for all the good things He provides.

Third, *morning, noon, and night, pause and remind yourself, "I am complete in Christ."* Remember that you're fully accepted by God because of the person and work of Jesus Christ—not because of your own worth or merit. Recall that you're totally free from the eternal punishment of sin. Acknowledge that Christ has broken the power of sin's dominance in your life, allowing you to walk in a manner worthy of His calling (see 1:10; Eph. 4:1). And rejoice in the fact that you are absolutely secure in His salvation and will be fully delivered from the presence of sin when Christ returns.

By consistently sharing encouragement with others, regularly expressing your gratitude to God, and continually recalling the all-sufficiency of Christ, you'll be watering the roots of your faith that nourish spiritual growth.

Living Forgiven . . . and Free
COLOSSIANS 2:11-23

NASB

[11] and in Him you were also circumcised with a circumcision made without hands, in the removal of the body of the flesh by the circumcision of Christ; [12] having been buried with Him in baptism, in which you were also raised up with Him through faith in the working of God, who raised Him from the dead. [13] When you were dead [a]in your transgressions and the uncircumcision of your flesh, He made you alive together with Him, having forgiven us all our transgressions, [14] having canceled out the certificate of debt consisting of decrees against us, which was hostile to us; and He has taken

NLT

[11] When you came to Christ, you were "circumcised," but not by a physical procedure. Christ performed a spiritual circumcision—the cutting away of your sinful nature.* [12] For you were buried with Christ when you were baptized. And with him you were raised to new life because you trusted the mighty power of God, who raised Christ from the dead.

[13] You were dead because of your sins and because your sinful nature was not yet cut away. Then God made you alive with Christ, for he forgave all our sins. [14] He canceled the record

it out of the way, having nailed it to the cross. [15] When He had [a]disarmed the rulers and authorities, He made a public display of them, having triumphed over them through [b]Him.

[16] Therefore no one is to [a]act as your judge in regard to food or drink or in respect to a festival or a new moon or a Sabbath [b]day— [17] things which are a *mere* shadow of what is to come; but the [a]substance [b]belongs to Christ. [18] Let no one keep [a]defrauding you of your prize by delighting in [b]self-abasement and the worship of the angels, [c]taking his stand on *visions* he has seen, [d]inflated without cause by his fleshly mind, [19] and not holding fast to the head, from whom the entire body, being supplied and held together by the joints and [a]ligaments, grows with a growth [b]which is from God.

[20] If you have died with Christ [a]to the elementary principles of the world, why, as if you were living in the world, do you submit yourself to decrees, such as, [21] "Do not handle, do not taste, do not touch!" [22] (which all *refer to* things destined to perish [a]with use)—in accordance with the commandments and teachings of men? [23] These are matters which have, to be sure, the [a]appearance of wisdom in [b]self-made religion and self-abasement and severe treatment of the body, *but are* of no value against fleshly indulgence.

2:13 [a]Or *by reason of* 2:15 [a]Or *divested Himself of* [b]Or *it;* i.e. the cross 2:16 [a]Lit *judge you* [b]Or *days* 2:17 [a]Lit *body* [b]Lit *of Christ* 2:18 [a]Or *deciding against you* [b]Or *humility* [c]Or *going into detail about* [d]Or *conceited* 2:19 [a]Lit *bonds* [b]Lit *of God* 2:20 [a]Lit *from* 2:22 [a]Or *by being consumed* 2:23 [a]Lit *report;* Gr *logos* [b]Or *would-be religion*

of the charges against us and took it away by nailing it to the cross. [15] In this way, he disarmed* the spiritual rulers and authorities. He shamed them publicly by his victory over them on the cross.

[16] So don't let anyone condemn you for what you eat or drink, or for not celebrating certain holy days or new moon ceremonies or Sabbaths. [17] For these rules are only shadows of the reality yet to come. And Christ himself is that reality. [18] Don't let anyone condemn you by insisting on pious self-denial or the worship of angels,* saying they have had visions about these things. Their sinful minds have made them proud, [19] and they are not connected to Christ, the head of the body. For he holds the whole body together with its joints and ligaments, and it grows as God nourishes it.

[20] You have died with Christ, and he has set you free from the spiritual powers of this world. So why do you keep on following the rules of the world, such as, [21] "Don't handle! Don't taste! Don't touch!"? [22] Such rules are mere human teachings about things that deteriorate as we use them. [23] These rules may seem wise because they require strong devotion, pious self-denial, and severe bodily discipline. But they provide no help in conquering a person's evil desires.

2:11 Greek *the cutting away of the body of the flesh.* 2:15 Or *he stripped off.* 2:18 Or *or worshiping with angels.*

Strange as it may sound, one of the most challenging aspects of life is actually learning how to live our lives. There are far too many Christians merely proceeding from one day to the next. They don't know how to truly live. Yes, their hearts may be beating, their minds may be racing, and their senses may be active, but they don't realize the full meaning of Jesus' words "I came that they may have life, and have it abundantly" (John 10:10).

Instead of receiving all the benefits that are theirs to claim, many settle for a lifestyle that is anything but fulfilling and gratifying. This isn't true only of our current generation; it's been going on for centuries. It can even be traced back to the era in which the apostle Paul lived and ministered. For example, the Christians in the ancient city of Colossae needed Paul's strong words of warning because they lacked an understanding of what it meant to live as fully forgiven people.

Additionally, the Colossian believers were being seduced by those who criticized them for what they ate and drank, what holy days they observed, and what rituals and regulations they followed. Instead of living like fully forgiven people who were truly free, they were being held captive by the rules and requirements of legalistic Judaizers and ascetic Gnostics. As it was in those days, so it is today. Many believers in our own time are failing to live forgiven . . . and free.

— 2:11-15 —

The saving gospel message centers on the person and work of Jesus Christ. In Colossians 2:9-10 Paul powerfully articulated his thoughts on the person of Christ. He is the God-man, in whom "the fullness of Deity dwells in bodily form" (2:9). As such, He is "the head over all rule and authority" (2:10). In 2:11-15 Paul emphasizes the saving work of Christ and how the forgiveness of sins is personally applied to every believer.

In 2:11 Paul begins with a metaphor that would have been familiar to Jewish believers and anyone who knew the Old Testament Law: circumcision. As instituted by God, the ritual of cutting away a male's foreskin served to identify the male child as a participant in God's covenant with Abraham. In Genesis 17:10-11, God said to Abraham, "This is My covenant, which you shall keep, between Me and you and your descendants after you: every male among you shall be circumcised. And you shall be circumcised in the flesh of your foreskin, and it shall be the sign of the covenant between Me and you."

In time, this distinguishing feature became symbolic of the Israelite people, the covenant, and the culture. Many Jews thought that the covenant sign of circumcision entitled them to blessings from God and exemption from the divine judgment rightly deserved by the Gentiles. However, Paul taught that in Christ neither circumcision nor uncircumcision had any eternal significance—only salvation by grace alone through faith alone in Christ alone (see Gal. 6:15).

When Paul uses the analogy of circumcision in Colossians, he does so knowing that his readers would recall its significance as a physical act that identified the recipients as having a special covenant relationship with God. It was the external sign of a spiritual reality. In Colossians 2:11, however, Paul doesn't have literal circumcision in mind when he says to the mostly Gentile believers in Colossae, "In Him you were also circumcised with a circumcision made without hands." Rather, he is referring to "the removal of the body of the flesh by the circumcision of Christ."

Several interpretations have been posited regarding the meaning of this last phrase. I think the best way to understand it is to take "body of the flesh" as a reference to Christ's body when He suffered and died on the cross. Believers participate in His death spiritually by identifying with Him through faith, and they participate physically by submitting to baptism as an external sign of a spiritual reality, thereby reenacting the events of Christ's burial and resurrection.[29] Thus in 2:12 Paul shifts from the spiritual reality (identification with the atoning death of Christ by faith) to a physical analogy ("having been buried with Him in baptism, in which you were also raised up with Him through faith in the working of God, who raised Him from the dead").

Being "in Christ" means that we share in what was accomplished through His death. By believing, we participate in His death, burial, and resurrection and receive the eternal benefits of His work in a new covenant relationship with God. We died to our former way of life when we turned from our sins, and we rose to a new lifestyle when we pledged to live as disciples of Christ in the new covenant community of the Spirit. These actions were symbolized by baptism.

In 2:13 Paul refers to the spiritual reality that stands behind the physical sign of baptism mentioned in 2:12. We were once dead in our transgressions, unclean, and separated from the covenant of God and His people—"uncircumcised" in the flesh. However, by grace through faith on the basis of the death and resurrection of Christ, we have been forgiven of all our sins. Our debt has been canceled. Any outstanding warrants against us have been suspended. They were "nailed to the cross" and abolished forever (see 2:14).

Furthermore, because we are now under the domain of the King of kings and Lord of lords, who is "the head over all rule and authority" (2:10), we have also been liberated from the power of demonic forces. How? They, too, were disarmed at the Cross (2:15). To illustrate Christ's vanquishing of wicked spiritual powers, Paul invokes the image of a victorious general leading a procession, parading his conquered enemies in shackles to humiliate them in their defeat. Paul uses this term for "triumph" only once elsewhere, in 2 Corinthians 2:14, where he writes, "But thanks be to God, who always leads us in triumph in Christ, and manifests through us the sweet aroma of the knowledge of Him in every place." Commentator William Barclay helps us see the picture Paul evoked for his readers when he used the word "triumph" for the kind of victory believers have in Jesus Christ:

> In a Triumph, the procession of the victorious general marched through the streets of Rome to the Capitol in the following order. First came the state officials and the senate. Then came the trumpeters. Behind them came those carrying the spoils taken from the conquered land. . . . Walking behind all these were the captive princes, leaders and generals in chains. . . . Then came the officers who attended the magistrates, the lictors bearing their rods, followed by the musicians with their lyres; then the priests swinging their censers with the sweet-smelling incense burning in them. After that came the general himself. He stood in a chariot drawn by four horses. . . . After him rode his family, and finally came the army wearing all their decorations and shouting *Io triumphe!*, their cry of triumph.[30]

Photo by Jebulon/Wikimedia Commons

Relief of a **Roman triumphal procession** on the Arch of Titus in Rome, Italy, depicting Titus's siege of Jerusalem in AD 70

Though the illustration is the same in 2 Corinthians 2:14 and Colossians 2:15, Paul's use of the image in Colossians differs slightly in that it focuses on the humiliating march of the vanquished, whereas the emphasis in 2 Corinthians is on the jubilant march of the victors. In any case, the believers in Colossae would have gotten the picture. Their permanent covenant relationship with Christ by grace through faith had been sealed and signified in baptism. And just as they were fully associated with Christ's death and resurrection, they were likewise fully associated with His conquest of sin, death, and demons. Believers are therefore reckoned among the triumphant victors!

They were forgiven . . . and free!

— 2:16-23 —

In 2:11-15 Paul emphasized the vertical aspect of Christ's person and work in securing forgiveness and liberation for those who trust in Him alone for salvation. In 2:16-23, Paul turns to the horizontal features of this salvation. He begins verse 16 with the conjunction *therefore*, pointing to the connection between the practical application that follows and the theological discussion of salvation just outlined. From here to the end of the chapter, Paul focuses his attention on three lingering threats to Christian freedom: Judaistic legalism (2:16-17), Gnostic mysticism (2:18-19), and dualistic asceticism (2:20-23).

Charles Ryrie defines legalism as "a fleshly attitude which conforms to a code for the purpose of exalting self."[31] Legalism always involves man-made rules and regulations enforced through guilt and shame. Legalists portray God as a severe judge ready to pounce at every infraction—and the leaders and teachers among the legalists have deputized themselves as God's agents to make sure everybody toes the line. The threat of legalism probably came not from the nascent Gnostic teachers but from Paul's original heel nippers, the Judaizers. These men wanted to soften Paul's radical emphasis on grace and liberty, mixing the Old Testament Law with the New Testament gospel. They believed the stipulations of the Mosaic Law—or at least some of them— were still in force for the Christian as a rule of life.

In response to this brand of old-fashioned legalism, Paul gave a brief but crushing critique. He instructed the Colossians to stand against anyone who would judge them regarding dietary laws or feast days (2:16). Though the people of God under the old covenant were obligated to observe these rules and regulations as part of their unique arrangement with God, these practices were merely a "shadow of what

EXCURSUS: WERE THE OLD TESTAMENT SAINTS SAVED BY OBEYING THE LAW?

COLOSSIANS 2:16-17

Colossians 2:16-17 says that the Old Testament laws regarding food and drink, festivals, new moons, and Sabbaths were "a mere shadow of what is to come," pointing forward to the reality of Jesus Christ. This leads to an important question: How were Old Testament saints saved? Were they saved by good works like eating and drinking only certain foods or religiously keeping the holy days prescribed in the Law of Moses? Did the old system save them temporarily until Christ came to save them permanently? Some people mistakenly believe that the Old Testament saints were saved and bound for heaven by obeying the Law and seeking forgiveness through animal sacrifices when they fell short. However, as Hebrews 10:4 says, "It is impossible for the blood of bulls and goats to take away sins."

Christians must understand that God never promised eternal life in heaven for those who were faithful to keep the dietary laws, religious rites and rituals, and the sacrificial system of the Mosaic Law. Rather, God said to Israel, "If you will indeed obey My voice and keep My covenant, then you shall be My own possession among all the peoples, for all the earth is Mine; and you shall be to Me a kingdom of priests and a holy nation" (Exod. 19:5-6). And in Deuteronomy 28:1-2, Moses declared, "Now it shall be, if you diligently obey the LORD your God, being careful to do all His commandments which I command you today, the LORD your God will set you high above all the nations of the earth. All these blessings will come upon you and overtake you if you obey the LORD your God." The blessings for obedience that are then listed in Deuteronomy 28:3-14

relate to their safe, secure, bountiful lives in the Promised Land. Not a single line offers Israel eternal salvation in heaven for obedience. Likewise, the list of curses that will come as a result of breaking the covenant contains no threat of eternal punishment in hell—only temporal judgments on earth, including death and destruction (Deut. 28:15-68).

How then were Old Testament saints born again, eternally saved, and sealed for heaven? The Bible makes it clear that eternal salvation has always come *by grace through faith* (Rom. 4:1-17). It has never been earned by works, by obeying the Law (see Gal. 2:21), or by offering animal sacrifices (see Heb. 10:4). Rather, eternal salvation is based on the atoning work of Christ (Rom. 3:21-26).

Of course, the Old Testament saints under the Mosaic covenant didn't have the full story that came with the revelation of Jesus Christ in the Incarnation, Crucifixion, and Resurrection. The Law provided "a mere shadow of what is to come" (Col. 2:17). However, they had prophecies, promises, and glimpses of the ultimate salvation that would come through the future Messiah (see Rom. 1:1-4; 1 Pet. 1:10-12). They could therefore exercise simple, childlike faith in God's goodness, mercy, and promises (see Gen. 15:6; Rom. 4:3). Their salvation, like ours, was by grace through faith, not by works. As theologian Charles Ryrie famously put it, "The *basis* of salvation in every age is the death of Christ; the *requirement* for salvation in every age is faith; the *object* of faith in every age is God; the *content* of faith changes in the various dispensations."[32]

is to come," the substance of which is Jesus Christ's person and work. For legalists to force the observance of these old rules and regulations on Gentile believers in Christ would be to go backward, mixing the old covenant with the new, grace with merit, faith with works. Paul's message for those threatened by legalism was simple: *You're forgiven and free. Live like it!*

Besides facing the threat of legalism, the Colossians also had to contend with mysticism (2:18-19). Fledgling Gnostic heresies thrived on speculations, spiritual experiences, and encounters with the invisible realm. Paul warns against those who sought to rob believers of their freedom by parading their own "self-abasement." These individuals projected a phony humility, claiming to have become the chosen channel of special revelations. All the while they used their feigned encounters with "the other side" to inflate their own egos and puff up their reputations as prophets and seers.

These frauds had strayed so far from the centrality of Jesus Christ that they were even promoting "the worship of the angels"! Paul may have had in mind an early version of the essentially polytheistic Gnostic notion of emanations—spirit beings that served as mediators between the earthly and heavenly realms. As these mystics turned the spotlight on themselves and their own fictitious revelations, they drew attention away from Jesus Christ and did damage to His body, the church.

Having confronted the threats of Judaistic legalism and Gnostic mysticism, Paul concludes this section with a sound rejection of dualistic asceticism (2:20-23). This form of asceticism believed that the soul could be purified by a harsh discipline of the body. It is associated with a dualistic view of humanity, in which the good, spiritual part of a person is trapped in the wicked, physical part (the body). Until a person escapes the prison of the flesh through death, they must punish the body, beating it into submission so the soul can thrive.

However, this kind of dualistic approach to spirituality resulting in asceticism is contrary to the Christian view of humanity and spirituality. Both aspects of humanity—material and immaterial—were originally created good (Gen. 1:26-27, 31; 2:7). However, after the Fall, the whole person—body and soul—fell into sin and death (Eph. 2:1-3). When we are saved by grace through faith, we are to worship, serve, and honor God not only with our minds but also with our bodies—indeed, with our whole selves (Matt. 22:37; Rom. 12:1-2).

The ascetics who were threatening the Colossians were trying to enslave unsuspecting saints with man-made decrees like "Do not handle, do not taste, do not touch!" (Col. 2:21). These rules led to "self-abasement and severe treatment of the body," but they did nothing to actually deliver them from fleshly desires (2:23). Such principles had no foundation in the teachings of Jesus or the apostles. There were no biblical passages these teachers could turn to in support of their rules and regulations. Their dualistic asceticism was propped up by "the appearance of wisdom in self-made religion" (2:23), that is, by sophisticated arguments that supported human traditions that were set forth as being from the mouth of God.

Paul's defense against the triple threat of legalism, mysticism, and asceticism in Colossians 2:16-23 was the same: the person and work of Jesus Christ. Against legalism, Jesus is the Liberator who forgave our sins through the Cross and freed us from the Law. Against mysticism, Jesus is the One in whom the fullness of Deity dwells bodily; He alone is the sole Mediator between God and humanity and the One through whom we have all wisdom, knowledge, and spiritual insight. Against asceticism, Jesus is the One who sprung us—through our association with His death—from the prison of worldly rules and regulations that can't please God.

APPLICATION: COLOSSIANS 2:11-23

Fully Forgiven . . . Forever Free

If you are in Christ, you are completely forgiven and totally free. It's not a matter of *if* or *when*. There are no strings attached to His forgiveness and no conditions on your liberty from the domination of sin, the dominion of demons, or the destruction of legalism, mysticism, and misdirected asceticism. How does this spiritual reality work its way out in the Christian's life? Let me share three practical directives.

First, *be strong in the Word of God and keep worshiping Christ*. When false teachers lead people astray, they take them down one or both of these paths: a neglect or rejection of Scripture, or a diminishing or dethronement of Christ. They'll divert you from a careful, faithful, personal study of the Word of God and distract you from the honor, worship, and obedience due to the Lord Jesus. To live forgiven and free, you need to keep your feet firmly planted on the unshakable foundation of

Scripture and your heart and mind focused on the person and work of Christ.

Second, *refuse and resist all substitutes.* False teachers who trade in spiritual bondage will try to swap out the authentic Scriptures for convincing forgeries—new revelations, authoritative interpretations, or supplemental sources of divine truth. I'm not talking about legitimate insights from orthodox commentators—gifted teachers who respect God's Word and preach truth. I'm referring to those who undermine the Word and offer up a powerless Jesus and a weak gospel.

I have been eminently blessed in my life in many ways, not the least of which has been the joy and privilege of serving under mentors and being influenced by those who have helped shape my thinking. Every one of my mentors has been strongly committed to the Word of God and a sincere worshiper of the Lord Jesus. I've been privileged to have them around me, especially in my formative years as I was just learning my way. They didn't point me to their own opinions based on their own authority; they stepped aside and pointed me to the Word of God and to Christ. They were the real thing. And by knowing what's real, I learned to refuse and resist all substitutes.

Third, *don't be afraid to risk living your life unshackled.* Remember that your true Master is Christ. We are bond-servants to Him and to no other. Only by submitting to the liberating lordship of Christ can we be free from the enslaving oppression of false teachers. When we seek to serve only Him, we won't even be tempted to shackle ourselves under the bondage of frauds. I love the way Paul wrote about this in Galatians: "Am I now seeking the favor of men, or of God? Or am I striving to please men? If I were still trying to please men, I would not be a bond-servant of Christ" (Gal. 1:10).

If I tried to please others by tolerating their twisted doctrines or accommodating their man-made traditions or legalistic rules and regulations, I would soon become a doormat. They wouldn't stop with just one or two demands. It would become an epidemic. I could never please them all or live up to their unending requirements. My goal is to please the Lord Jesus Christ. And He tells you and me to be free from sin, free from Satan, and free from legalism, mysticism, and misdirected asceticism.

In Christ we're fully forgiven and forever free. Let's live like it!

JESUS CHRIST, OUR LIFE (COLOSSIANS 3:1–4:1)

The overarching theme of Paul's letter to the Colossians is that *Jesus Christ is sufficient as our Lord, our Life, and our Leader.* In chapters 1 and 2 Paul developed the principle that Jesus Christ is sufficient as our Lord. In the second major section (3:1–4:1), Paul emphasizes the sufficiency of Christ as our Life.

Here Paul turns our attention to believers' heavenly calling and their longing for the ultimate salvation that will come at Christ's return (3:1-4). Though eternal life already began for us when we received salvation by grace through faith, we await the full realization of that eternal life in the future. In the meantime, we aren't called to keep our eyes in the sky or our heads in the clouds. The fact of our future glory should compel us to live new lives that follow the pattern of Christ in the here and now (3:5-17).

This new life in which we live as faithful imitators of Christ will affect all dimensions of our lives including marriage, family, and even employment (3:18–4:1). In contrast to the speculative and cerebral notions of budding Gnostic heresies, the Christian life is meant to impact our present life on earth in a practical way—lived out in the minute-by-minute here and now of everyday life. And in order to live this new life, we need to depend entirely on the sufficiency of Jesus Christ, who is our Life.

KEY TERMS IN COLOSSIANS 3:1–4:1

anakainoō (ἀνακαινόω) [341] "to make new," "to renovate," "to renew"

This word appears only twice in the New Testament (2 Cor. 4:16; Col. 3:10), but it encapsulates a central concept in Colossians. It refers to the fresh, new life that a believer receives when he or she is "born again" (see John 3:3; 1 Pet. 1:3). At the root of the verb *anakainoō* is the Greek term for "new," *kainos* [2537], which refers to a qualitative newness—not something merely different but altogether superior. There may be some continuity and similarity between the old and the new, but the new should never be equated with the old. In Colossians, the "old self" and its sinfulness is contrasted with the "new self" and its righteousness, emphasizing the renewed life believers are empowered to live in Christ (Col. 3:5-10).

zōē (ζωή) [2222] "life," often "spiritual life"

Most of us have been to a zoological garden, better known simply as a "zoo." But few of us know that the word zoo comes from the Greek word for "life." In the New Testament the word occasionally refers to physical human life (Acts 8:33; 17:25) or to animal life (Rev. 16:3), but the great majority of uses of zōē in the New Testament refer to the eternal life that comes from the Father, through the Son, by the Holy Spirit. In fact, Jesus Christ is called "our zōē" (Col. 3:4): He is the Source of our eternal life, both spiritually and physically, and He is the One who nourishes and sustains our life forever.

Spot-On Advice from a Seasoned Mentor
COLOSSIANS 3:1-14

NASB

¹Therefore if you have been raised up with Christ, keep seeking the things above, where Christ is, seated at the right hand of God. ²ªSet your mind on the things above, not on the things that are on earth. ³For you have died and your life is hidden with Christ in God. ⁴When Christ, who is our life, is revealed, then you also will be revealed with Him in glory.

⁵Therefore ªconsider the members of your earthly body as dead to ᵇimmorality, impurity, passion, evil desire, and greed, which ᶜamounts to idolatry. ⁶For it is because of these things that the wrath of God will come ªupon the sons of disobedience, ⁷and in them you also once walked, when you were living ªin them. ⁸But now you also, put them all aside: anger, wrath, malice, slander, *and* abusive speech from your mouth. ⁹ªDo not lie to one another,

NLT

¹Since you have been raised to new life with Christ, set your sights on the realities of heaven, where Christ sits in the place of honor at God's right hand. ²Think about the things of heaven, not the things of earth. ³For you died to this life, and your real life is hidden with Christ in God. ⁴And when Christ, who is your* life, is revealed to the whole world, you will share in all his glory.

⁵So put to death the sinful, earthly things lurking within you. Have nothing to do with sexual immorality, impurity, lust, and evil desires. Don't be greedy, for a greedy person is an idolater, worshiping the things of this world. ⁶Because of these sins, the anger of God is coming.* ⁷You used to do these things when your life was still part of this world. ⁸But now is the time to get rid of anger, rage, malicious behavior, slander,

since you laid aside the old [b]self with its *evil* practices, [10]and have put on the new self who is being [a]renewed to a true knowledge according to the image of the One who created him— [11]*a renewal* in which there is no *distinction between* Greek and Jew, circumcised and uncircumcised, [a]barbarian, Scythian, slave and freeman, but Christ is all, and in all.

[12]So, as those who have been chosen of God, holy and beloved, put on a heart of compassion, kindness, humility, gentleness and [a]patience; [13]bearing with one another, and forgiving each other, whoever has a complaint against anyone; just as the Lord forgave you, so also should you. [14]Beyond all these things *put on* love, which is [a]the perfect bond of unity.

3:2 [a]Or *Be intent on*   3:5 [a]Lit *put to death the members which are upon the earth* [b]Lit *fornication* [c]Lit *is*   3:6 [a]Two early mss do not contain *upon the sons of disobedience*   3:7 [a]Or *among these*   3:9 [a]Or *Stop lying* [b]Gr *anthropos*   3:10 [a]Lit *renovated*   3:11 [a]I.e. those who were not Greeks, either by birth or by culture   3:12 [a]I.e. forbearance toward others   3:14 [a]Lit *the uniting bond of perfection*

and dirty language. [9]Don't lie to each other, for you have stripped off your old sinful nature and all its wicked deeds. [10]Put on your new nature, and be renewed as you learn to know your Creator and become like him. [11]In this new life, it doesn't matter if you are a Jew or a Gentile,* circumcised or uncircumcised, barbaric, uncivilized,* slave, or free. Christ is all that matters, and he lives in all of us.

[12]Since God chose you to be the holy people he loves, you must clothe yourselves with tenderhearted mercy, kindness, humility, gentleness, and patience. [13]Make allowance for each other's faults, and forgive anyone who offends you. Remember, the Lord forgave you, so you must forgive others. [14]Above all, clothe yourselves with love, which binds us all together in perfect harmony.

3:4 Some manuscripts read *our*.   3:6 Some manuscripts read *is coming on all who disobey him*.   3:11a Greek *a Greek*.   3:11b Greek *Barbarian, Scythian*.

True or false? *Experience is the best teacher.* Many of us have heard this statement throughout our lives. It sounds right, doesn't it? But it's false. The truth is similar, but with an important qualification added: *Guided* experience is the best teacher.

Think about it. The experience of cooking without any prior knowledge will likely result in a meal nobody wants to eat. But if you have a seasoned chef coaching you, you'll be cooking gourmet meals in no time. Likewise, the experience of trying to drive a car without any training will probably result in an accident. But behind-the-wheel lessons from an experienced driver will help you get safely from point A to point B.

This is also true in relation to the whole of our lives. When we are young, our parents and teachers guide us, challenge us, correct us, and stretch us. They help us overcome our weaknesses and enhance our strengths. Through their guidance we grow and mature, entering into more specific areas of interest and giftedness. These wise mentors equip us to live skillfully and experience life fully.

In the first century, the apostle Paul was a qualified, experienced mentor whose wise advice was reliable. His counsel was trustworthy. His warnings were constructive. His instructions were insightful. Those who attended to his teaching were sure to grow under his guided experience.

Colossians 3:1-14 provides a perfect example of Paul's inspired leadership regarding how to live out the new life in Christ. He tells us what to think about as we seek to live life to the fullest (3:1-4). He instructs us on what distractions we need to get rid of (3:5-9). Then, knowing that we all form some bad habits through the years, he shows us what we need in order to gain a fresh start (3:10-11). Finally, he wraps up by outlining a list of essential virtues that we're to "put on" as part of the new life (3:12-14).

These are the words of a master mentor. We do well to heed them.

— 3:1-4 —

Picture Paul as your personal spiritual trainer, standing before you saying, "Okay, I want to get into your head, because everything we do begins there. It's the center of our thoughts, our emotions, and our will. Let's start with properly exercising the mind." So in Colossians 3:1, Paul urges those who have been "raised up with Christ" to direct their minds upward, "seeking the things above, where Christ is, seated at the right hand of God."

If we're associated with Christ's death and resurrection, we're also associated with His victorious ascension to the right hand of God. We're spiritually united with Him, and our thoughts and attitudes should be constantly drawn upward, not downward (3:2). And if we're associated with Him in His death, resurrection, and ascension (3:3), our minds should also anticipate the next stage in the work of Christ—His return (3:4).

However, Paul isn't suggesting we live each day in a superspiritual, out-of-touch la-la land, ignoring our lives on earth and paying attention only to the things to come. Richard Melick nicely brings out the practical point of Paul's image:

> This command called the Colossians to focus on matters related to the rule of Christ in the world. Since he is the sovereign one, his concerns should occupy the Christian. . . . Believers' values and loves were to be focused on the rule of Christ, and consecrated energies were to be devoted to making that rule a reality on earth.

Coach 'Em Up!

COLOSSIANS 3:1-2

I have a good friend named Skip Hall who coached football for thirty years, helping lead teams to three Rose Bowls and the Orange Bowl. He has vast experience in coaching, recruiting, team building, and consulting. Although he decided to step away from coaching, he still promotes and practices the lessons he learned through decades of successful coaching.

Skip once said to me, "Chuck, let me tell you one of the greatest things I ever learned as a coach. I needed to coach 'em up. You don't coach 'em down. You don't land on 'em constantly with all the things they're doing wrong. You coach 'em up, not down. You've got the same calling. As a pastor, never forget, Chuck, the importance of coaching 'em up."

Skip's advice is golden. It applies to coaching, teaching, mentoring, parenting, pastoring, and leading. In fact, nearly two thousand years ago, Paul followed the same principle of positive, upward-focused guidance when he encouraged the Colossians to look up, focus on Christ, and put on new life. Take your eyes off the drag-you-down world around you—the things that will only discourage, depress, and disappoint. Instead, set your sights on the things above.

This principle was driven home for me in a profound way when a member of our church staff suffered from brain cancer. He had been battling it for a long time and was putting up a brave fight. He was an encouragement to all of us. When he finally lost the earthly battle against the disease, I reflected on his courageous ability to keep looking up all the way to the end. What's remarkable is that he continued to urge us to set our sights high. He told us, "I just want you to remember, if I don't survive this, help everybody around you to keep looking up."

That brave saint coached us up to the very end.

... The task of the Colossian church was to call people to Christ and away from earthly things. It was to call people to life.[1]

Next time the world gets us down or we're in a funk and can't seem to get out of it, we need to check our spiritual eyesight. What's our focus? Are we looking backward, downward, and inward—fixated on things below, obsessing over things on this horizontal plane, and surrendering to the world's values and loves? Or are we setting our gaze on things above, where Christ, "who is our life" (3:4), sits victorious, ready to return from heaven and rescue us from this wicked world? A worldly focus will drag us deeper into the mire, but an upward focus—a focus on Christ's values and loves—will lift us out of it.

— 3:5-9 —

If we hire a physical fitness trainer to whip us into shape, we can be sure they will insist that we get rid of some things that slow our progress, set us back, or work against positive results. We'll no doubt be told to cut down on sweets, trim the fat, and avoid high-sugar drinks.

It's no different in our spiritual training. In Colossians 3:5-9, our spiritual mentor Paul gives us a handful of things we need to lay aside as we pursue a life that reflects the "things above." These sinful attitudes and actions will be the cause of God's wrath coming upon this world (3:6), so they have no place in the lives of believers destined for eternity with Him. They are—and should continue to be—things of our past, things we once practiced but have abandoned for the sake of conformity to Christ. We can categorize these attitudes and actions into three groups.

First, Paul tells us to get rid of *sensuality* (3:5). This group of behaviors includes four practices that we are to consider our bodies to be "dead to": "immorality, impurity, passion, [and] evil desire." The term *immorality* is a translation of the Greek word *porneia* [4202]. *Porneia* is a general term for sexual immorality of any kind, including premarital and extramarital sexual relations, prostitution, and homosexuality.

"Impurity" refers to anything that is unclean, unwholesome, and corrupting. This includes anything that pollutes our minds—especially inappropriate or suggestive images. Moving to the interior, "passion" and "evil desire" have to do with dwelling on immoral or impure things—coddling unwholesome desires, obsessing over illicit cravings, and longing for things that are forbidden to Christians. These sensual thoughts and behaviors are disastrous to a healthy Christian life.

We can't even tinker or toy with these things. We can't dabble in these things and hope to remain untainted. There's only one stance a Christian should take with sensual things: Consider himself or herself dead to them (3:5). You may have heard the saying "He's dead to me," referring to a complete and total break in relationship with someone. Paul urges believers to make this kind of break with sensual things.

Second, Paul tells us to get rid of *materialism* (3:5). This includes greed and idolatry. The first relates to inner motivation, the second to outer manifestation. Greed is the driving desire to have more . . . and *more* . . . and *MORE*—a desire that can never be satiated. If you let greed get a foothold, it won't be long before you're worshiping and serving the very things you thought would satisfy you. Richard Foster pulls no punches when he writes, "Compulsive extravagance is a modern mania. The contemporary lust for 'more, more, more' is clearly psychotic; it has completely lost touch with reality."[2]

That's the world in which we live. Enough is never enough. A promotion is never high enough. A salary is never large enough. Things are never plentiful enough. So we end up worshiping those things that utterly fail to bring us lasting contentment or pleasure. We are a very spoiled people—and very deceived. The more we have, the more we want. We need to get rid of such out-of-control materialism.

Third, Paul tells us to get rid of *negative emotionalism* (3:8-9). This includes anger, wrath, malice, slander, abusive speech, and lying. In short, we need to set aside uncontrolled negative emotions. And this involves not only the sudden, angry outbursts in which we lose our cool and say things that shouldn't be said but also the long, quiet, stewing, seething, lingering bitterness that devours us from within. Christians seeking to live a new life in Christ need to stop the habits of uncontrolled temper, fits of rage, verbal abuse, malicious behavior, and hurtful, deceptive speech.

Isn't it interesting that Paul writes these things to Christians? It's easy for us to think that we who have accepted Christ as Savior, who have the Spirit living within us, will be free from negative emotionalism. But let me tell you, some of the harshest, angriest, and most insulting letters I've ever received have come from fellow Christians. The ugliest words ever said to my face came from so-called brothers and sisters in Christ. Our spiritual life coach, the apostle Paul, says, "Put them all aside . . . since you laid aside the old self with its evil practices" (3:8-9). These things should be in our past, not in our present—and certainly not in our future!

— 3:10-11 —

In 3:5-9 Paul listed the vices we ought to lay aside as we seek to live the abundant Christian life. Before providing in 3:12-14 the opposite list of virtues we ought to put on, he supplies two transitional verses that explain the source of these new character traits. Our old life without Christ came to an end when we "laid aside the old self with its evil practices" (3:9); now our new life in Christ has begun as we "put on the new self who is being renewed" (3:10).

This new life in Christ begins not with self-reformation or our turning over a new leaf. It isn't a pull-yourself-up-by-the-bootstraps kind of reform. The new birth is not something we can cause to happen ourselves. Rather, as the apostle John says, the new birth comes by the Holy Spirit (John 3:3-8). Similarly, Peter says, "Blessed be the God and Father of our Lord Jesus Christ, who according to His great mercy has caused us to be born again to a living hope through the resurrection of Jesus Christ from the dead" (1 Pet. 1:3). God the Father showed mercy, Christ made the provision, and the Holy Spirit makes it happen.

The new nature we have received through the new birth makes it possible for us to be "renewed to a true knowledge according to the image of the One who created [us]" (Col. 3:10). Each of us who is a believer has been placed into an eternal relationship with God. Each has begun the journey of becoming like Him. Every Christian, regardless of racial, ethnic, national, or cultural background, is transformed into the likeness of Christ in the same way—by grace alone through faith alone in Christ alone (3:11). Jesus Christ is sufficient as our Life.

— 3:12-14 —

The radical transformation in our relationship with God that begins when we are born again calls for a radical change in our external actions. Using an image of changing clothes, Paul weaves together the threads of a new garment of righteousness to match our identity as "those who have been chosen of God, holy and beloved" (3:12). Held together by love, the bond of unity (3:14), Paul's sampling of virtues constitutes a complete reversal of the three categories of wicked practices described in 3:5-9 that characterized our lives without Christ. Instead of sensuality, materialism, and negative emotionalism, we are to have compassion, kindness, humility, gentleness, patience, tolerance, forgiveness, forbearance, love, and unity (3:12-14). Of course, Paul could have added many more qualities to this list. His purpose isn't to give an exhaustive checklist, however, but rather to provide a general pattern of the Spirit-enabled, Christ-honoring lives we should live as the children of God.

What a magnificent pattern for our new garment of righteousness! What a grand blend of the qualities we all need in our extreme makeover from wicked, hell-bound sinners to righteous, heaven-bound saints! And when these virtues begin to characterize our new lives in Christ, everybody benefits. God uses each of us to touch the lives of others, to encourage them in their relationships with the Lord. We must think of ourselves not simply as recipients of God's renovating work but also as spiritual mentors for others on the same journey.

APPLICATION: COLOSSIANS 3:1-14

Beginning Your Wardrobe Change

Despite our differences, one thing we all share in common is the struggle against our "old self with its evil practices" (3:9). However, each of us faces unique weaknesses and temptations as we progress toward living lives according to the "new self" created by the Spirit after the likeness of Christ (3:10). Let's take a few moments to think critically about where we are in this spiritual wardrobe change.

The following chart contrasts the kinds of vices of the old life we are to lay aside with the types of virtues of the new life we are to put on. My lists don't completely match word for word Paul's own sketch of these conflicting lifestyles in Colossians 3:1-14, but they provide us with a helpful diagnostic tool to evaluate our lives. I want you to read through each list and honestly mark or write down any of the vices or virtues you think tend to characterize your daily life. Don't highlight those things that you only occasionally see in your life, but mark those that have become habits—whether good or bad.

LAY ASIDE THESE VICES		PUT ON THESE VIRTUES	
fornication	dissensions	love	thankfulness
homosexuality	envy	charity	joy
adultery	drunkenness	purity	peace
impure	anger	holiness	goodness
thoughts	bearing	compassion	self-control
hatred	grudges	kindness	faithfulness
lust	deviousness	humility	godliness
pornography	stealing	gentleness	perseverance
materialism	lying	patience	faith
greed	slander	tolerance	hope
strife	cursing	forgiveness	teachability
jealousy	vanity	mercy	courage
rage	pride	graciousness	prudence
bitterness	boasting	generosity	contentment
	arrogance		

Now, for each vice that needs to be discarded, find at least one virtue that would counter it or cancel it out. For example, if you struggle with the vice of greed, you could cultivate the virtues of charity, generosity, and contentment.

Finally, consider other specific ways to begin laying aside the wicked deeds of the old self and putting on the righteous deeds of the new self. Remember, though, that you can't do this on your own. Experience isn't the best teacher; *guided* experience is. You need the empowering work of the Holy Spirit, the clear example of Jesus Christ, and the constant forgiveness that comes from God. You also need the strength that comes from team members—fellow believers on the same journey—and coaches—wise, trusted pastors, counselors, or mentors to help you along the way.

Wherever, Whatever, Whenever, However . . . Christ!
COLOSSIANS 3:15-4:1

NASB

15Let the peace of Christ ªrule in your hearts, to which ᵇindeed you were called in one body; and ᶜbe thankful. 16Let the word of ªChrist richly dwell within you, ᵇwith all

NLT

15And let the peace that comes from Christ rule in your hearts. For as members of one body you are called to live in peace. And always be thankful.

16Let the message about Christ, in

wisdom teaching and admonishing ᶜone another with psalms *and* hymns *and* spiritual songs, singing ᵈwith thankfulness in your hearts to God. ¹⁷Whatever you do in word or deed, *do* all in the name of the Lord Jesus, giving thanks through Him to God the Father.

¹⁸Wives, be subject to your husbands, as is fitting in the Lord. ¹⁹Husbands, love your wives and do not be embittered against them. ²⁰Children, be obedient to your parents in all things, for this is well-pleasing ᵃto the Lord. ²¹Fathers, do not exasperate your children, so that they will not lose heart.

²²Slaves, in all things obey those who are your masters ᵃon earth, not with ᵇexternal service, as those who *merely* please men, but with sincerity of heart, fearing the Lord. ²³Whatever you do, do your work ᵃheartily, as for the Lord ᵇrather than for men, ²⁴knowing that from the Lord you will receive the reward ᵃof the inheritance. It is the Lord Christ whom you serve. ²⁵For he who does wrong will receive the consequences of the wrong which he has done, and ᵃthat without partiality.

⁴:¹Masters, grant to your slaves justice and fairness, knowing that you too have a Master in heaven.

3:15 ᵃOr *act as arbiter* ᵇLit *also* ᶜOr *show yourselves thankful* 3:16 ᵃOne early ms reads *the Lord* ᵇOr *in* ᶜOr *one another, singing with psalms...* ᵈOr *by*; lit *in His grace* 3:20 ᵃLit *in* 3:22 ᵃLit *according to the flesh* ᵇLit *eyeservice* 3:23 ᵃLit *from the soul* ᵇLit *and not* 3:24 ᵃI.e. consisting of 3:25 ᵃLit *there is no partiality*

all its richness, fill your lives. Teach and counsel each other with all the wisdom he gives. Sing psalms and hymns and spiritual songs to God with thankful hearts. ¹⁷And whatever you do or say, do it as a representative of the Lord Jesus, giving thanks through him to God the Father.

¹⁸Wives, submit to your husbands, as is fitting for those who belong to the Lord.

¹⁹Husbands, love your wives and never treat them harshly.

²⁰Children, always obey your parents, for this pleases the Lord. ²¹Fathers, do not aggravate your children, or they will become discouraged.

²²Slaves, obey your earthly masters in everything you do. Try to please them all the time, not just when they are watching you. Serve them sincerely because of your reverent fear of the Lord. ²³Work willingly at whatever you do, as though you were working for the Lord rather than for people. ²⁴Remember that the Lord will give you an inheritance as your reward, and that the Master you are serving is Christ.* ²⁵But if you do what is wrong, you will be paid back for the wrong you have done. For God has no favorites.

⁴:¹Masters, be just and fair to your slaves. Remember that you also have a Master—in heaven.

3:24 Or *and serve Christ as your Master.*

In English we have a brief but meaningful expression that helps us characterize a person's values, loves, priorities, and passions, telling us what that person is all about. If a person dearly loves music, we say, "Music is his life." If someone finds fulfillment in training and motivating athletes, we say, "Coaching is her life." For a woman whose work means everything to her, who finds great joy in her career, we might say, "Her job is her life." Of a prolific author who cranks out one book after another, we might say, "Writing is his life."

Clearly, this idiom is a case of hyperbole—an exaggerated claim not intended to be taken literally. But it's still a very meaningful descriptor. When something represents what we call "our life," that something occupies a place in our heart and mind like nothing else. We think of it in the daytime and dream about it at night. We never grow weary of it. It consumes our time and energy—and often our money! It's our passion, our driving force, our consuming interest . . . *our life!*

If you were to ask the apostle Paul to fill in the blank, "_____ is my life," there's no question what he would answer. Without taking a breath. Without hesitation. In fact, he answers it for us in Philippians 1:21: "To me, to live is Christ." And in Colossians 3:4, as Paul was looking forward to the future coming of Christ, he remarked that Christ "is our life." Paul's answer would have been clear, and his life choices reflected it. In fact, his inner passion for Christ and the external outworking of that passion were so much in harmony that nobody who knew him would have had to pause to answer that question. His life provided the answer: "Wherever I may be, whatever I may be doing, whenever it may be happening, however I may feel, *Christ is my life.*"

Could you say that about yourself? More importantly, if your spouse, children, parents, employer, co-workers, or employees were to fill in the blank for you ("_____ is his/her life"), would "Christ" occupy that place?

As we work through Colossians 3:15-4:1, I want us to think about the idea of having Christ as the center and source of our lives. Along the way we'll see how He can rule, fill, permeate, and be displayed in various areas of our lives. The peace of Christ is to rule in our hearts (3:15). The message of Christ is to fill our lives (3:16-17). The presence of Christ is to permeate our homes (3:18-21). And the life of Christ is to be displayed in our work (3:22–4:1).

Wherever, whatever, whenever, however . . . Christ is our Life.

— 3:15 —

Isaiah 9:6 prophesied that the coming Messiah would be called "Prince of Peace." Christ's entire life and ministry were characterized by imparting peace to others. Although Isaiah 9 looks forward to the universal peace that will be established on earth when the Messiah takes His throne and reigns in His kingdom, even now as He sits at the right hand of the Father in heaven and intercedes for His people, He imparts peace to us. Christ said, "Peace I leave with you; My peace I give to you; not as the world gives do I give to you. Do not let your heart be troubled, nor let it be fearful" (John 14:27). In Philippians 4:6-7 Paul describes the very personal and practical implication of our relationship with the Prince of Peace: "Be anxious for nothing, but in everything by prayer and supplication with thanksgiving let your requests be made known to God. And the peace of God, which surpasses all comprehension, will guard your hearts and your minds in Christ Jesus." I suggest that you read those verses again—aloud.

We can't establish lasting world peace or relieve the suffering and anguish of this fallen world. Nor can we prevent chaos from happening in and around our lives. However, we can experience the reality of the peace Christ imparts today. The peace given to us by Christ is this:

1. An inner quietness in the midst of swirling chaos
2. A calm sense of tranquility in the center of tribulation
3. A feeling of harmony amid the world's blaring discord
4. An experience of ease and rest in our hearts and minds

That's the kind of incomprehensible peace Christ gives.

When Christ becomes our Life, His peace—not our circumstances—becomes the determining factor in our attitudes and actions. Colossians 3:15 says, "Let the peace of Christ rule in your hearts." Focus on the verb *rule*. It's a translation of a Greek word rarely used in the New Testament: *brabeuō* [1018]. It literally means to "be in control of someone's activity by making a decision."[3]

When the peace of Christ—the peace He gives to us—governs how we interpret our experiences and respond to our challenges, two things will happen. First, our relationships with others in the body of Christ will be healthier as we refuse to let minor things bother us. We'll infuse our relationships with peace. Second, we'll have gratitude even in the midst of challenging circumstances. When our natural tendency might be to complain about things that happen to us, we'll "be thankful," knowing that God is in control (3:15). In fact, thankfulness will become an abiding characteristic at the core of our lives (3:16-17).

— 3:16-17 —

Paul turns from the peace of Christ to the Word of Christ, the message of His love, grace, mercy, and salvation. When Christ is our Life, we'll be immersed in His Word. Paul says, "Let the word of Christ richly dwell within you" (3:16). The phrase "richly dwell within you" conveys an

WORSHIP THROUGH MUSIC IN THE EARLY CHURCH

COLOSSIANS 3:16

Around the year AD 111, a Roman governor named Pliny reported to the emperor Trajan that the mysterious Christians "met regularly before dawn on a fixed day to chant verses alternately among themselves in honour of Christ as if to a god."[4] This description reflects a kind of fixed style of antiphonal singing still used in some churches today. However, had Pliny dug a little deeper in his investigation, he probably would have learned that music in early Christian worship was more diverse, as suggested by Paul's mention of "psalms and hymns and spiritual songs" in Colossians 3:16 and Ephesians 5:19.

The singing of psalms, most likely from the Old Testament Psalter, was common in Jewish worship, both corporately and individually (see 1 Chr. 15:16). Jesus and the disciples concluded the Last Supper by "singing a hymn" (Matt. 26:30). While in prison, Paul and Silas were "praying and singing hymns of praise to God" while other prisoners listened on in amazement (Acts 16:25).

In corporate worship, the gathered church would sing psalms and other songs of worship to God (1 Cor. 14:15, 26). Douglas Moo suggests that Paul's threefold distinction between "psalms and hymns and spiritual songs" may indicate different types of worship through music in the gathered setting. He notes, "It is attractive to identify 'psalms' as songs based on Scripture, 'hymns' as songs about Christ, and 'songs' as spontaneous compositions 'prompted by the Spirit.'"[5]

Another scholar contends that in the New Testament period "musical practice, along with liturgical practice in general, was not yet fixed."[6] It seems the early church made room for spontaneous, heartfelt musical praise. James writes, "Is anyone cheerful? Let him sing praise" (Jas. 5:13, ESV). The Greek term *psallō* [5567], meaning "to praise," was originally related to the plucking of a stringed instrument, but by the time of the New Testament the term was also used for singing with or without accompaniment (Rom. 15:9; 1 Cor. 14:15; Eph. 5:19).[7]

The term *psallō* is used numerous times in the Greek translation of the Old Testament (the Septuagint) and includes in its meaning the playing of musical instruments (e.g., Pss. 33:2-3; 149:3). Since the collection known as Psalms was

Photo © Zev Radovan/BibleLand Pictures

The **harp** was a common instrument used as accompaniment in the first century. Paul's description of music in Colossians 3:16 allows for great diversity of expression, likely including various instruments.

probably a major source for early Christian worship, it is likely that the earliest Christians followed the musical instructions in the psalms they were reading and singing, making melodies with their voices and with instruments. However, as Andrew McGowan notes, "The earliest explicit reference to use of the biblical Psalter in Christian gatherings is from the second century, where 'psalms of David' are included, with other songs, in the eucharistic meals shared 'according to custom' as described in an apocryphal romance (*Acts of Paul* 9)."[8]

The flexibility, freedom, and spontaneity of the New Testament church with regard to music should encourage us to employ a wide range of tasteful, Christ-focused, and God-honoring means to worship Him as we proclaim His Word in song.

image of permanent residence. God's Word shouldn't be like a friend who pops by for an occasional visit or a relative who stays in the guest room temporarily. God's Word is to move in, take residence, and become an integral part of our lives. *The Message* translation paraphrases this expression thus: "Let the Word of Christ—the Message—have the run of the house. Give it plenty of room in your lives" (3:16, MSG).

The idea is that every aspect of our lives should be informed by and infused with the Word. Turn it loose. This would include instances of formal "teaching and admonishing one another"—things like personal Bible reading and study, family devotions, participation in church, listening to solid preaching, and tuning in to good broadcasts and podcasts. But Paul also describes the deep permeation of the Word that is manifested in "psalms and hymns and spiritual songs," which are sung "with thankfulness in your hearts to God" (3:16; cf. Eph. 5:19).

Besides teaching one another through songs of worship, we're to let the Word fill our entire lives. Whatever we do "in word or deed" we should do in the name of the Lord Jesus with thanksgiving (Col. 3:17). As we open our mouths, we should ask ourselves, "Is what I'm saying consistent with the message of Christ? Is it honoring to Him?" Before we take any actions—even things that seem neutral or insignificant—we should consider, "Am I demonstrating my allegiance to Christ?"

— 3:18-21 —

When Christ is our Life, His peace will be the decisive factor in what we think and feel (3:15). And the truth of His Word will saturate everything we say and do (3:16-17). Christ also impacts the relationships in our homes, as Paul demonstrates by addressing wives, husbands, children, and fathers (3:18-21).

Regarding the role of a wife's submission to the headship of her husband, Christ serves as the perfect example. Though equal in nature to the Father, sharing in the same divinity, power, glory, and authority, the Son submitted to the Father's will to accomplish God's plan of redemption, humbling Himself in obedience (Phil. 2:5-8). This is the kind of humble submission wives are called to imitate. Note that Paul is speaking here only about the marriage relationship (wives and husbands), not about the general relationship between men and women. Wives are not told to be in submission to *every* man they encounter but rather to their own husbands in the family unit. Let me add one more clarification: Paul is not condoning passive submission to domestic abuse. Wives who are stuck in abusive relationships with their husbands should seek help from supportive church leadership or legal authorities.

At this point we need to emphasize that in Christ we all have equal dignity, so Paul's statement has nothing to do with inferiority. In Galatians 3:28, Paul says, "There is neither Jew nor Greek, there is neither slave nor free man, there is neither male nor female; for you are all one in Christ Jesus." Such a statement was profoundly countercultural in the first century. It was a time when many Jews felt superior to Gentiles, while Gentiles frequently looked on Jews with suspicion and disdain. Sometimes slave traders considered slaves to be mere pieces of property, like cattle, whose value was directly linked to their physical strength, health, or skills. And many men wrongly believed that women were physically, mentally, and emotionally inferior to them. Paul's statements in Colossians 3 concerning husbands and wives—as well as his remarks regarding servants and masters—suggest that in the eyes of God all are equal. While different groups of people play distinct and complementary roles in an orderly society, God shows no partiality.

As wives fulfill their unique roles in the family "as is fitting in the Lord" (3:18), husbands are called to exceed the world's expectations in two ways. First, they are to love their wives (3:19). Some husbands reading this might be thinking, *Whew! I got off easy this time.* Not so! Paul is not referring to the passion of romantic love or even to the warm affection of a two-way relationship. He uses the term *agapē* [26]—the kind of love that seeks the highest good of the other, even at the price of one's own comfort, safety, and benefit. This is unconditional, self-sacrificial love, the quality of love that God shows His undeserving children.

Second, husbands are instructed not to "be embittered against" their wives (3:19). How natural it would be for husbands to become resentful of their wives if they poured all their time, energy, and emotions into such selfless love, only to discover that there's no equal return on the investment! But this is exactly what husbands are called to do. Whether a man's wife submits to, honors, or cherishes him, the husband's responsibility is to cherish and honor his wife regardless, with nothing less than true *agapē*.

In the first century, not unlike the present, it was common for husbands to treat their wives harshly or to ignore and neglect them until they needed them to meet their needs. What Paul was advocating for stood in stark contrast to what was taking place around them. The Christian man's love for his wife—like the Christian woman's submission to her husband—often went against the grain of personal preference, natural tendencies, and cultural expectations.

When Christ is the Life of our families, not only will the marriage relationship reflect mutual love, respect, and unity, but so will the parenting relationship. Children must be obedient to their parents. In light of what Paul has just said, children should already have a model to follow in their godly mother who shows deference and submission to the leadership of her husband. In fact, this may be one of the reasons God has ordered the husband-wife relationship this way—to provide an everyday example of what respect for authority is supposed to look like.

Children also have a perfect example of submission and obedience to parents in the life of Christ. He "continued in subjection" to His earthly parents, Joseph and Mary (Luke 2:51). This is ironic, isn't it? God the Son incarnate, who created the whole universe and everything in it—including Joseph and Mary—voluntarily submitted to His own creatures to fulfill a greater purpose in the plan of God. Children, too, must treat their parents with respect in order to be "well-pleasing to the Lord" (Col. 3:20).

The ultimate responsibility for carrying out discipline when children step out of line falls on the father as the head of the home. No dad is called to be a harsh, unloving, ironfisted dictator. Nor is he to relinquish his authority and become a passive, timid, permissive parent who fails to provide leadership or exercise discipline when necessary. Fathers (and mothers) are to set standards, provide guidance, and discipline their children with patience, kindness, and love.

Paul warns fathers not to "exasperate" their children, crushing their spirits and causing them to lose heart (3:21). The Greek term *erethizō* [2042] means "to arouse" or "to provoke," mostly in a bad sense"[9] The idea is that through overbearing actions, a father can push a child over the edge, not only failing to impart wisdom but actually goading the child into anger, resentment, and bitterness! He can do this by being overly critical or by disciplining too harshly or too often. A wise father will balance instruction and discipline with fun and laughter. And he will never tire of telling his children "I love you" and reinforcing it with affectionate actions.

— 3:22-4:1 —

When Christ is our Life, His peace fills our hearts (3:15), His Word permeates our every moment (3:16-17), and His presence transforms our families (3:18-21). In 3:22–4:1 Paul explores how the power of Christ also impacts our work.

In light of his first-century context, Paul was addressing the pervasive institution of slavery and how servants and masters were to live under the mutual lordship of Christ. Before we seek to apply his principles to the twenty-first-century context of employment, let me make a couple comments about Paul's treatment of slavery in relation to his first-century context.

First, Paul probably had in mind something akin to domestic servants—day-to-day workers in a household. There would be a logical connection between Paul's discussion of family life and that of household servants. To leave the issue of servants out of the discussion would have been to ignore a common fixture of the first-century household.

Second, by describing how Christian masters and servants were to relate to each other Paul was not conveying support for the entire institution of slavery in perpetuity. In fact, in 1 Corinthians 7:21 he tells slaves, "If you are able also to become free, rather do that." And a couple verses later he warns those who had a choice, "Do not become slaves of men" (1 Cor. 7:23). Elsewhere, Paul specifically condemns "slave traders" (1 Tim. 1:10, NLT). The Greek term rendered "slave traders" refers to those who acquire another person through means like kidnapping in order to sell that person into slavery.[10] An example of this today is human trafficking.

Thankfully, most societies today have officially banned slavery and diligently seek to avoid slave-like conditions. For those of us in modern Western cultures, Paul's words to slaves and masters can best be

Photo by Giovanni Dall'Orto/Wikimedia Commons

Household servants who carried out everyday domestic duties were common in the first century. It is estimated that in some places one-third of the population was regarded as belonging to the slave class.

applied to those in employee-employer relationships. While the institutions of ancient slavery and modern employment have major differences, some practical principles governing both establishments are similar. Whether you are a contract worker, an hourly wage earner, a salaried employee, a manager, or a business owner, Paul's principles for servants and masters in Colossians 3:22–4:1 can apply to you.

For employees, Paul's principles are clear. We're to do as we're instructed, diligently and with integrity, even when we aren't being observed by our bosses (3:22). Our respect for the authority of our bosses should be a reflection of our commitment to Christ, who desires us to live peaceful, humble lives of integrity. This should result in a positive attitude of cheerful service, as if we're working for the Lord and striving for a heavenly reward rather than laboring for human employers simply for earthly gain (3:23-24). We shouldn't cheat our bosses or wrong them in any way, knowing that we're ultimately accountable to Christ (3:25). We should have a reputation for diligence, loyalty, punctuality, and responsibility. We should be models in terms of our attitude and integrity, becoming a positive influence in the workplace.

For employers, Paul offers a reminder that masters, like all others, are under the authority of a heavenly Master, the Lord Jesus Christ, to whom they must give an account (4:1). No person, however high on the organizational chart or however powerful in an institution, is without accountability. As such, we who serve in leadership roles must do so with two prevailing qualities: justice and fairness. We must be just in our expectations and decisions, following the example of Christ. God shows no favoritism; neither should we. God rewards faithfulness; so should we. God justly exacts proper punishment for wrong; so should we. We must also be fair—fair in our wages, fair in our use of words, fair in our evaluations and critiques, and fair in our treatment of employees, whether they are men or women, young or old, executives or laborers. Christ's Golden Rule is paramount in work relationships: "Treat people the same way you want them to treat you" (Matt. 7:12).

APPLICATION: COLOSSIANS 3:15–4:1

Fill In the Blank

All of us are born with the words "_____ is my life" written on our hearts and minds. Throughout our lives we try to fill in the blank with different things, forming our identities around people, hobbies, interests, obsessions, ideologies, and experiences. Some fill in the blank with things that are dangerous and destructive, for example, "partying," "drinking," or "sex." For others, it's something harmless that has turned into an obsession, such as "eating," "golfing," "traveling," or "going to movies." Still others center their lives on more noble pursuits like "my spouse," "my family," "my ministry," or "my career." Whatever we place in that blank comes to define us, dominate us, and determine our thoughts and actions.

In over fifty years of ministry, I've seen the tragic results of people filling in the blank with various worldly sources of fulfillment. On the other hand, I've witnessed some amazing things take place as individuals have filled in the blank with big, bold, permanent letters that spell **"CHRIST."**

Many who were incessant worriers, filled with anxiety and fear, have been filled with the peace of Christ. Many who had lived uncertain, insecure, confused lives have found that the Word of God gives them assurance, security, and direction. Many whose marriages and family relationships were a disaster have found that the presence of Christ brings healing, restoration, and reconciliation. And many who hated their jobs, resented their bosses, or had messed up in their leadership roles have experienced the power of Christ, which has brought humility, justice, and fairness.

What about you? I asked this question at the beginning of this section. Let me ask it again. This time think it through. Maybe even ask somebody this question about you. If your spouse, children, parents, employer, co-workers, or employees had to fill in the blank ("_____ is his/her life"), would **"CHRIST"** occupy that place?

If so, do you see the evidence in the four realms of life Paul discusses in Colossians 3:15–4:1: your heart and mind, your daily life, your family, and your employment? Do you need to turn these areas over to Christ in a prayer of surrender, letting Him completely fill in the blank rather than sharing that privileged space with something else? If you do, do it now. And remind yourself every day of the centrality of Christ.

Wherever, whatever, whenever, however . . . make Christ your Life.

JESUS CHRIST, OUR LEADER (COLOSSIANS 4:2-18)

Jesus Christ is sufficient as our Lord, our Life, and our Leader. For baby Christians under attack from false teachers who were rejecting Christ's person and reducing His power, that message was the perfect defense. In the first section of Colossians Paul underscored the sufficiency of Christ as our Lord (1:1–2:23). In the second section he highlighted the sufficiency of Christ as our Life (3:1–4:1). Now, in the remainder of the final chapter of this short but formidable book, Paul emphasizes the sufficiency of Christ as our Leader (4:2-18).

Paul ended the previous section by pointing out that we all have a "Master in heaven" (4:1). Now he wraps up this letter by outlining a number of practical, personal ways that Christ's leadership is to manifest itself in our lives. Christ directs our paths, navigating us through ministry opportunities and obstacles (4:2-6). And when we serve Him as bond-servants, we have to depend on our fellow laborers, acknowledging that we all serve one Leader and have one goal: the widespread proclamation of His message (4:7-18). Only when we depend on Christ as our sufficient Leader will we be able to fulfill this goal.

KEY TERMS IN COLOSSIANS 4:2-18

doulos (δοῦλος) [1401] "bond-servant"; **syndoulos (σύνδουλος)** [4889] "fellow bond-servant"

Though the word *doulos* can refer simply to a slave or household servant, as it does in Colossians 3:22 and 4:1, Paul uses it in ministry contexts to describe a "bond-servant" of Jesus Christ (see Phil. 1:1). In Colossians, Epaphras is called a "bondslave" (*doulos*) of Jesus Christ (4:12). Bond-servants or bondslaves are "duty-bound only to their owners or masters, or those to whom total allegiance is pledged."[1] The compound word *syndoulos* emphasizes that servants of Christ are not alone. We have been placed in the body of Christ to serve our heavenly Leader *together*, all being accountable to the same Master.

> ***synergos* (συνεργός)** [4904] "fellow laborer," "co-worker"
> Since bond-servants have been called into fellowship under the same
> Master, Jesus Christ, they are to carry out the work of ministry together.
> The Greek word *synergos*, appearing in Colossians 4:11, is translated in
> the NASB as "fellow worker." The term reminds us that ministry is not
> an independent enterprise but a team effort. In Colossians Paul refers
> to nearly a dozen fellow laborers in ministry. Paul knew he could never
> accomplish the hard work of ministry alone as a sole *ergos*. He was a
> *synergos*—a member of a team of co-workers committed to the same
> Leader and pursuing the same calling together.

The Big Deal about "Little" Things
COLOSSIANS 4:2-6

NASB

²Devote yourselves to prayer, keeping alert in it with *an attitude of* thanksgiving; ³praying at the same time for us as well, that God will open up to us a door for the word, so that we may speak forth the mystery of Christ, for which I have also been imprisoned; ⁴that I may make it clear in the way I ought to speak.

⁵ᵃConduct yourselves with wisdom toward outsiders, ᵇmaking the most of the opportunity. ⁶Let your speech always be ᵃwith grace, *as though* seasoned with salt, so that you will know how you should respond to each person.

4:5 ᵃLit *Walk* ᵇLit *redeeming the time* 4:6 ᵃOr *gracious*

NLT

²Devote yourselves to prayer with an alert mind and a thankful heart. ³Pray for us, too, that God will give us many opportunities to speak about his mysterious plan concerning Christ. That is why I am here in chains. ⁴Pray that I will proclaim this message as clearly as I should.

⁵Live wisely among those who are not believers, and make the most of every opportunity. ⁶Let your conversation be gracious and attractive* so that you will have the right response for everyone.

4:6 Greek *and seasoned with salt.*

In our world of information overload, where tweets, posts, pins, and texts are thrown around like empty disposable wrappers, it's easy to believe that words are unimportant, weak, meaningless, vaporous, and hollow.

This notion is completely false!

Contrary to the familiar expression, talk is *not* cheap. Words do matter—especially spiritual words.

As we'll see in these five insightful verses from Paul's letter to the

Colossians, our speech has two dimensions: the vertical and the horizontal. Both dimensions represent powerful lines of communication—not worthless chatter or squandered syllables, but living, active, effectual articulations. Our *vertical* speech is directed to God. Believers are to be committed to prayer. Rather than using prayer as a casual and relaxed type of communication, we are challenged to be devoted in our practice of it. And our *horizontal* speech (our interpersonal communication) is equally significant because it occurs amid those who don't have a relationship with God.

We'll discover in examining this passage that the words we speak and the actions we take—even the seemingly little things—mean a lot and can accomplish far more than we imagine. Our words and actions may not seem all that significant in the moment, but we often later realize that lives have been changed by them. The apostle Paul certainly finds these things important. He underscores the importance of prayer for "insiders" (4:2-4) and the significance of our actions and words toward "outsiders" (4:5-6).

— 4:2-4 —

In these three verses, Paul addresses the vertical dimension as he writes about words directed to God in prayer. He offers three pieces of sound advice that we can apply to our prayer lives.

First, *be devoted in prayer* (4:2). Prayer is to be active, not passive; bold, not weak; specific, not general; attentive, not lazy; continuous, not sporadic. Hebrews 4:16 says, "Let us draw near with confidence to the throne of grace." We don't come groveling, pleading, begging, or bargaining. Entering God's presence boldly but with proper humility, we acknowledge that He has the power to give us what we ask but the right to answer however He pleases. And we can know that however He answers—"Yes," "No," "Wait," or "Here's something better"—He's going to work everything out for our good, not for our harm (Rom. 8:28). So with an attitude of thanksgiving—even for prayers God has not yet answered—we're to exercise diligence and vigilance. We're to pray with an alert mind and a thankful heart.

Second, *be visionary in prayer* (Col. 4:3-4). Paul doesn't hesitate to ask the Colossians to pray for him and his fellow workers, giving some specifics unique to his particular circumstances and directly related to his eager desire to fulfill his calling to preach Christ with clarity. I find it interesting that Paul doesn't ask them to pray for his physical release from prison. He doesn't ask that they conduct an hour-by-hour prayer vigil until he's released from his house arrest. Rather, he asks that doors of opportunity might be opened right where he has found himself. Though he was experiencing very limiting circumstances, Paul had massive ministry vision. And as I read the closing lines of the book of Acts, I have every reason to believe the Colossians *did* pray for this and that God granted it. Acts 28:30-31 says of Paul, "He stayed two full years in his own rented quarters and was welcoming all who came to him, preaching the kingdom of God and teaching concerning the Lord Jesus Christ with all openness, unhindered." It seems that their prayers were answered!

Third, *be specific in prayer* (Col. 4:3-4). Note how specific Paul was in his request for the Colossians' prayers. He didn't ask them to pray for missionaries in general, but for himself and his co-workers specifically. He didn't ask them to pray for God to make Himself known across the globe but to grant Paul open doors to proclaim the gospel in his particular circumstance. He didn't ask them to pray that God would open the hearts and minds of unbelievers around the world to respond to His revelation but to give Paul clarity of expression when he preached the word to those around him.

These few statements concerning the vertical words that can be expressed on behalf of insiders provide a pattern for us to follow when we pray for others who are engaged in the frontline battle for souls. Name the people for whom you're praying. Ask for open doors. Pray for their specific situations, challenges, and opportunities. Ask that God would help them make the most of their limited resources and overcome setbacks. We need to pray continually, pray passionately, and pray specifically.

— 4:5-6 —

In Colossians 4:2-4 Paul reminded us that our words matter in our vertical orientation in prayer toward God on behalf of insiders. Now, in 4:5-6, he turns to how our words and actions make a difference on behalf of outsiders. In discussing our walk (4:5) and our talk (4:6) Paul addresses the two most observed aspects of our witness to the lost.

Never forget that although those on the outside—that is, unbelievers who are without Christ—are lost, they don't lack a keen sense of seeing and hearing. They're very perceptive, discerning, and observant when it comes to how we who claim to know Christ behave and speak. Sometimes the scrutiny with which they examine our lives is a little unfair. Christians typically don't claim to be completely free from sin, just completely forgiven of it. Nevertheless, our works and our words can either draw a watching world closer to God or drive them farther away.

We need to pay attention to our walk, and we need to conduct ourselves with wisdom toward those on the outside. The word translated "conduct" in the NASB (4:5) is the Greek word *peripateō* [4043], meaning "to walk around." It refers to all the actions of a person's daily life. Only God can see our hearts, so people will size us up and evaluate the quality of our faith through how we conduct ourselves.

This is why Paul calls us to walk "with wisdom." *Wisdom* is one of the great words of Scripture. The Greek term *sophia* [4678], which we translate as "wisdom," means "the capacity to understand and function accordingly."[2] In Colossians alone it's used six times. In one instance Paul refers to worldly human "wisdom" stemming from false religion and asceticism (2:23)—the antithesis of the "spiritual wisdom" found only in Christ (1:9, 28; 2:3; 3:16; 4:5).

When we live our lives under the leadership of Christ alone, who is our source of true spiritual wisdom, we will experience numerous positive effects:

- It will help us know when to speak and when to be silent.
- It will give us insight into how to relate to others with tactfulness.
- It will equip us to discern the best course of action with skeptics and critics.
- It will grant us opportunities to give advice and counsel in the midst of people's struggles.

In short, conducting ourselves with wisdom will help us make the most of every opportunity. We won't squander the encounters we have with those who desperately need Christ. It will make our lives winsome, persuasive, and convincing—even before we open our mouths to share the saving truths of the person and work of Jesus Christ. But when we live foolishly and hypocritically, we can turn outsiders away. Warren Wiersbe illustrates this point well:

This story has often been told about Dr. Will H. Houghton, who pastored the Calvary Baptist Church in New York City and later served as president of Chicago's Moody Bible Institute till his death in 1946. When Dr. Houghton became pastor of the Baptist Tabernacle in Atlanta, a man in that city hired a private detective to follow Dr. Houghton and report on his conduct. After a few weeks, the detective was able to report to the man that Dr. Houghton's life matched his preaching. As a result, that man became a Christian.[3]

Still addressing the issue of how we conduct ourselves in the horizontal dimension to those on the outside, Paul next discusses our talk (4:6). We can't win people to Christ merely by being kind, smiling pleasantly, and living like we should. We need to have winning words coupled with our wise walks. Paul puts it this way: "Let your speech always be with grace." We understand the "grace" part. Our words should be thoughtful, charming, and winsome—not rude, arrogant, or caustic. This has to do with the *manner* of our speech, not the *content*. Of course, some people are going to be offended by the gospel message no matter how lovingly we present it. People often do not like being told they are lost sinners in need of a Savior and that they are absolutely helpless to save themselves. Yet, in our words and actions, we should strive to present the truths of the gospel "with grace." As Paul says elsewhere, "Give no offense either to Jews or to Greeks or to the church of God; just as I also please all men in all things, not seeking my own profit but the profit of the many, so that they may be saved" (1 Cor. 10:32-33).

In Colossians 4:6 Paul emphasizes his point by way of illustration, saying that our speech should be "seasoned with salt." In the ancient world, as today, salt was used as a preservative to keep food from spoiling. But this doesn't seem to be Paul's primary focus. Though a positive response to the gospel does preserve the eternal lives of believers, Paul's main emphasis in the metaphor here is that we respond to each person appropriately. It is the *quality* of our speech that's in view. Paul probably has in mind another common use of salt—as a seasoning to add zest to food. Skilled cooks will tell you that salt isn't supposed to be used to add flavor to tasteless, bland food but to enhance the natural flavor of food. Thus Paul likely means that our words should be lively and zestful, attractive and thought-provoking, winsome, and even humorous.[4]

I like how William Barclay puts it:

It is all too true that Christianity in the minds of many is connected with a kind of sanctimonious dullness and an outlook in which laughter is almost a heresy. . . . Christians must commend their message with the charm and the wit which were in Jesus himself. There is too much of the Christianity which stodgily depresses people and too little of the Christianity which sparkles with life.[5]

APPLICATION: COLOSSIANS 4:2-6

Our Talk and Our Walk

We've considered the power of seemingly "little" things—our talk and our walk. Paul has prompted us in Colossians 4:2-6 to give more thought to the words we speak and the things we do. These may at times seem insignificant to us, but our daily words and actions expressed under the leadership of Christ are a big deal in our vertical and horizontal relationships. As we wrap up this section, let me share four specific principles that we can all apply in our lives.

First, *strengthen your commitment to pray*. Be devoted. Be visionary. And be specific. Honestly, I don't know of any work harder than prayer—devoted, passionate, focused prayer. Passive, purposeless prayer is easy. It's simple to lip-sync prayers, mumbling mere words while our minds are in neutral. How difficult it is to shift our hearts and minds into four-wheel drive and plow through specific prayer requests with power and compassion! It's easy to occasionally belt out prayers when people are around who expect us to pray. But how difficult it is to be committed to prayer behind the scenes when nobody is looking, offering up requests to Someone we can't see and hear. It takes faith. It takes perseverance. And it takes commitment. Commit to praying more tomorrow than you did yesterday, more next week than you do this week. Then build from there.

Second, *ask God for greater wisdom in your walk*. James says, "If any of you lacks wisdom, let him ask of God, who gives to all generously and without reproach, and it will be given to him" (Jas. 1:5). And Paul reminds us that Jesus Christ Himself is the wisdom of God (1 Cor. 1:24). We are given wisdom by means of the Holy Spirit who indwells us. We can simply pray something like this: "Lord, by your Holy Spirit and according to the character of Jesus Christ, help me to be wise in my walk. Enable me to be sensible in my interactions with people, to cultivate tact, and to think before I respond."

Third, *pay closer attention to "outsiders."* I don't mean that we nitpick their words and actions that don't conform to our Christian standards. We're wrong to expect unbelievers to live like Christians, but they are right to expect Christians to live like Christ. Remember that they're watching you. They're listening to you. They're curious about your faith and whether it's real to you. If your commitment to Christ isn't real to you, it won't be worth considering for them. If it isn't changing you, it won't be challenging to them.

Fourth, *work on becoming more winsome and friendly.* Your words do matter. Think before you speak. Banish cynicism and sarcasm. Don't be a grump or a prude. Listen to yourself and try to imagine how your manner of speech is coming across to others. Is it bland and boring or zesty and interesting? Is it all about you and your life, or is it all about Christ and the new life? Answer the questions they're asking, not the issues you're personally interested in. Be gracious in your words and actions. Learn how to meet and accept people where they are and speak in a language they can understand.

A Friendly Farewell
COLOSSIANS 4:7-18

NASB

7 As to all my affairs, Tychicus, *our* beloved brother and faithful servant and fellow bond-servant in the Lord, will bring you information. 8 *For* I have sent him to you for this very purpose, that you may know about our circumstances and that he may encourage your hearts; 9a and with him Onesimus, *our* faithful and beloved brother, who is one of your *number.* They will inform you about the whole situation here.

10 Aristarchus, my fellow prisoner, sends you his greetings; and *also* Barnabas's cousin Mark (about whom you received ªinstructions; if he comes to you, welcome him); 11 and *also* Jesus who is called Justus; these are the only fellow workers for the kingdom of God who are

NLT

7 Tychicus will give you a full report about how I am getting along. He is a beloved brother and faithful helper who serves with me in the Lord's work. 8 I have sent him to you for this very purpose—to let you know how we are doing and to encourage you. 9 I am also sending Onesimus, a faithful and beloved brother, one of your own people. He and Tychicus will tell you everything that's happening here.

10 Aristarchus, who is in prison with me, sends you his greetings, and so does Mark, Barnabas's cousin. As you were instructed before, make Mark welcome if he comes your way. 11 Jesus (the one we call Justus) also sends his greetings. These are the only Jewish believers among my co-workers; they are working with me

NASB

from the circumcision, and they have proved to be an encouragement to me. [12]Epaphras, who is one of your number, a bondslave of Jesus Christ, sends you his greetings, always laboring earnestly for you in his prayers, that you may [a]stand [b]perfect and [c]fully assured in all the will of God. [13]For I testify for him that he has [a]a deep concern for you and for those who are in Laodicea and Hierapolis. [14]Luke, the beloved physician, sends you his greetings, and *also* Demas. [15]Greet the brethren who are in Laodicea and also [a]Nympha and the church that is in [b]her house. [16]When [a]this letter is read among you, have it also read in the church of the Laodiceans; and you, for your part read [a]my letter *that is coming* from Laodicea. [17]Say to Archippus, "Take heed to the ministry which you have received in the Lord, that you may [a]fulfill it."

[18a]I, Paul, write this greeting with my own hand. Remember my [b]imprisonment. Grace be with you.

4:9 [a]Lit *along with Onesimus*   4:10 [a]Or *orders*
4:12 [a]Or *stand firm* [b]Or *complete* or *mature* [c]Or
made complete   4:13 [a]Or *much toil* or *great
pain*   4:15 [a]Or *Nymphas* (masc) [b]One early ms
reads *their*   4:16 [a]Lit *the*   4:17 [a]Or *continually
fulfill*   4:18 [a]Lit *The greeting by my hand of Paul*
[b]Lit *bonds*

NLT

here for the Kingdom of God. And what a comfort they have been!

[12]Epaphras, a member of your own fellowship and a servant of Christ Jesus, sends you his greetings. He always prays earnestly for you, asking God to make you strong and perfect, fully confident that you are following the whole will of God. [13]I can assure you that he prays hard for you and also for the believers in Laodicea and Hierapolis.

[14]Luke, the beloved doctor, sends his greetings, and so does Demas. [15]Please give my greetings to our brothers and sisters* at Laodicea, and to Nympha and the church that meets in her house.

[16]After you have read this letter, pass it on to the church at Laodicea so they can read it, too. And you should read the letter I wrote to them.

[17]And say to Archippus, "Be sure to carry out the ministry the Lord gave you."

[18]HERE IS MY GREETING IN MY OWN HANDWRITING—PAUL.

Remember my chains.

May God's grace be with you.

4:15 Greek *brothers.*

"Friendship is a sheltering tree," observed the great poet Samuel Taylor Coleridge.[6] How right he was. Think about it. Friends reach out to us and offer us refuge like the branches of a tree. They give us shade, shelter, provision, and protection. They invite us to a familiar place of refreshment, retreat, and repose.

In particular, true friends provide three things vital for a quality life. Friends provide companionship, without which we'd be lonely and isolated. They provide comfort—a pat on the back, a shoulder to cry on, and kind words of consolation when we need them. And they provide the accountability and perspective we need to keep us on the straight path. By sharing our lives with others outside our immediate families, our world enlarges, our hearts are strengthened, and our minds are sharpened with fresh insight.

One psychologist notes the importance of friendship to our overall health:

I have discovered that friendship is the springboard to every other love. Friendships spill over onto the other important relationships of life. People with no friends usually have a diminished capacity for sustaining *any* kind of love. They tend to go through a succession of marriages, be estranged from various family members, and have trouble getting along at work. On the other hand, those who learn how to love their friends tend to make long and fulfilling marriages, work well on business teams, and enjoy their children.[7]

If we look to Christ as our Leader and example, we see that He, too, had friends who labored with Him—some very close, others more on the periphery of His ministry. He had the "more than five hundred brethren" to whom He appeared after His resurrection (1 Cor. 15:6). He had the seventy whom He sent out in pairs to preach (Luke 10:1). And He had the twelve disciples who were with Him day in and day out (Matt. 10:2-4). Within that group were three individuals (Peter, James, and John) with whom He had an especially personal bond (Mark 5:37; 9:2; 14:33). And even among these three, he seemed to have an especially intimate friendship with one, "the disciple whom He loved"—John (John 19:26; 21:20). All of these and many others were involved in Jesus' life and ministry. They provided companionship not only for Jesus Himself but also for one another. These concentric circles of friends were like sheltering trees, giving comfort and accountability.

In the closing twelve verses of the book of Colossians, the apostle Paul names no fewer than ten friends who had been a vital part of his life and ministry. Among these friends are those who stayed with him through thick and thin, those who prayed for him and supported him, and even one who strayed, for whom Paul continued to be concerned.

Let's examine Paul's friendly farewell to the Colossian Christians, exploring his close circle of friends and gleaning wisdom and insight for our own lives, lived under the leadership of Jesus Christ.

— 4:7-9 —

Paul first mentions two close friends, one of whom carried not only this letter to the Colossian church but also a letter to the church in Ephesus (Eph. 6:21-22).

Tychicus (Col. 4:7-8). Paul regarded Tychicus as a much-loved brother, a faithful minister, and a fellow servant. He is portrayed as consistent, loyal, trustworthy, and reliable—someone who was intimately familiar with Paul's condition. This wasn't the only time Tychicus served as one of Paul's trusted personal envoys. In Titus 3:12 Paul says, "When I send Artemas or Tychicus to you, make every effort to come to me at Nicopolis, for I have decided to spend the winter there." Being from Asia Minor himself (see Acts 20:4), Tychicus knew the culture and could be trusted to represent Paul well.

Onesimus (Col. 4:9). As we will see when we discuss the single-chapter book of Philemon, Onesimus was a runaway slave from Colossae who had come to know Christ when he had encountered Paul in Rome. He had fled from his owner, Philemon, who was the recipient of the letter now bearing his name. When he escaped from his service to Philemon, Onesimus traveled west, all the way to Italy, ending up by God's providence in Paul's rented home in Rome. This encounter led to his conversion to Christ, resulting in a desire to make things right with his owner, Philemon. Paul describes Onesimus as a "faithful and beloved brother" (4:9).

I find it interesting that Onesimus, who was legally a slave, was simply called a "brother" in Christ, while Tychicus, who was free, was called a "fellow bond-servant" (literally, "slave") in the Lord (4:7). Surely Paul recognized the irony. Perhaps he was intentionally trying to put things in perspective. Though the unity believers have in Christ as brothers and sisters doesn't cancel out social distinctions, we must regard those distinctions as secondary to our primary identity as members of the same family, regardless of our ethnicity, social status, or gender (see Gal. 3:28).

In any case, at the end of Colossians 4:9 we're told that both these men—the veteran minister Tychicus and the new convert Onesimus—would represent Paul to the church in Colossae. They would give an oral report about what was happening to him in Rome. Paul depended on them as his hands, feet, and mouth while he was stuck in Rome under house arrest.

— 4:10-14 —

Next Paul mentions six more friends who were remaining with him in Rome: Aristarchus, Mark, Jesus (Justus), Epaphras, Luke, and Demas. The first three are Jews; the second three are Gentiles. Paul has mentioned one of them earlier in the letter—Epaphras (1:7). Two of them—Mark and Luke—are well known to us as Gospel writers. Three of them are probably new to most of us—Aristarchus, Justus, and Demas.

Aristarchus (4:10). Aristarchus is mentioned in Acts 20:4 as one who, along with Sopater, Secundus, Gaius, Timothy, Tychicus, and Trophimus, was traveling with Paul during his ministry in Greece, Macedonia, and Asia Minor. Luke also joined that group at some point (Acts 20:5-6). We're told that Aristarchus was originally from Thessalonica (Acts 20:4). In Colossians 4:10, Paul calls him his "fellow prisoner." We can't be sure whether Aristarchus had been placed under house arrest with Paul[8] or whether he was a "fellow prisoner" elsewhere. (The same uncertainty also applies to Epaphras; see Phlm. 1:23.)

In any case, Aristarchus had shared some harrowing ministry experiences with Paul. He and Gaius were "dragg[ed] along" by the rushing mob during a riot in Ephesus (Acts 19:29). He was also with Paul during the long and treacherous voyage by ship to Italy when Paul went to appeal his case to Caesar (Acts 27:2). On that journey he survived a shipwreck in the Adriatic Sea and ended up on the island of Malta (Acts 27:14–28:1). The fact that Aristarchus was still with Paul in Rome when he wrote this letter to the Colossians demonstrates the tenacious loyalty he had toward Paul and toward their mutual leader, Jesus Christ. The trials and hardships they experienced together served to strengthen their bond.

Mark (Col. 4:10). Paul refers to John Mark as "Barnabas's cousin." It's likely that the Colossians had heard of Barnabas, but they may not have been as familiar with the young man who had earlier abandoned Paul and Barnabas midway through the first missionary journey (Acts 13:5, 13), and whose departure had later caused a break in the relationship between Paul and Barnabas (Acts 15:37-40). Now, some years later, Mark had been reconciled with Paul and was serving alongside him in Rome. In fact, toward the end of his life, Paul would request Mark's presence, for he was "useful to me for service" (2 Tim. 4:11). Though the friendship between the young John Mark and Paul had been strained early on, both of them grew through their struggles—Mark grew in maturity and fortitude, and Paul grew in patience and forgiveness.

Jesus (Justus) (Col. 4:11). The third of the three Jewish believers in Christ mentioned here happened to share the same name as the Lord, the Hebrew name *Joshua*. His Latin name was Justus, a name shared by two other men in the book of Acts (Acts 1:23; 18:7). We know nothing about this Justus except that he, Aristarchus, and Mark were "fellow workers for the kingdom of God" and were an encouragement to Paul (Col. 4:11).

A LETTER TO THE LAODICEANS?

COLOSSIANS 4:16

Paul expected and desired his epistles not only to be read out loud to the churches to which they were sent but also to be copied and passed around to neighboring churches. In fact, this is why we have a collection of New Testament writings. Already by the mid-60s, the apostle Peter could refer to "all [Paul's] letters" (2 Pet. 3:15-16). Not only was Peter evidently aware of a collection of Paul's writings in circulation among the churches in Asia Minor, but he even seemed to consider these letters on par with authoritative Scripture.

But if the churches were faithfully copying, distributing, and collecting Paul's letters, why do we have the letters to the Ephesians, Philippians, Colossians, and Philemon, but not the letter to the Laodiceans? In Colossians 4:16 Paul instructed the Colossians, "When this letter [Colossians] is read among you, have it also read in the church of the Laodiceans; and you, for your part read my letter that is coming from Laodicea."

At first glance, this verse may suggest that a letter to the Laodiceans had been written by Paul, sent to that church, read by the Colossians, but then subsequently lost. But is that really what this passage is saying? If we look closely at the original Greek text, we see that Paul is actually referring to a letter "from Laodicea" (*ek Laodikeias*). In fact, the word *my* isn't part of the original text. It simply says, "the letter from Laodicea." Thus it may not be a letter Paul addressed *to* the Laodiceans, but a letter that the Colossians should expect to be coming *from* them.

Some scholars believe there was a (now lost) letter to Laodicea.[9] Others, meanwhile, believe Paul could be referring to his letter to the Ephesians, which he may have sent along with Tychicus when he sent the letters of Colossians and Philemon (see Eph. 6:21).[10] If this is the case, we may envision a scenario like the following:

Paul sent Tychicus, together with Onesimus, to deliver three of the so-called Prison Epistles—Ephesians, Colossians, and Philemon—to their destinations. When they first arrived at the port city of Ephesus, they delivered the letter addressed to the Ephesians and shared news of Paul as well as additional instructions (see Eph. 6:21). Before the carriers departed for Colossae, the church in Ephesus was instructed to send copies of their letter to other churches with which they had relationships. Those churches, in turn, were to send copies to other churches.

The church at Laodicea was undoubtedly the largest among the three sister churches mentioned by Paul in Colossians—Laodicea, Hierapolis, and Colossae. Thus Paul would have known that eventually the letter to the Ephesians would make its way through the network of churches to the small church of Colossae. Note that Paul didn't instruct the Colossians to send their letter to Hierapolis. He knew that the church in Laodicea—likely the larger, more central church—would have sent this letter to Hierapolis, since they would have been responsible to make sure the smaller churches in the vicinity received copies of all the apostolic writings they had.

As intriguing as the idea may be of someday finding a lost epistle to the Laodiceans, it's likely that no such letter from Paul ever existed and that the letter mentioned in Colossians 4:16 has been in our Bibles from the very beginning—as the letter to the Ephesians!

Epaphras (4:12-13). Among any group of Christian friends there are usually one or two who are known for their faithful intercession. In Paul's circle of friends, Epaphras filled this role. Originally a member of the Colossian church and, in fact, the one who had brought the gospel to them (1:7; 4:12), he was an all-in servant of Jesus Christ who prayed earnestly and specifically not just for the Colossians but also for the neighboring congregations in Laodicea and Hierapolis (4:12-13). Paul probably had such a deep knowledge of the Colossians' spiritual condition not simply because he and Epaphras had discussed it but also because he had heard Epaphras's passionate prayers and deep concern for them.

Luke (4:14). Like Aristarchus, Luke had been with Paul through many ups and downs in ministry over a long period of time. Here we're told that Luke had been trained as a physician. How great is that! Not only could he attend to the spiritual and practical needs of those with whom and to whom he was called to minister, but he could also address medical needs. It may be that Luke served as Paul's personal physician, helping him cope with the lingering condition he referred to as a "thorn in the flesh" (2 Cor. 12:7).[11] We also know that Luke was a gifted researcher and writer, being personally responsible for the Gospel of Luke and the book of Acts.

Demas (Col. 4:14). In Colossians the only thing we learn about Demas is that he sends greetings; in Philemon, we are merely told that he was a "fellow worker" with Paul (Phlm. 1:24). However, he is also mentioned in 2 Timothy 4:10: "Demas, having loved this present world, has deserted me and gone to Thessalonica." All of us have known friends whose camaraderie cooled and whose faithfulness waned. They began to drift, ultimately becoming absent. Whereas John Mark had a similar lapse in his youth but returned to service, Demas had apparently lapsed in his later years, and we're not told if he ever repented and returned.

— 4:15-18 —

Finally, Paul sends greetings to the believers in Laodicea and to two more friends—a woman named Nympha and a man named Archippus.

Nympha (Col. 4:15). In the early centuries of church history, when Christianity was an illegal religion in the Roman Empire, churches met in private homes.[12] Usually the owners of these homes were wealthy members of the congregation who had large enough houses to host a sizable group. The message to the church in Laodicea recorded in Revelation 3:14-22 indicates that Laodicea was a wealthy church, having enough material goods to be self-sufficient. Nympha may have been a wealthy matron of the church in Laodicea who opened her doors and served the entire congregation.[13] Women were deeply involved both in the ministry of Jesus (Matt. 27:55-56; Luke 8:1-3; 10:38-39) and in the ministry of Paul (Acts 16:14-15, 40; Rom. 16:1-6, 12, 15). The women listed by Paul were not just committed servants of the church, but also faithful friends of the apostle.

Archippus (Col. 4:17). In Philemon 1:2 Paul calls Archippus "our fellow soldier," implying that he was a hardworking, committed, faithful minister of Christ. In Colossians, Paul has a specific message for Archippus: "Take heed to the ministry which you have received in the Lord, that you may fulfill it" (4:17). We don't know what kind of ministry Paul was addressing here, but regardless, he sought to extend encouraging, strengthening words to Archippus, essentially saying, "Stay at it!" Perhaps Archippus was one of the pastoral leaders of the church in Colossae, and these words were meant to encourage him in defending the faith against the threat of budding Gnostic heresy.

Paul wraps up his letter to the Colossians with a touching, handwritten farewell. As was his custom, he took the stylus from his secretary—in this case probably Timothy, who assisted him in writing—and provided his own personal signature: "I, Paul, write this greeting with my own hand. Remember my imprisonment. Grace be with you" (4:18). With these brief words, he asks for their prayers of concern and intercession ("Remember my imprisonment") and prays a blessing over them ("Grace be with you").

It is fitting that Paul's farewell demonstrates his priority on prayer, reminding us again that our sufficiency comes not from ourselves but from Jesus Christ, who is sufficient as our Lord, our Life, and our Leader.

APPLICATION: COLOSSIANS 4:7-18

There Are No Nobodies

A number of major figures in my life have impacted me—and thousands of others—in big ways. Their influence on Christianity around the world has been felt far and wide. I'm thinking of people like Ray Stedman, Howard Hendricks, Stanley Toussaint, John Walvoord, Charles Ryrie, S. Lewis Johnson, Bruce Waltke, Grant Howard, Earl Radmacher, and Dwight Pentecost. If you've never heard of some of them, a quick Internet search will show just how instrumental they were in shaping a whole generation of Christians. These men taught me about the Bible, Hebrew, Greek, theology, and ministry. Some of them became close, personal, lifelong friends. I'll never cease to be thankful for their investment in me, my family, and my ministry.

But I have to be honest. As much as those great men molded me in profound ways, there's another list of men and women whose names probably wouldn't yield a single entry in an online search. To the world at large, they're nobodies. They didn't invent anything, write a bestselling novel, star in a blockbuster movie, go platinum in record sales, or run for president, and history has forgotten them—except for names etched in headstones or brief summaries of their lives in newspaper obituaries. But when I close my eyes and review the newsreels of my life, those nobodies make the headlines.

People like Richard Nieme, my wonderful high school speech and drama teacher, who taught me how to speak without stuttering.

And Bob Newkirk, the Navigator representative serving on the island of Okinawa during the sixteen months I was stationed there in the Marine Corps, who urged me to be more engaged in memorizing Scripture, leading, teaching, and evangelizing.

There was Billy Haughton, a former Marine, who believed in me during my student days in seminary. He was there for me when I struggled with several personal issues.

And then there was Dr. Richard Seume, who became the chaplain at Dallas Theological Seminary after I graduated. He influenced me to trust God without fearing the unknown (which led to my moving to California, where my ministry began to blossom).

I must also mention Lawson Ridgeway, a very successful Dallas businessman, who took me under his wing, loved me unconditionally, and invited me to teach a life-changing Bible class in his home. Because Lawson gave me that enviable opportunity I would have never had otherwise, I learned how to communicate to real people living on the ragged edge of the real world.

These valuable men, whom the world may consider nobodies, proved to be of inestimable benefit to me during the maturing years of my life. If I could actually quantify influence, I'd conclude that their effect on me—through both words and actions—equaled that of the "big names."

And this is probably true for you, too. In fact, it's always been true. A nobody taught the reformer Martin Luther his theology. A nobody visited evangelist Dwight L. Moody at a shoe store and spoke to him about Christ. A nobody financed William Carey's ministry to India. A nobody faithfully prayed for Billy Graham for over twenty years. A nobody found the Dead Sea Scrolls and revolutionized biblical studies in the twentieth century. And a nobody refreshed the apostle Paul in a Roman prison as he wrote his last letter to Timothy.

Think about it. The visible 10 percent of the iceberg wouldn't be seen without the 90 percent of its mass that is obscured under the water. The executive branch of the US government would be paralyzed if the president didn't have the support of a competent cabinet and several wise counselors. And a pastor couldn't preach the Word week in and week out without the behind-the-scenes work of numerous yet anonymous nobodies. Without the nobodies of this world, there would be no somebodies.

Now that I think about it, even using the word *nobodies* doesn't seem right. Those men and women laboring behind the scenes are all *somebodies*—anonymous somebodies, yes, but somebodies nonetheless.

In the body of Christ, there are no nobodies. As Francis Schaeffer once put it, "There are no little people."[14] Not in your life, not in mine.

Take a few minutes to write up your own list of somebodies who have been (and are) instrumental in your life. Thank God for each one of them. Write them notes of encouragement and gratitude. Remind them: There are no nobodies. Express how valuable they have been in your life.

INSIGHTS ON PHILEMON

Paul's letter to Philemon has great practical value for us today. It illustrates for us the reality and importance of second chances, the equality that believers have in Christ, and the power of the gospel to transcend cultural and social boundaries. In short, Paul's postcard to Philemon reminds us about the profoundly Christ-centered concepts of freedom, forgiveness, mercy, and grace.

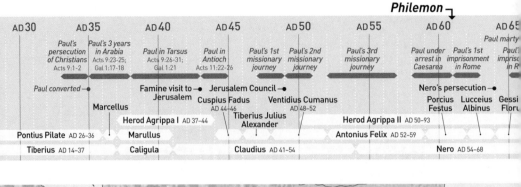

Philemon

AD 30	AD 35	AD 40	AD 45	AD 50	AD 55	AD 60	AD 65
	Paul's persecution of Christians Acts 9:1-2	Paul's 3 years in Arabia Acts 9:23-25; Gal 1:17-18	Paul in Tarsus Acts 9:26-31; Gal 1:21	Paul in Antioch Acts 11:22-26	Paul's 1st missionary journey	Paul's 2nd missionary journey	Paul's 3rd missionary journey	Paul under arrest in Caesarea	Paul's 1st imprisonment in Rome	Paul marty	Paul's impriso in R

Paul converted

Famine visit to Jerusalem

Jerusalem Council

Cuspius Fadus AD 44-46

Ventidius Cumanus AD 48-52

Nero's persecution

Marcellus

Tiberius Julius Alexander

Porcius Festus

Lucceius Albinus

Gessi Flort

Herod Agrippa I AD 37-44

Herod Agrippa II AD 50-93

Pontius Pilate AD 26-36

Marullus

Antonius Felix AD 52-59

Tiberius AD 14-37

Caligula

Claudius AD 41-54

Nero AD 54-68

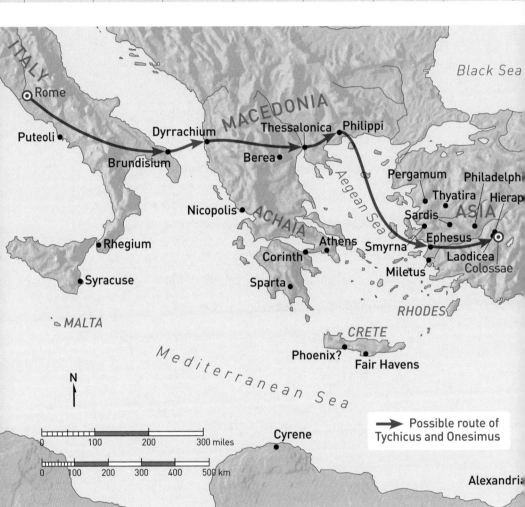

The Setting of Philemon. This is a possible route for Onesimus's journey from Rome to Colossae, where he returned to his master, Philemon.

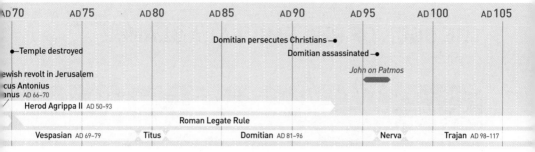

AD 70 — AD 75 — AD 80 — AD 85 — AD 90 — AD 95 — AD 100 — AD 105

Domitian persecutes Christians —●

●— Temple destroyed   Domitian assassinated —●

Jewish revolt in Jerusalem   *John on Patmos*

cus Antonius

anus AD 66–70

Herod Agrippa II AD 50–93

Roman Legate Rule

Vespasian AD 69–79   Titus   Domitian AD 81–96   Nerva   Trajan AD 98–117

PHILEMON

INTRODUCTION

It is the year AD 110. The emperor Trajan waits in Rome for a shipment from the East. Originating in Antioch of Syria and sent as a special gift to the emperor to win his favor, the cargo was being transported under the guard of ten Roman legionaries. They made it as far as the port city of Smyrna on the western coast of Asia Minor. There the group stopped as the soldiers rested from their long journey and weighed their options for completing the trip to Rome.

What is their precious cargo? Ignatius of Antioch—once the revered bishop of Antioch who had been a personal associate of the apostle John, now a shackled prisoner headed to Rome to be fed to the lions. His crime? Refusing to denounce Jesus Christ as Savior and Lord, God and King.

But the hiatus in Smyrna gave Ignatius an opportunity to meet with Christian leaders eager to spend time with the famous pastor of the even more famous church of Antioch. The Roman soldiers saw no reason to prevent the harmless, old bishop of Antioch from receiving visitors. He wasn't a flight risk, and he had been nothing but compliant with even their most unreasonable orders.

Among Ignatius's visitors was the renowned Polycarp, head of the church in Smyrna, where the party had halted. Years earlier the apostle John himself had appointed Polycarp to the position of bishop (perhaps equivalent to a senior pastor today) in Smyrna. Also among the visitors were representatives from three churches south of Smyrna: Tralles, Magnesia, and Ephesus. Each of these churches sent leaders to meet Ignatius and lend support and encouragement during this trying time. The church in Tralles sent their bishop Polybius,[1] while the Magnesians sent the bishop Damas along with other leaders.[2] It's not likely

THE BOOK OF PHILEMON AT A GLANCE

SECTION	GREETING	PREPARATION OF THE APPEAL
PASSAGE	1:1-3	1:4-7
THEMES		Philemon's love
		Praise of Philemon
		Philemon's faith
		Philemon's ministry
KEY TERMS	Refresh	Appeal

THE APPEAL		SOURCE OF THE APPEAL	BENEDICTION
1:8-16		1:17-21	1:22-25
Onesimus's conversion	A new relationship	Paul's love	
Plea for Onesimus		Promise of Paul	
Was unsaved, now born again	Retrospect: A slave	Surety of a partner	
Was useless, now useful	Prospect: A brother	Charge to my account	
Useful			

that either of those names would have carried much weight, even in those days. But the bishop of the renowned city of Ephesus was well known, as was the church there. Paul had written one of his Prison Epistles to the Ephesians, and Timothy had served there as pastor near the end of Paul's ministry. Furthermore, the apostle John lived out his last days in Ephesus.

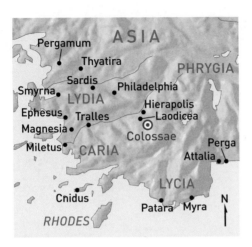

Western Asia Minor. The churches of Ephesus, Magnesia, and Tralles were just south of where Ignatius was staying in Smyrna.

Who was the bishop of this prominent church in the early second century? A man named Onesimus. In a letter sent to the church in Ephesus to encourage them in their faithfulness to Christ, Ignatius described their bishop, Onesimus, as "a man of inexpressible love," adding, "Blessed is the one who has graciously granted you, who are worthy, to obtain such a bishop."[3]

In the year AD 60 Onesimus was a runaway slave who had possibly stolen from his master, Philemon, and had fled to Rome, probably hoping to blend in and make a new life for himself. But while Onesimus was in Rome, the apostle Paul was also there under house arrest. Through the providential plan of God, Onesimus came to know Christ through Paul's ministry and was convicted of his sin against his master, Philemon.

Therefore, Paul sent Onesimus back to his master in Colossae as a traveling companion of Tychicus—now not merely as a runaway slave but as a brother in Christ (1:16). In his letter to Philemon, Paul interceded on behalf of Onesimus: "I appeal to you for my child Onesimus, whom I have begotten in my imprisonment, who formerly was useless to you, but now is useful both to you and to me. I have sent him back to you in person . . . whom I wished to keep with me, so that on your behalf he might minister to me in my imprisonment for the gospel" (1:10-13).

On their way to Colossae, Tychicus and Onesimus likely carried three letters: Ephesians, Colossians, and Philemon. By the time they reached Colossae, Tychicus and Onesimus had already spent some days in Ephesus, delivering Paul's letter, informing the Ephesians of news about Paul, and encouraging them (Eph. 6:21-22). The church there had undoubtedly seen the same qualities in Onesimus that Paul had experienced in Rome. Clearly he had made a positive impression on them.

Fast-forward fifty years to AD 110. That same former slave, Onesimus, now probably about seventy years old, is settled into a permanent ministry in Ephesus as the bishop.[4] As the leader he earnestly contends for the faith against false teachers, building up that body in faith and love. In his letter to the church in Ephesus, Ignatius says, "Onesimus himself highly praises your good discipline in God, because you all live according to the truth and that no heresy dwells among you, but you do not even so much as hear anyone unless he speaks truthfully about Jesus Christ."[5]

> **QUICK FACTS ON PHILEMON**
>
> **Who wrote it?** Paul, with Timothy (Phlm. 1:1).
> **Where was it written?** Rome, where Paul was under house arrest (Acts 28:16, 30-31).
> **When was it written?** Around AD 61, during Paul's house arrest in Rome while he awaited a hearing before Caesar (Acts 28:16-31).
> **Why was it written?** To appeal to Philemon for the forgiveness and freedom of runaway slave Onesimus.

THE UNIQUE OCCASION OF PHILEMON

This personal "postcard" addressed primarily to the Colossian Christian named Philemon was composed and sent at the same time as the letter to the church in Colossae. Both came from Paul, written with the secretarial help of Timothy (Col. 1:1; Phlm. 1:1). Paul probably sent these two letters, with the letter to the Ephesians, via Tychicus, who was accompanied by Onesimus (see Eph. 6:21; Col. 4:7).

This brief letter is the shortest of Paul's extant writings—just twenty-five verses in our Bibles. But don't let its size fool you. Although brief in comparison to Paul's other New Testament letters, it contains a magnificent study in forgiveness. It is a warm appeal to Philemon, a slave owner, that he accept back into his household the runaway slave Onesimus, who had become a Christ follower because of Paul's preaching. Just as Jesus Christ acts as the Advocate for Christians before God, Paul acted as Onesimus's advocate before Philemon.

Paul's letter to Philemon follows a simple outline but contains a significant request. In the heart of the letter (Phlm. 1:8-16), Paul appeals to Philemon for the forgiveness and freedom of Onesimus. Paul could have flexed his apostolic authority and demanded that Philemon receive Onesimus, show him forgiveness, cancel his debt, and send him back to Paul to serve him in ministry. Instead, Paul kindly and gently asks Philemon to make the right choice by his own free will. In fact, Paul offers to repay all of Onesimus's debts himself!

Clearly, Paul's letter to Philemon has great practical value for us today. It illustrates for us the reality and importance of second chances, the equality that believers have in Christ, and the power of the gospel to transcend cultural and social boundaries. In short, Paul's postcard to Philemon reminds us about the profoundly Christ-centered concepts of freedom, forgiveness, mercy, and grace . . . *especially grace.*

KEY TERMS IN PHILEMON

***anapauō* (ἀναπαύω)** [373] "to refresh," "to give rest," "to relieve"

Paul uses this verb twice in his short letter to Philemon. He first mentions that Philemon is a source of refreshment to the hearts of the saints because of his love (1:7). Then, in his petition on behalf of Onesimus, Paul requests that Philemon be a source of refreshment to his heart as well (1:20). In this case Paul is not only asking for mental or emotional relief for his concern over Onesimus's fate, but he is also hoping that Philemon will provide tangible, physical relief to him by allowing Onesimus to return and help Paul in ministry.

***parakaleō* (παρακαλέω)** [3870] "to appeal," "to urge," "to beseech"

Parakaleō is a verbal form of a noun used of the Holy Spirit—"Paraclete" (*paraklētos* [3875]; see John 16:7). *Paraklētos* portrays the image of a person standing alongside another in order to provide counsel through gentle encouragement. A good encourager challenges without condemnation, instructs without lecturing, inspires without condescending, and helps another toward excellent choices. Like a coach encouraging and challenging an athlete to reach a particular goal, Paul urges Philemon to act in accordance with the ultimate Paraclete, the Holy Spirit.

***onēsimos* (ὀνήσιμος)** [3682] "useful," "profitable," "beneficial"

Besides being the proper name (Onesimus) of the runaway slave who is the primary subject of the letter to Philemon, the Greek word *onēsimos* is an adjective that means "useful" or "profitable."[6] In Philemon 1:11 Paul plays on the meaning of Onesimus's name when he says that formerly the slave had been "useless" (*achrēstos* [890]), but was now "useful" (using a synonym, *euchrēstos* [2173]), living up to the meaning of his name.

A Study in Forgiveness
PHILEMON 1:1-25

NASB

¹Paul, a prisoner of Christ Jesus, and Timothy ᵃour brother,

To Philemon our beloved *brother* and fellow worker, ²and to Apphia ᵃour sister, and to Archippus our fellow soldier, and to the church in your house: ³Grace to you and peace from God our Father and the Lord Jesus Christ.

⁴I thank my God always, making mention of you in my prayers, ⁵because I hear of your love and of the faith which you have toward the Lord Jesus and toward all the ᵃsaints; ⁶*and I pray* that the fellowship of your faith may become effective ᵃthrough the knowledge of every good thing which is in you ᵇfor Christ's sake. ⁷For I have come to have much joy and comfort in your love, because the ᵃhearts of the ᵇsaints have been refreshed through you, brother.

⁸Therefore, though I have ᵃenough confidence in Christ to order you *to do* what is proper, ⁹yet for love's sake I rather appeal *to you*—since I am such a person as Paul, ᵃthe aged, and now also a prisoner of Christ Jesus—

¹⁰I appeal to you for my child ᵃOnesimus, whom I have begotten in my ᵇimprisonment, ¹¹who formerly was useless to you, but now is useful both to you and to me. ¹²I have sent him back to you in person, that is, *sending* my very heart, ¹³whom I wished to keep with me, so that on your behalf he might minister to me in my ᵃimprisonment for the gospel;

NLT

¹This letter is from Paul, a prisoner for preaching the Good News about Christ Jesus, and from our brother Timothy.

I am writing to Philemon, our beloved co-worker, ²and to our sister Apphia, and to our fellow soldier Archippus, and to the church that meets in your* house.

³May God our Father and the Lord Jesus Christ give you grace and peace.

⁴I always thank my God when I pray for you, Philemon, ⁵because I keep hearing about your faith in the Lord Jesus and your love for all of God's people. ⁶And I am praying that you will put into action the generosity that comes from your faith as you understand and experience all the good things we have in Christ. ⁷Your love has given me much joy and comfort, my brother, for your kindness has often refreshed the hearts of God's people.

⁸That is why I am boldly asking a favor of you. I could demand it in the name of Christ because it is the right thing for you to do. ⁹But because of our love, I prefer simply to ask you. Consider this as a request from me—Paul, an old man and now also a prisoner for the sake of Christ Jesus.*

¹⁰I appeal to you to show kindness to my child, Onesimus. I became his father in the faith while here in prison. ¹¹Onesimus* hasn't been of much use to you in the past, but now he is very useful to both of us. ¹²I am sending him back to you, and with him comes my own heart.

¹³I wanted to keep him here with me while I am in these chains for preaching the Good News, and he would have helped me on your

NASB

¹⁴but without your consent I did not want to do anything, so that your goodness would not be, in effect, by compulsion but of your own free will. ¹⁵For perhaps he was for this reason separated *from you* for a while, that you would have him back forever, ¹⁶no longer as a slave, but more than a slave, a beloved brother, especially to me, but how much more to you, both in the flesh and in the Lord.

¹⁷If then you regard me a partner, accept him as *you would* me. ¹⁸But if he has wronged you in any way or owes you anything, charge that to my account; ¹⁹I, Paul, am writing this with my own hand, I will repay it (not to ᵃmention to you that you owe to me even your own self as well). ²⁰Yes, brother, let me benefit from you in the Lord; refresh my heart in Christ.

²¹Having confidence in your obedience, I write to you, since I know that you will do even more than what I say.

²²At the same time also prepare me a lodging, for I hope that through your prayers I will be given to you.

²³Epaphras, my fellow prisoner in Christ Jesus, greets you, ²⁴*as do* Mark, Aristarchus, Demas, Luke, my fellow workers.

²⁵The grace of the Lord Jesus Christ be with your spirit.ᵃ

1:1 ᵃLit *the*   1:2 ᵃLit *the*   1:5 ᵃOr *holy ones*
1:6 ᵃOr *in*   ᵇLit *toward Christ*   1:7 ᵃLit *inward parts*   ᵇOr *holy ones*   1:8 ᵃLit *much*   1:9 ᵃOr *an ambassador*   1:10 ᵃI.e. useful   ᵇLit *bonds*
1:13 ᵃLit *bonds*   1:19 ᵃLit *say*   1:25 ᵃOne early ms adds *Amen*

NLT

behalf. ¹⁴But I didn't want to do anything without your consent. I wanted you to help because you were willing, not because you were forced. ¹⁵It seems you lost Onesimus for a little while so that you could have him back forever. ¹⁶He is no longer like a slave to you. He is more than a slave, for he is a beloved brother, especially to me. Now he will mean much more to you, both as a man and as a brother in the Lord.

¹⁷So if you consider me your partner, welcome him as you would welcome me. ¹⁸If he has wronged you in any way or owes you anything, charge it to me. ¹⁹I, PAUL, WRITE THIS WITH MY OWN HAND: I WILL REPAY IT. AND I WON'T MENTION THAT YOU OWE ME YOUR VERY SOUL!

²⁰Yes, my brother, please do me this favor* for the Lord's sake. Give me this encouragement in Christ.

²¹I am confident as I write this letter that you will do what I ask and even more! ²²One more thing— please prepare a guest room for me, for I am hoping that God will answer your prayers and let me return to you soon.

²³Epaphras, my fellow prisoner in Christ Jesus, sends you his greetings. ²⁴So do Mark, Aristarchus, Demas, and Luke, my co-workers.

²⁵May the grace of the Lord Jesus Christ be with your spirit.

2 Throughout this letter, *you* and *your* are singular except in verses 3, 22, and 25.   9 Or *a prisoner of Christ Jesus.*   11 Onesimus means "useful."
20 Greek *onaimen,* a play on the name Onesimus.

The setting of Paul's letter to Philemon is certainly different from our own. Most likely none of us has ever been or will ever be enslaved. But literally millions of people in that era would have never known freedom.

Historians believe that slaves in Roman society may have constituted between 25 and 40 percent of the population.⁷ A perusal of history books will reveal estimates of between forty-five and sixty million slaves in the Roman Empire during the middle of the first century. They were an indispensable fixture in the daily social and economic realities of Roman culture. As Aristotle once wrote, "The slave is a living tool."[8] The land was crawling with these living, two-legged tools that were generally considered a cut below humanity. Any master had the right to control the life and death of his slaves.

It was in this environment that the slave Onesimus ran away from his master, Philemon, and found his way to Paul. In this brief letter, we catch a glimpse of the early church working out how to live the gospel in the midst of an unredeemed culture. As we learn how Paul appealed to Philemon to forgive and free Onesimus, we find an example not only of how we should treat others but also of how we have been shown forgiveness ourselves. This makes the story even sweeter and more relevant to us.

— 1:1-3 —

Paul's warm greeting in Philemon 1:1-3 reveals some important things about the recipient of Paul's request on behalf of Onesimus. First, Philemon was not simply a fellow member of the body of Christ, a "beloved brother"; he was also a "fellow worker" (1:1). The Greek term *synergos* [4904], translated "fellow worker," was used to refer to those who were involved in official ministry leadership (Rom. 16:3, 9, 21; 2 Cor. 8:23; Phil. 2:25; 4:3). It seems quite likely, then, that Philemon was serving in a leadership role in the church at Colossae. Paul refers to "the church in [his] house" in Philemon 1:2. Philemon was more than a church member; he was a church leader.

Second, Paul's language strongly suggests he had a prior personal relationship with Philemon—and possibly his family as well. Philemon was not simply a "brother" but was "beloved" to Paul (1:1). And Paul greets "Apphia our sister," who was likely the wife of Philemon, and "Archippus our fellow soldier," who may have been Philemon's son.[9] We know that Archippus was a fellow minister in the church of Colossae (Col. 4:17). In any case, the warm tone of this greeting reveals that Paul knew Philemon well.

Third, though this letter is addressed specifically to Philemon, Paul also extends the greeting (and the letter) to "the church" (Phlm. 1:2). By broadening his audience to all the believers in Colossae, Paul subtly communicates that even though the matter of Onesimus's fate is a personal one to be handled by Philemon, such decisions cannot be separated from the accountability of the family and the church, both of which would be impacted by Philemon's actions.

— 1:4-16 —

Before getting to the delicate matter of what to do about Onesimus, Paul praises Philemon. He indicates that he regularly thanks God for Philemon in prayer (1:4). He commends him for his faith in Christ and love for the saints (1:5). He prays that Philemon's faith would grow in its effectiveness (1:6). And he rejoices in the encouragement that has come from the fruitful ministry of Philemon among the saints at Colossae (1:7).

Paul isn't flattering Philemon to soften him up for the big ask in the next paragraph. He's serious about his high regard for his friend. He knows this man, and he considers his reputation praiseworthy. Paul is well acquainted with his ministry of love, faith, fellowship, knowledge, goodness, joy, comfort, and refreshment. Whatever hard feelings Philemon may understandably have toward the runaway slave Onesimus—and whatever legal right he might have to drop the hammer on him—Paul's words of commendation remind Philemon of his true Christian character of grace and mercy. And, as James writes, "Mercy triumphs over judgment" (Jas. 2:13).

In Philemon 1:8 Paul pivots to his main purpose with the use of the word *therefore*, which connects what precedes with what follows: "In light of your Christlike character, Philemon, I want to ask something of you." Though, as an apostle, Paul could pull rank on Philemon, he instead appeals to Philemon from a position of humility (1:8-9). He doesn't begin with "Thus saith St. Paul the Apostle, handpicked by the Lord Jesus Christ, recipient of visions, author of inspired Scripture!" Rather, he refers to himself as "Paul, the aged, and now also a prisoner of Christ Jesus" (1:9). And he doesn't order Philemon to obey, but instead he appeals to him, twice using the word *parakaleō* [3870], a word of gentle encouragement (1:9-10).

In 1:10 Paul first mentions the content of his heartfelt request. Paul arranged the Greek word order in a way that placed the name at the end. Originally, Philemon would have read the statement like this: "I appeal to you on behalf of my child, whom I begat during my imprisonment—Onesimus." The mention of that name may have caused Philemon to stiffen up. Maybe he did a double take, pulling the paper close to his nose to make sure he read that right. *Onesimus?* Philemon would have been rightly perplexed by this sentence. The Onesimus Philemon knew was "useless" (1:11)—an outlawed runaway slave who probably robbed Philemon of money or property before he fled (see 1:18)! What could motivate Paul to intercede on behalf of a thief and fugitive?

RUNAWAY SLAVES

PHILEMON 1:16

Under Roman law, masters had complete control over the lives of their slaves. While many slave owners treated their slaves brutally, others were not cruel at all. Slaves were expensive to purchase and keep, and they also possessed many of the legal rights of free citizens. Slaves in the Roman Empire had access to money, could marry and rear families, and were tried in court according to the same laws as those who were free.[10]

However, for runaway slaves—like Onesimus—the situation was different. Roman law made running away an offense sometimes punishable by death! In those cases, the master could register the runaway's name and description with local officials who would place them on a wanted list. Usually, a captured runaway was returned to his or her owner, who might fit the slave with an iron collar or tattoo them with a sign that they were a *fugitivus*—"runaway."[11]

Photo by Giovanni Dall'Orto/Wikimedia Commons

Though many slaves in the Roman Empire enjoyed relative freedom in their service to their masters, rebellious or **runaway slaves** would often be forced to wear iron collars to mark them as delinquent and prevent them from fleeing.

Many slaves, however, chose never to run away—not because of possible punishment, but because they often fared better than free people.[12] While many free people slept in the streets of Roman cities or in cheap rooms with their families, slaves usually lived within the homes of their masters, often in a top-floor room of the master's city house or country villa. Slaves were also provided food and clothing, and in some cases, as much as five denarii a month as spending money.[13] Their free counterparts, who labored for a living, had to live off what they earned without assistance.

Paul acknowledges that Onesimus had been useless to Philemon, but something had changed—he was now "useful both to you and to me" (1:11). It may not be evident, but there's a play on words in 1:11: The name Onesimus literally means "useful." Onesimus obviously hadn't lived up to the meaning of his name. It would be like a woman named Grace who holds a grudge, or a man named Earnest who can't tell the truth! The slave named "Useful" had been nothing but trouble until the Lord Jesus got ahold of his heart and transformed his life.

I can almost picture Philemon's eyebrows rising as he read how Paul described the new and improved Onesimus. Not only was he now "useful" (1:11)—he was a born-again child in the faith (1:10). He was Paul's "very heart" (1:12), whom Paul had become so fond of he wished to keep him in Rome to continue ministering for the gospel (1:13). As such, Onesimus was no longer to be regarded as just a slave, but "more than a slave, a beloved brother" to both Paul and Philemon (1:16). In fact, Paul floats the idea that maybe it had all been part of God's sovereign plan that Onesimus ran away for a short time—now Philemon could "have him back forever" as a brother in Christ who would be a co-heir of eternal life (1:15).

Paul's point was clear: The Onesimus standing before Philemon, his family, and the church in Colossae was not the same young man who had run away. He had been saved by the grace and mercy of the Lord Jesus Christ. He had proven himself a faithful, devoted minister of the gospel with Paul in Rome. Surely Philemon, who had also experienced the forgiveness and freedom that come from Christ, could understand the great principle of 2 Corinthians 5:17: "Therefore if anyone is in Christ, he is a new creature; the old things passed away; behold, new things have come."

— 1:17-21 —

Having explained to Philemon the transformation Onesimus had experienced, Paul appeals to Philemon to grant Onesimus not only forgiveness but also freedom. It would be proper for Philemon to extend forgiveness to Onesimus. After all, it is a fundamental principle of brotherly love to "be kind to one another, tender-hearted, forgiving each other, just as God in Christ also has forgiven you" (Eph. 4:32). It doesn't appear that Paul expected anything less from Philemon than to extend full and complete forgiveness to his runaway slave. He expected Philemon to accept Onesimus as he would accept Paul—as a "beloved brother" (Phlm. 1:16-17).

But freedom? That would go above and beyond Philemon's obligation, which may be why Paul doesn't actually outright ask Philemon to free Onesimus.[14] But as we look closely, we can infer that Paul hoped Philemon would read between the lines:

1. Onesimus had been useful to Paul for ministry (1:11, 13).
2. Paul regarded Onesimus as his "very heart" and "a beloved brother" (1:12, 16).
3. Paul wished that he could keep Onesimus with him (1:13).
4. Paul would need Philemon's consent to keep Onesimus (1:14).
5. Paul desired that Philemon would do this out of his free will (1:14).
6. Paul was willing to pay back what Onesimus may have cost Philemon (1:18-19).
7. Paul reminded Philemon that he owed Paul his "own self" (1:19).
8. Paul asked that he would benefit from Philemon "in the Lord" (1:20).
9. Paul expected that Philemon would do "even more" than what he said (1:21).

Paul employs another clever play on words in 1:20, when he says, literally, "May I benefit (*oninēmi*) from you in the Lord."[15] He uses a word that shares the same root as the name Onesimus. The message behind this pun may be, "Let me have Onesimus—the 'beneficial one' in the Lord."

Even if Philemon wasn't paying attention to what Paul was hinting at, I'm sure Apphia or his fellow worker Archippus would have helped him realize it. And if neither of them got the picture, perhaps at least one of the members of the church in Colossae would have said something like, "You know, Phil, I wonder if Paul would like you to send Onesimus back to minister with him. That'd be a pretty nice thing to do, don't you think?"

Two things assure me that Philemon forgave Onesimus, accepted him as a brother in Christ, freed him from his slavery, canceled his debt, and perhaps even paid for his return trip to the apostle Paul. First, we have the book of Philemon in the canon of Scripture. I suspect that had Philemon balked at Paul's request and decided to double down on his rejection of Onesimus as "useless," this letter probably wouldn't have been preserved and copied far and wide. Second, if the aged Onesimus serving as bishop of Ephesus around AD 110 was the same Onesimus as in the letter to Philemon, it's likely that he was granted his freedom from bond-service to Philemon to become a lifelong bond-servant of Jesus Christ.

Philemon wasn't obligated to cancel Onesimus's debt or to free him from service. But was he obligated to forgive him as a brother in Christ? Yes. Conversion to Christ doesn't mean all our financial debts or contractual obligations are suspended. Paul himself acknowledged this when he promised to pay whatever financial loss Philemon had incurred because of Onesimus. He wrote, "Charge that to my account . . . I will repay it" (1:18-19). I doubt that Philemon wrote up an itemized statement and mailed it off to Paul. Moved by Paul's passionate plea on behalf of the useless-turned-useful Onesimus, Philemon probably wrote across his former slave's tally of wrongs, "PAID IN FULL"—just as Christ had done for Philemon years earlier.

— 1:22-25 —

In his closing remarks, Paul expresses his hope that he will be released in answer to their prayers. If he is released, he intends to visit Philemon and the church in Colossae. In fact, so confident is he in his deliverance from bondage in Rome that he says, "Prepare me a lodging" (1:22). What optimism!

Besides instilling hope that Philemon would likely be seeing his old friend Paul soon, this statement would also put some gentle pressure on Philemon to make a favorable decision regarding Onesimus. Had he expected Paul to be languishing in prison for many more years, it might have been easier for Philemon to drag his feet, getting a few more years of service out of the runaway slave to help settle his account. But the prospect of Paul's arrival in Colossae within months, even if it was just a prospect, would have encouraged a timely decision to "do what is proper" (1:8).

Prior to a formal blessing of grace (1:25), this brief letter to Philemon ends with greetings from Epaphras, Mark, Aristarchus, Demas, and Luke (1:23-24)—fellow workers of Paul also mentioned at the end of Colossians (Col. 4:10-14). Not only were there faithful witnesses to the handling of the matter of Onesimus in Colossae, but there was also a sizable circle of saints with Paul in Rome who knew Onesimus and would be eager to learn of Philemon's decision on the matter. There's nothing like a little loving accountability to urge a believer to "do even more" than what's required (Phlm. 1:21).

A Tale of a Modern-Day Slave

PHILEMON 1:17-21

I knew of a young man named Ed who had been on the run from the age of seventeen. Constantly in trouble with the law, Ed would get restless every time pressure mounted, and he would be on the run again. The older he got, the more complicated his problems grew until he finally worked up the reckless courage to steal a car and write bad checks in order to stay on the move.

One semester Ed ended up at a college in Michigan where he became close friends with the dean. Being a strong Christian, the dean talked to him about Christ. And this young man became a Christian. But old habits are hard to break. Once the pressure mounted again, Ed stole another car and took off.

However, earlier that week, before Ed stole the car, he was in his house taping some rock music off the radio. He climbed into the shower while the music was being recorded. But, for some reason, while he was in the shower the radio switched frequency and changed to a Christian radio program called Insight for Living. He didn't know anything about the program or about the man who was teaching on the radio at the time, nor would he have been interested in either. When he got out of the shower and heard that it was a religious broadcast, he reached over and switched off both the recorder and the radio.

Afterward, Ed was in that stolen car, fleeing to Canada. He popped in the cassette that he had recorded and "accidentally" listened to the conclusion of my message on Philemon, the runaway slave. Ed heard me say, "Some of you are on the run right now. From what, I don't know. It's time to stop, to turn around, to face the issue, and to make it right."

Sometime later Ed found himself in San Diego, and he still couldn't get that message out of his mind. Then he heard someone mention my name and found out about the church where I preached. And he called us. The result was that Ed finally turned his life around and stopped running.

Though we live in a world very different from Philemon's, God's Word is still leading slaves to forgiveness and freedom.

APPLICATION: PHILEMON 1:1-25

Finding Forgiveness and Freedom in Philemon

The tiny book of Philemon contains a powerful example of Paul's selfless, Christlike intercession on behalf of another. It also provides a grand testimony of the transforming power of God's grace in the life of a redeemed sinner. Beyond these applicable elements, I see five beautiful analogies between the themes of Philemon and our own salvation.

First, *every Christian was once a fugitive.* Like Onesimus, we were cowering from God's law and trying to outrun the consequences of our actions. Scripture says that "all have sinned and fall short of the glory of God" (Rom. 3:23). And like Onesimus, we can't escape the fact of our own enslavement to sin and death.

Second, *our guilt was great and our penalty was severe.* Paul wrote that "the wages of sin is death" (Rom. 6:23). Had Onesimus been left without grace and mercy, he would have been subject to possible punishment by death. In fact, that sentence loomed over him. It was exactly what he deserved under the law. The same was true for all of us. The penalty of our own sin against God was severe and our guilt weighed heavily.

Third, *grace grants us a stay of judgment and the intercession of an Advocate.* Had Philemon chosen to give Onesimus what he deserved, it would have been death. But instead he chose grace. He chose forgiveness. He chose freedom. The grace of God for each of us accomplishes the same. Our judgment has been set aside, and we now have a "mediator also between God and men, the man Christ Jesus" (1 Tim. 2:5).

Fourth, *our debt has been paid by Christ.* Just as Paul offered to step up to the bar of judgment to pay for Onesimus's crime and purchase his freedom, the Lord Jesus Christ took all of our sin, shame, and guilt upon Himself and paid for it on the cross. Isaiah 53:5-6 sums it up well:

But He was pierced through for our transgressions,
He was crushed for our iniquities;
The chastening for our well-being fell upon Him,
And by His scourging we are healed.
All of us like sheep have gone astray,
Each of us has turned to his own way;
But the LORD has caused the iniquity of us all
To fall on Him.

Finally, as a result, *our rightful Owner accepts us back and adopts us into His family*. We have a new relationship with our God and Creator. Though we were once in a relationship of enmity with God and subject to His just wrath, we have now been forgiven and cleansed by the blood of Christ. In Romans 6:23 Paul says, "The wages of sin is death, but the free gift of God is eternal life in Christ Jesus our Lord." And as Romans 5:10 declares, "If while we were enemies we were reconciled to God through the death of His Son, much more, having been reconciled, we shall be saved by His life."

As a result of the book of Philemon, I have a whole new appreciation for my forgiveness, freedom, and fellowship in the family of God. It reminds me that we were all untrustworthy fugitives, every one of us. But like Onesimus, I was rescued by the good news of Jesus Christ, and it resulted in an end to my running, the complete forgiveness of my debt, and my adoption into the family of God.

There are two kinds of slaves reading these words right now. The first are those who have stopped running and have found rest, refreshment, and a new life in Christ. The second are those who are still running—running from God, running from the horrible consequences of sin, and running from the forgiveness and freedom available right now. My hope is that the grace of the Lord Jesus Christ will emancipate all the runaway slaves who are reading this. And to those who have been freed: My prayer is that you will be useful to the Master who paid the price for your redemption and that you will be willing to submit yourself to Him as a bond-servant.

ENDNOTES

PHILIPPIANS

INTRODUCTION

1. See Charles R. Swindoll, *Swindoll's Living Insights New Testament Commentary*, vol. 8, *Galatians, Ephesians* (Carol Stream, IL: Tyndale House, 2015), 165.
2. See Eduard Verhoef, *Philippi: How Christianity Began in Europe—The Epistle to the Philippians and the Excavations at Philippi* (London: Bloomsbury, 2013), 2.
3. Robert P. Lightner, "Philippians," in *The Bible Knowledge Commentary: New Testament Edition*, ed. John F. Walvoord and Roy B. Zuck (Wheaton, IL: Victor Books, 1983), 647–648.
4. Chaido Koukouli-Chrysantaki, "Colonia Iulia Augusta Philippensis," in *Philippi at the Time of Paul and after His Death*, ed. Charalambos Bakirtzis and Helmut Koester (Eugene, OR: Wipf and Stock, 1998), 22; see also Verhoef, *Philippi*, 2.
5. See Richard R. Melick, Jr., *Philippians, Colossians, Philemon*, The New American Commentary: An Exegetical and Theological Exposition of Scripture, vol. 32, ed. David S. Dockery (Nashville: B & H Publishing, 1991), 25–26. See also Verhoef, *Philippi*, 10.
6. Koukouli-Chrysantaki, "Colonia Iulia Augusta Philippensis," 24–25.
7. Verhoef, *Philippi*, 13.
8. This is suggested by Luke's change from the first-person plural *we*, last appearing prior to the arrest of Paul and Silas (Acts 16:16-17), to the third-person plural after their departure from Philippi (Acts 16:40). See Melick, *Philippians, Colossians, Philemon*, 28.
9. Translation is that of Rick Brannan, *The Apostolic Fathers in English* (Bellingham, WA: Lexham Press, 2012).
10. See G. Walter Hansen, *The Letter to the Philippians*, The Pillar New Testament Commentary, ed. D. A. Carson (Grand Rapids: Eerdmans, 2009), 20–25.
11. Ibid., 47.

JOY IN LIVING (PHILIPPIANS 1:1-30)

1. Walter Bauer et al., *A Greek-English Lexicon of the New Testament and Other Early Christian Literature*, 3rd ed. (Chicago: University of Chicago Press, 2000), 213.
2. Ella Wheeler Wilcox, "The Winds of Fate," in *The Best Loved Poems of the American People*, ed. Hazel Felleman (Garden City, NY: Doubleday, 1936), 364.
3. Kenneth S. Wuest, *Wuest's Word Studies from the Greek New Testament*, vol. 2 (Grand Rapids: Eerdmans, 1973), 27.
4. See Michael J. Svigel, *RetroChristianity: Reclaiming the Forgotten Faith* (Wheaton: Crossway, 2012), 179–182.
5. Ibid., 184–192.
6. Bauer et al., *Greek-English Lexicon*, 383.

7   Hansen, *Letter to the Philippians*, 52.
8   Wilcox, "The Winds of Fate," in *Best Loved Poems*, 364.
9   Viktor E. Frankl, *Man's Search for Meaning*, rev. ed. (New York: Simon and Schuster, 1984), 86.
10 Ibid., 87.
11 Markus Bockmuehl, *The Epistle to the Philippians*, Black's New Testament Commentary, ed. Henry Chadwick (London: A. & C. Black, 1997), 87.
12 Hansen, *Letter to the Philippians*, 85.
13 Ralph P. Martin, *Philippians: An Introduction and Commentary*, Tyndale New Testament Commentaries, vol. 11, ed. Leon Morris (Downers Grove, IL: InterVarsity, 1987), 87.
14 Bauer et al., *Greek-English Lexicon*, 846
15 Martin, *Philippians*, 93.
16 F. F. Bruce, *Philippians*, Understanding the Bible Commentary Series (San Francisco: Harper and Row, 1983), 57.

JOY IN SERVING (PHILIPPIANS 2:1-30)

1   Bauer et al., *Greek-English Lexicon*, 659.
2   Hansen, *Letter to the Philippians*, 135.
3   See Melick, *Philippians, Colossians, Philemon*, 93.
4   H. A. Ironside, *Philippians and Colossians*, An Ironside Expository Commentary (Grand Rapids: Kregel, 2007), 38.
5   See discussion in Hansen, *Letter to the Philippians*, 122–127. See also the discussion on early Christological hymns in this commentary on Colossians 1, pages 122–129.
6   Melick, *Philippians, Colossians, Philemon*, 101.
7   Bauer et al., *Greek-English Lexicon*, 133.
8   Ibid.
9   Hansen, *Letter to the Philippians*, 123.
10 Brannan, *Apostolic Fathers*.
11 Charles Wesley, "And Can It Be?," *Hymnal for Worship and Celebration* (Waco, TX: Word Music, 1986), no. 203.
12 The early Christian writing *The Shepherd of Hermas* uses the term to refer to an empty jar (*Mandates* 11.15).
13 J. Scott Horrell, with Nathan D. Holsteen and Michael J. Svigel, "God in Three Persons: Father, Son, and Holy Spirit," in *Exploring Christian Theology*, vol. 1, *Revelation, Scripture, and the Triune God*, ed. Nathan D. Holsteen and Michael J. Svigel (Minneapolis: Bethany House, 2014), 163.
14 Mark Twain, *Pudd'nhead Wilson: A Tale* (London: Chatto & Windus, 1894), 197.
15 See Hansen, *Letter to the Philippians*, 172.
16 See Wuest, *Wuest's Word Studies*, 75.
17 Gerald F. Hawthorne and Ralph P. Martin, *Philippians*, rev. ed., Word Biblical Commentary, vol. 43 (Grand Rapids: Zondervan, 2015), 148.
18 William Barclay, *The Letters to the Philippians, Colossians, and Thessalonians*, The New Daily Study Bible (Louisville: Westminster John Knox, 2003), 55.
19 Bauer et al., *Greek-English Lexicon*, 481.
20 Ibid., 759.
21 Excerpted in Eusebius, *Ecclesiastical History*, 7.22, cited in Philip Schaff and Henry Wace, eds., *Nicene and Post-Nicene Fathers*, Second Series, vol. 1, *Eusebius: Church History, Life of Constantine the Great, and Oration in Praise of Constantine* (New York: Christian Literature Publishing Company, 1890), 307.
22 Patrick J. Healy, "Parabolani," in *The Catholic Encyclopedia*, vol. 11, *New Mexico—Philip*, ed. Charles G. Herbermann et al. (New York: Encyclopedia Press, 1913), 467.

23 See Barclay, *Letters to the Philippians, Colossians, and Thessalonians*, 7.

24 Joseph M. Scriven, "What a Friend We Have in Jesus," *Hymnal for Worship and Celebration* (Waco, TX: Word Music, 1986), no. 435.

25 Marcus Tullius Cicero, *On Friendship*, trans. Andrew P. Peabody (McLean, VA: Trinity Forum, 2004), 19.

JOY IN SHARING (PHILIPPIANS 3:1-21)

1 Bauer et al., *Greek-English Lexicon*, 602–603.

2 Ibid., 213.

3 Ibid., 44–45.

4 Henry George Liddell, Robert Scott, et al., *A Greek-English Lexicon*, 10th ed. (Oxford: Clarendon Press, 1996), 1616.

5 Melick, *Philippians, Colossians, Philemon*, 131.

6 Nathan D. Holsteen and Michael J. Svigel, eds., *Exploring Christian Theology*, vol. 2, *Creation, Fall, and Salvation* (Minneapolis: Bethany House, 2015), 253.

7 Melick, *Philippians, Colossians, Philemon*, 138.

8 Bauer et al., *Greek-English Lexicon*, 373.

9 H. D. M. Spence-Jones, ed., *Philippians*, The Pulpit Commentary (New York: Funk & Wagnalls, 1909), 114.

10 Bauer et al., *Greek-English Lexicon*, 1065.

11 Ibid., 996.

12 Gordon D. Fee, *Paul's Letter to the Philippians*, The New International Commentary on the New Testament (Grand Rapids: Eerdmans, 1995), 355.

13 Stuart Briscoe, *Bound for Joy* (Ventura, CA: Regal, 1975), 129.

14 Bauer et al., *Greek-English Lexicon*, 845.

15 Ibid.

JOY IN RESTING (PHILIPPIANS 4:1-23)

1 Bauer et al., *Greek-English Lexicon*, 632.

2 Barry D. Jones, *Dwell: Life with God for the World* (Downers Grove, IL: InterVarsity, 2014), 34.

3 Ironside, *Philippians and Colossians*, 86.

4 Hansen, *Letter to the Philippians*, 286.

5 Jones, *Dwell*, 34.

6 Bauer et al., *Greek-English Lexicon*, 152.

7 John R. W. Stott, *The Message of 1 Timothy and Titus*, The Bible Speaks Today (Downers Grove, IL: InterVarsity, 1996), 149.

8 Alfred Plummer, *A Commentary on St. Paul's Epistle to the Philippians* (London: Robert Scott, 1919), 107.

COLOSSIANS

INTRODUCTION

1 For a discussion on the location of Paul's writing of Colossians, see Douglas J. Moo, *The Letters to the Colossians and to Philemon*, The Pillar New Testament Commentary (Grand Rapids: Eerdmans, 2008), 41–46.

2 Richard R. Losch, *The Uttermost Part of the Earth: A Guide to Places of the Bible* (Grand Rapids: Eerdmans, 2005), 71.

3 Moo, *Letters to the Colossians and to Philemon*, 26.

[4] Troy Martin and Todd Still, "Colossians," in *The Blackwell Companion to the New Testament*, ed. David E. Aune (Malden, MA: Wiley-Blackwell, 2010), 493.

[5] Ibid.

[6] Melick, *Philippians, Colossians, Philemon*, 163.

[7] Josephus, *Antiquities of the Jews* 12.3.4, in *The New and Complete Works of Josephus*, rev. and exp. ed., trans. William Whiston, ed. Paul L. Maier (Grand Rapids: Kregel, 1999), 397.

[8] Walter Bauer et al., *A Greek-English Lexicon of the New Testament and Other Early Christian Literature*, 3rd ed. (Chicago: University of Chicago Press, 2000), 934.

JESUS CHRIST, OUR LORD (COLOSSIANS 1:1–2:23)

[1] Bauer et al., *Greek-English Lexicon*, 892–894.

[2] Timothy is mentioned in the salutations of several of Paul's letters, indicating the close association Paul had with this apprentice-turned-colleague (2 Cor. 1:1; Phil. 1:1; Col. 1:1; 1 Thes. 1:1; 2 Thes. 1:1; Phlm. 1:1).

[3] Warren W. Wiersbe, *The Bible Exposition Commentary*, vol. 2 (Wheaton, IL: Victor Books, 1996), 110.

[4] See R. Kent Hughes, *Colossians and Philemon: The Supremacy of Christ*, Preaching the Word (Westchester, IL: Crossway Books, 1989), 22.

[5] See Irenaeus, *Against Heresies* 1.16; Tertullian, *On the Soul* 34.

[6] Justin Martyr, *Apologies* 1.26. See discussion on this statue in Leslie William Barnard, ed., *St. Justin Martyr: The First and Second Apologies*, Ancient Christian Writers, vol. 56 (New York: Paulist Press, 1997), 136, note 181.

[7] For a detailed discussion of the main features of Gnostic theology, see Kurt Rudolph, *Gnosis: The Nature and History of Gnosticism*, trans. Robert McLachlan Wilson (Edinburgh: T. & T. Clark, English, 1983), 53–274.

[8] Bauer et al., *Greek-English Lexicon*, 1039.

[9] Ibid., 612.

[10] Edward Perronet, "All Hail the Power of Jesus' Name," *Hymnal for Worship and Celebration* (Waco, TX: Word Music, 1986), no. 96.

[11] See Melick, *Philippians, Colossians, Philemon*, 210–211.

[12] Pliny, *Lib.* 10.96.7. Translation from Betty Radice, *Pliny: Letters and Panegyrics*, vol. 2, *Letters VIII–X*, Loeb Classical Library, ed. G. P. Goold, vol. 59 (Cambridge, MA: Harvard University Press, 1969).

[13] For a close, scholarly analysis, see Jack T. Sanders, *The New Testament Christological Hymns: Their Historical Religious Background*, Society for New Testament Studies Monograph Series, vol. 15, ed. Matthew Black (Cambridge, UK: Cambridge University Press, 1971).

[14] David L. Allen, *Hebrews*, The New American Commentary: An Exegetical and Theological Exposition of Holy Scripture, vol. 35, ed. E. Ray Clendenen, Kenneth A. Mathews, and David S. Dockery (Nashville: Broadman & Holman, 2010), 120.

[15] Horrell, "God in Three Persons," 159.

[16] See Melick, *Philippians, Colossians, Philemon*, 216–217.

[17] Hughes, *Colossians and Philemon*, 31.

[18] See Melick, *Philippians, Colossians, Philemon*, 237–240.

[19] Moo, *Letters to the Colossians and to Philemon*, 152–153.

[20] Eugene Peterson, *Five Smooth Stones for Pastoral Work* (Atlanta: John Knox Press, 1980), 93.

[21] Bauer et al., *Greek-English Lexicon*, 679.

[22] Ibid., 558.

[23] Ibid., 17.

[24] See F. F. Bruce, *The Epistles to the Colossians, to Philemon, and to the Ephesians*, The New International Commentary on the New Testament (Grand Rapids: Eerdmans, 1984), 91.

25 Bauer et al., *Greek-English Lexicon*, 955.
26 Melick, *Philippians, Colossians, Philemon*, 252.
27 Hughes, *Colossians and Philemon*, 71.
28 Gerard van Groningen, *First Century Gnosticism: Its Origins and Motifs* (Leiden: Brill, 1967), 177.
29 For a more detailed explanation of this view, see Moo, *Letters to the Colossians and to Philemon*, 199.
30 William Barclay, *The Letters to the Corinthians*, The New Daily Study Bible, 3rd rev. ed. (Louisville: Westminster John Knox, 2002), 218.
31 Charles C. Ryrie, *Balancing the Christian Life* (Chicago: Moody, 1969), 159.
32 Charles C. Ryrie, *Dispensationalism* (Chicago: Moody, 1995), 115.

JESUS CHRIST, OUR LIFE (COLOSSIANS 3:1–4:1)

1 Melick, *Philippians, Colossians, Philemon*, 281–282.
2 Richard Foster, *The Challenge of the Disciplined Life: Christian Reflections on Money, Sex & Power* (San Francisco: HarperSanFrancisco, 1985), 5.
3 Bauer et al., *Greek-English Lexicon*, 183.
4 Pliny, *Lib.* 10.96.7.
5 Moo, *Letters to the Colossians and to Philemon*, 290.
6 James McKinnon, *Music in Early Christian Literature*, Cambridge Readings in the Literature of Music (Cambridge, UK: Cambridge University Press, 1987), 8.
7 Bauer et al., *Greek-English Lexicon*, 1096.
8 Andrew B. McGowan, *Ancient Christian Worship: Early Church Practices in Social, Historical, and Theological Perspective* (Grand Rapids: Baker Academic, 2014), 114.
9 Bauer et al., *Greek-English Lexicon*, 391.
10 Ibid., 76.

JESUS CHRIST, OUR LEADER (COLOSSIANS 4:2-18)

1 Bauer et al., *Greek-English Lexicon*, 260.
2 Ibid., 934.
3 Wiersbe, *Bible Exposition Commentary*, 147–148.
4 See Moo, *Letters to the Colossians and to Philemon*, 331.
5 Barclay, *Letters to the Philippians, Colossians, and Thessalonians*, 195.
6 Samuel Taylor Coleridge, "Youth and Age," in *The Poems of Samuel Taylor Coleridge,* new ed., eds. Derwent Coleridge and Sara Coleridge (London: Edward Moxon, 1859), 321.
7 Alan Loy McGinnis, *The Friendship Factor: How to Get Closer to the People You Care For,* rev. and exp. ed. (Minneapolis: Fortress, 2004), 2.
8 Melick, *Philippians, Colossians, Philemon*, 328.
9 Ibid., 332; Moo, *Letters to the Colossians and to Philemon*, 351.
10 See N. T. Wright, *Colossians and Philemon: An Introduction and Commentary,* Tyndale New Testament Commentaries, vol. 12 (Downers Grove, IL: InterVarsity, 1986), 164–165.
11 See my discussion of identifying Paul's "thorn in the flesh" in Charles R. Swindoll, *Swindoll's Living Insights New Testament Commentary,* vol. 7, *1 & 2 Corinthians* (Carol Stream, IL: Tyndale House, 2017), 469–470.
12 Wright, *Colossians and Philemon*, 163.
13 On the text-critical issue of whether Nympha was a woman or a man, see Todd D. Still, "Colossians," in *The Expositor's Bible Commentary: Ephesians–Philemon*, vol. 12, rev. ed., eds. Tremper Longman III and David E. Garland (Grand Rapids: Zondervan, 2006), 355–356. The best evidence, as followed by the NASB translation, suggests that Nympha was a woman.

14 Francis A. Schaeffer, *No Little People* (Downers Grove, IL: InterVarsity, 1974; repr., Wheaton, IL: Crossway, 2003), 21.

PHILEMON

1 Ignatius, *Trallians* 1.1. All translations from Ignatius's writings are taken from Brannan, *Apostolic Fathers.*
2 Ignatius, *Magnesians* 2.1.
3 Ignatius, *Ephesians* 1.3.
4 Though we can't be certain that the Onesimus of Colossians and Philemon is the same Onesimus who served as bishop of Ephesus fifty years later, several scholars have argued in favor of this idea, and I find the notion compelling. See, for example, John Knox, *Philemon among the Letters of Paul* (London: Collins, 1960), 79–80; Bruce, *Epistles to the Colossians, to Philemon, and to the Ephesians*, 202.
5 Ignatius, *Ephesians* 6.2.
6 Henry George Liddell, Robert Scott, Henry Stuart Jones, et al., *A Greek-English Lexicon*, 9th ed., rev. and exp. (Oxford: Clarendon Press, 1996), 1231.
7 Sam Tsang, *From Slaves to Sons: A New Rhetoric Analysis on Paul's Slave Metaphors in His Letter to the Galatians* (New York: Peter Lang, 2005), 22.
8 Aristotle, *The Nicomachean Ethics* 8.11 in Jonathan Barnes, ed., *The Complete Works of Aristotle: The Revised Oxford Translation*, vol. 2, Bollingen Series 71:1 (Princeton: Princeton University Press, 1984), 1835.
9 Melick, *Philippians, Colossians, Philemon*, 350.
10 Arthur A. Rupprecht, "Slave, Slavery," in *The Zondervan Pictorial Encyclopedia of the Bible*, vol. 5, *Q–Z*, ed. Merrill C. Tenney (Grand Rapids: Regency, 1976), 459.
11 See Christopher H. Fuhrmann, *Policing the Roman Empire: Soldiers, Administration, and Public Order* (Oxford: Oxford University Press, 2012), 29–30.
12 See Moo, *Letters to the Colossians and to Philemon*, 371–372.
13 Rupprecht, "Slave, Slavery," 460. A denarius was the daily wage of a free laborer (see Matt. 20:2).
14 For a discussion of the scholarly opinions on whether Paul was requesting that Philemon release Onesimus from slavery, see Moo, *Letters to the Colossians and to Philemon*, 369–374.
15 Wright, *Colossians and Philemon*, 195.